A CANOEING AND KAYAKING GUIDE TO THE OZARKS

formerly Ozark Whitewater

DEDICATION

*This book is dedicated to Jim Raymond, who inspired me in my initial
days of canoeing and outdoor activity and who remained an inspiration
during the many years I was fortunate enough to share in his dedication to
canoeing, teaching, and great fun. Jim gave all associated with him many
gifts that can never be repaid, and we will remember him fondly when we
"raft up" on the river or gather around the campfire with "Old Grandad
and popcorn." Jim was the granddad of our canoe club and we miss him.*

A CANOEING AND KAYAKING GUIDE TO THE OZARKS

TOM KENNON

MENASHA RIDGE PRESS
Birmingham, Alabama

Published by Menasha Ridge Press
Distributed by Publishers Group West
Printed in the United States of America
Third edition 2004

Library of Congress Cataloging-in-Publication Data:

Kennon, Tom, 1953–
A canoeing and kayaking guide to the Ozarks/by Tom Kennon.
p. cm.
Rev. ed. of: Ozark whitewater. 1st ed. c1989.
Includes bibliographical references.

ISBN 978-0-89732-521-9 (pbk.); ISBN 978-0-89732-827-2 (ebook); ISBN 978-1-63404-251-2 (hardcover)
    1. White-water canoeing—Arkansas—Guidebooks.
    2. White-water canoeing—Missouri—Guidebooks.
    3. White-water canoeing—Ozark Mountains Region—Guidebooks. 4. Arkansas—Guidebooks. 5. Missouri—Guidebooks.
    6. Ozark region—Guidebooks. I. Kennon, Tom, 1953– Ozark White-water. II. Title.

GV776.A8K4595 2004
797.122'09767—dc22   2003071006

Cover photo © Comstock Images / Alamy
Interior photos © Thomas G. Kennon except where noted
Cover design by Bud Zehmer
Text design by Ann Marie Healy

Menasha Ridge Press
An imprint of AdventureKEEN
2204 First Avenue South, Suite 102
Birmingham, Alabama 35233
www.menashridge.com

DISCLAIMER

While every effort has been made to insure the accuracy of this guidebook, river and road conditions can change greatly from year to year. This book is intended as a general guide. Whitewater paddling is an assumed-risk sport. The decision to run a river can only be made after an on-the-spot inspection, and a run should not be attempted without proper equipment and safety precautions. The author and publisher of *A Canoeing and Kayaking Guide to the Ozarks* are not responsible for any personal or property damage that may result from your activities. By using any part of this guide, you recognize and assume all risks and acknowledge that you are responsible for your own actions.

Table *of* Contents

Map Index   viii
Map Legend   ix
Acknowledgments   x
Preface   xi

introduction

An Overview of the Ozarks   1
Using This Guide   3
River Hydrology   7
Safety   10
Conservation and the Law   13
Legal Rights of Canoeists   14

part**One**

THE EASTERN OZARKS

Archey Creek   15
Big Creek   17
Cadron Creek   19
Cove Creek   22
Middle Fork of the Little Red River   24
North Sylamore Creek   27
Salado Creek   29
South Fork of the Spring River   31
Spring River   33
Strawberry River   36
White River   38

part**Two**

THE CENTRAL OZARKS

Big Piney Creek   44
Buffalo National River   50
Crooked Creek   60
East Fork of the Illinois Bayou   63
Falling Water Creek   65
Hailstone River   67
Hurricane Creek   70
Illinois Bayou   73

Little Piney Creek	75
Middle Fork of the Illinois Bayou	77
North Fork of the Illinois Bayou	80
Richland Creek	82
Shoal Creek	87
Spadra Creek	89

part**Three**

THE WESTERN OZARKS

Cedar Creek and West Cedar Creek	91
Clear Creek	94
Cove Creek	97
Frog Bayou	99
Illinois River	104
King's River	106
Lee Creek	112
Little Mulberry Creek	116
Middle Fork of the White River	119
Mulberry River	122
Osage Creek	129
Upper White River	130
War Eagle Creek	132
West Fork of the White River	134

part**Four**

THE OUACHITAS

Alum Fork of the Saline River	137
Baker Creek	139
Big Creek (Oklahoma)	141
Brushy Creek	143
Caddo River	145
Cossatot River	148
Eagle Fork Creek	154
Jack Creek	156
Little Missouri River	158
Lower Ouachita River	162
North Fork of the Saline River	165
Ouachita River	167
Saline River	172
South Fourche Lafave River	174
Sugar Creek	176

part**Five**

THE MISSOURI OZARKS

Bryant's Creek	179
Current River	182
Eleven Point River	188
Jack's Fork River	193
North Fork of the White River	198

part**Six**

THE ST. FRANCIOS MOUNTAINS

Big Creek	201
Castor River	204
Marble Creek	206
St. Francis River	208
Turkey Creek	213

appendices

Appendix A: Clubs and Organizations	216
Appendix B: Additional Books and Videos	220
Appendix C: Maps	222
Appendix D: Recommended Web sites	224
Appendix E: USGS Waterline	226
Index	228

Map Index

Archey Creek	15
Big Creek	18
Cadron Creek	21
Cove Creek	23
Middle Fork of the Little Red River	25
North Sylamore Creek	27
Salado Creek	29
South Fork of the Spring River	31
Spring River	34
Strawberry River	37
White River	39, 41
Big Piney Creek	45
Buffalo National River	51, 54, 58
Crooked Creek	60
East Fork of the Illinois Bayou	63
Falling Water Creek	66
Hailstone River	68
Hurricane Creek	71
Illinois Bayou	73
Little Piney Creek	75
Middle Fork of the Illinois Bayou	78
North Fork of the Illinois Bayou	80
Richland Creek	84
Shoal Creek	87
Spadra Creek	89
Cedar Creek and West Cedar Creek	92
Clear Creek	95
Cove Creek	98
Frog Bayou	100
Illinois River	105
King's River	106, 109
Lee Creek	114
Little Mulberry Creek	117
Middle Fork of the White River	120
Mulberry River	124
Osage Creek	126
Upper White River	131
War Eagle Creek	133
West Fork of the White River	135
Alum Fork of the Saline River	137
Baker Creek	139
Big Creek (Oklahoma)	142

Brushy Creek	143
Caddo River	146
Cossatot River	149
Eagle Fork Creek	154
Jack Creek	156
Little Missouri River	160
Lower Ouachita River	163
North Fork of the Saline River	165
Ouachita River	169
Saline River	172
South Fourche Lafave River	174
Sugar Creek	177
Bryant's Creek	180
Current River	184, 186
Eleven Point River	188
Jack's Fork River	194
North Fork of the White River	198
Big Creek	202
Castor River	205
Marble Creek	206
St. Francis River	208
Turkey Creek	214

Map Legend

301 90	129 70 BUS 23	10 1121	54 150
Interstates	U.S. Hwys.	State Hwys.	County Hwys./ Streets & Roads

FS 475-A	....	Pope Co.	ARKANSAS	N	Ben Hur ◉
Forest Service Rd./ unpaved road	Trail	County Line	State Line	North Indicator	City

Lake Ft. Smith *Frog Bayou*	A	A A	ALT	⬇	NATIONAL PARK
River, Creek, Lake or Pond	Put-in Point	Section Continues	Alternate Put-in Point	Take-out Point	Park or City Boundaries

Acknowledgments

The author wishes to acknowledge the many people who contributed valuable information for this book. It is impossible to mention everyone, but several people deserve special thanks.

The following people contributed to the earlier edition of *Ozark Whitewater:*

Jim Raymond helped with his great knowledge of the Buffalo National River, the Jack's Fork River, and the Eleven Point River. David Smallwood's information on the Hailstone River and Richland Creek was extremely helpful. Gordon and Margaret Bartelt contributed advice on the North Fork and the Alum Fork of the Saline. Carry and Debbie Moore lent valuable advice about Shoal Creek, Little Piney Creek, and the Ozark National Forest in general. The USGS and USFS employees were very helpful. Finally, there were many people in the Bluff City Canoe Club that accompanied me on countless wild adventures and exploratory trips; they include Jack Chambers, Ken and Lois Kuiken, John Edgar, Jim and Harriet Surprise, Lou Ingram, and Henry Hall.

The addition of new runs and new rivers in *A Canoeing and Kayaking Guide to the Ozarks* was made possible through help and feedback from the many fine members of the Arkansas Canoe Club. Several people deserve special recognition:

Larry Pearce helped remove inconsistencies from my descriptions and added helpful input on the creeks and rivers we've paddled together over the years, including Frog Bayou, Cedar Creek, Sugar Creek, and the Middle Fork of the White River.

Jim Simmons helped greatly by lending his paddling and safety expertise to this book. Jim was among the first to run Oklahoma's Big Creek and convinced us to try it. Jim added valuable insight throughout the book, including the sections on Brushy Creek and the Cossatot River.

Ted Smethers contributed information on the lower Ouachita River. Ted has been a driving force in getting recreational releases from Remmel Dam for the upper Rockport Ledge play spot.

Cowper Chadbourn was gracious enough to add his insight and knowledge on the Cossatot River and Richland Creek. Cowper also added the deck boater's perspective on both the Cossatot River and Richland Creek by providing vital information about play spots and routes for deck boaters.

Walter Felton was very helpful concerning the Cossatot River, and Marcell Jones concerning Hurricane Creek.

Finally, I want to thank my family, who put up with this project the first and now a second time. My wife has commented several times that she has enough material to write a book, *A Thousand Reasons Why I Have to Go Paddling This Weekend.*

Preface

The story behind this book begins in 1974, when I was first introduced to the sport of whitewater paddling. I could not find information about rivers in Arkansas, however, so I decided to gather it for myself. In 1978, I wrote and published a book entitled *Arkansas Whitewater Rivers* that described 14 of the more popular rivers in Arkansas. In 1988, Menasha Ridge Press published *Ozark Whitewater,* a collection of the original 14 rivers plus 33 additional waterways. *A Canoeing and Kayaking Guide to the Ozarks* adds 17 new creeks and rivers, plus complete updates of the 47 rivers described in its predecessor. Many of the classic runs feature new sections, including Big Piney Creek, Frog Bayou, the Cossatot, and the Ouachita River.

The Ozarks cover parts of Oklahoma, Kansas, Missouri, Arkansas, and Illinois. While streams in Arkansas—and to a lesser extent Missouri—are the emphasis of this book, two new streams in Oklahoma, Big Creek and Big Eagle Creek, have been added. All but ten of the 64 streams described herein are found in Arkansas. The route's classifications range from class I to class IV, with the majority of the streams falling into class II or III.

Paddling has continued to increase in popularity over recent decades, meaning more people paddle the streams each year. Safety remains a major focus of paddling clubs and individuals, so it is fitting that this guide includes an expanded chapter on the subject of safety. Likewise, the sections on conservation and on paddler's river-access rights remain timely.

In contrast to my early days as a paddler, when data about water levels was scarce, the Internet has made available vast amounts of information on water levels, forecasted and current, as well as past precipitation models. A chapter on finding and using this pertinent knowledge is included.

A short introductory section, "Using This Guide," explains the logic behind *A Canoeing and Kayaking Guide to the Ozarks* and how to use the guide efficiently. Readers will find a new, easy-to-use data sidebar with important information about each run on a river. Difficulty, time, distance, gauge, minimum level, scenery, water quality, gradient, and the GPS coordinates for the put-in are listed in the sidebar.

The main body of the book discusses 64 Ozark whitewater rivers, which are divided into six chapters according to geography: the Eastern Ozarks, the Central Ozarks, the Western Ozarks, the Ouachitas Mountain, the Southeastern Missouri Ozarks, and the St. Francios Mountains in Missouri.

Maps are vital tools in planning a paddling trip, so a listing of the better maps available for the Ozark area is included in the

appendices. Topographic and county maps offer the best detail of a river and the roads around a river, while national forest maps provide a good overview of the area.

A listing of area and national paddling organizations is also included, as well as contact information for some of the more prominent conservation groups in the Ozarks. In the appendices, a listing of some of the best Internet sites has been added. The paddler can start with the sites listed and find almost all the information available on area creeks and rivers. Finally, there is an updated listing of suggested reading material that relates to the Ozarks and paddling in general.

I hope that this expanded river guide will help you find the perfect route for an enjoyable paddling adventure in the Ozark area. The sport of whitewater paddling has evolved over the years, and *A Canoeing and Kayaking Guide to the Ozarks* is intended for novice and veteran paddlers alike who want essential information on paddling in the Ozarks.

A concerted effort was made to insure the accuracy of all information in this book, but stream and road conditions are very dynamic and change often. Comments and suggested changes for profiles or maps are welcome and appreciated.

Tom Kennon
A Canoeing and Kayaking Guide to the Ozarks
P.O. Box 43673
Birmingham, Alabama 35243

Introduction

An Overview of the Ozarks

The mountainous Interior Highlands of northwest Arkansas extend north into Missouri and west into Oklahoma. Bordered to the south and east by the Gulf Coastal Plain, the Interior Highlands are home to the whitewater, or clear-running, streams in these otherwise flat states. Formed by uplifting, folding, and faulting in the earth's crust between 300 and 350 million years ago, the Highlands geological region is further divided into the Ozark and the Ouachita Mountains. The basic dividing line between these mountain ranges is the Arkansas River Valley, running from Fort Smith east to Little Rock with the Ozarks to the north.

The Ozarks comprise three divisions: the Salem Plateau, the Springfield Plateau, and the Boston Mountains. The Salem and Springfield Plateaus are in the northern reaches of the Ozarks, and the Boston Mountains are in the southern reaches of the Ozarks. The difficulty of the region's rivers is directly related to their location within these divisions. Class I and II rivers are generally found in the Salem and Springfield Plateaus, where surface rocks of limestone and dolomite are less resistant to erosion by water. The more challenging streams are found in the Boston Mountains, the highest of the three plateaus with elevations up to 2,500 feet. Typically, streambeds in the Boston Mountains are made of sandstone, which erodes so as to produce rapids.

The St. Francois Mountains, located in southeast Missouri, represent a departure from the typical Ozark landscape common to the other Missouri streams in this guide. Their igneous bedrock is much more resistant to erosion than the sedimentary rock found in most of the Ozarks. This results in several rivers that have very good gradients and whitewater. Among them is the St. Francis River described in Part Seven, "The Whitewater Runs of the St. Francois Mountains."

The Ouachita Mountains, south of the Arkansas River Valley and west of the Gulf Coastal Plain, are similar to the Ozarks in geological age and origin. Unlike the Ozarks, the Ouachitas are a series of east-west-trending ridges: the Fourche Mountains in the north, the Central Ouachita Mountains, and the Athens Piedmont Plateau in the south. River difficulty can be correlated to the subdivisions of the Ouachitas as with those of the Ozarks. Class I and II rivers are generally found in the Fourche Mountains, while

some of the most difficult rivers in Arkansas are in the Central Ouachitas. The streams in this area tend to cut through mountains consisting of igneous, sedimentary, novaculite, sandstone, and shale; this produces more severe drops and rapids. Examples are the Cossatot River, the Little Missouri River, and Baker Creek.

Plants and wildlife are abundant in the Interior Highlands. The northern Ozarks have some of the best stands of hardwood oak and hickory forest, while short-leaf pine is more prevalent in the southern reaches of the Ozarks. The cover on the Ouachita Mountains consists of mixed short-leafed pine and upland-hardwood forests. Deer, turkey, beaver, and black bear all inhabit the Interior Highlands.

The climate of the Ozarks is generally pleasant, but the temperature swings from 0 °F in the most severe winters to 100 °F and higher in the hottest summers. Most of the time, however, the severe swings are not a factor. Average high temperatures in the summer are in the upper 80s and average lows are in the high 60s. The average highs in the winter are in the 60s, with lows in the 30s. Rainfall averages 45 inches in most parts of the Ozarks. Snow is a factor only in the months of January, February, and early March and rarely exceeds three inches.

Using This Guide

Each part of this guide covers the waterways of a single watershed or geographic region. A brief overview of each river proceeds individual river-run profiles, the overview is accompanied by a list of maps covering the river. Each profile begins with an at-a-glance data sidebar that lists the following data: difficulty, distance, time, gauge, level, scenery, water quality, gradient, latitude, and longitude. Each profile also includes a brief description, shuttle information, and gauge information.

TOPOGRAPHIC MAPS: U.S. Geological Survery (USGS) topographic maps, or topos, are listed following the overview of each river in the order that the river flows. Topographic maps are very helpful in determining the gradient of a stream or a stream section. For ordering information, see Appendix C (page 222).

COUNTY MAPS: County maps are also listed for each waterway in the order the stream flows. County maps are available from the Arkansas State Highway Commission, The Missouri Highway Planning Commission, and the Oklahoma Highway Department. See Appendix C (page 222) for ordering information.

difficulty	Class I—VI
distance	Miles
time	Hours
gauge	Name or location
level	Feet
scenery	A—C
water	Excellent—poor
gradient	Feet per mile
latitude	GPS data
longitude	GPS data

DIFFICULTY: The first line of the data sidebar gives the difficulty of a stream section using the International Scale of River Difficulty. The scale divides waterways into six classes and, with the addition of "+" and "-", a total of 18 levels. This helps paddlers better determine the relative difficulty of a given section. If the majority of the run is one class but there is one significant rapid in a higher class, it is noted with parentheses.

Class I easy: Fast-moving water with riffles and small waves but few obstructions, all obvious and easily missed with minimal training. The risk to swimmers is slight; self-rescue is easy.

Class II novice: Straightforward rapids with wide, clear channels, which are evident without scouting. Occasional maneuvering may be required, but trained paddlers easily avoid the rocks and medium-sized waves. Swimmers are seldom injured, and group assistance, while helpful, is seldom needed.

Class III intermediate: Rapids with moderate, irregular waves, which may be difficult to avoid and can swamp an open canoe. Complex maneuvers in fast currents and good boat control in

tight passages or around ledges are often required; large waves or strainers may be present but are easily avoided. Strong eddies and powerful current effects can be found, particularly on large-volume rivers. Scouting is advisable for inexperienced parties. Injuries while swimming are rare; self-rescue is usually easy but group assistance may be required to avoid long swims.

Class IV advanced: Intense, powerful-but-predictable rapids requiring precise boat handling in turbulent water. Depending on the character of the river, it may feature large, unavoidable waves and holes or constricted passages demanding fast maneuvers. A fast, reliable eddy turn may be needed to initiate maneuvers, scout rapids, or rest. Rapids may require "must-know" moves above dangerous hazards. Scouting may be necessary on an initial run. The risk of injury to swimmers is moderate to high, and water conditions may make self-rescue difficult. Group assistance for rescue is often essential and requires practiced skills. A strong Eskimo roll is highly recommended.

Class V expert: Extremely long, obstructed, or very violent rapids that expose a paddler to added risk. Drops may contain large, unavoidable waves and holes or steep, congested chutes with complex, demanding routes. Rapids may continue for long distances between pools, demanding a high level of fitness. What few eddies exist may be small, turbulent, or difficult to reach. At the high end of the scale, several of these factors coexist. Scouting is recommended but may be difficult. Swims are dangerous, and rescue is often difficult even for experts. A very reliable Eskimo roll, proper equipment, extensive experience, and practiced rescue skills are essential. Because of the large range of difficulty that exists beyond class IV, class V is an open ended, multiple-level scale designated using decimals: 5.0, 5.1, 5.2, etc. Each of these levels is an order of magnitude more difficult than the previous. For example, increasing difficulty from class 5.0 to class 5.1 is a similar order of magnitude as increasing from class IV to class V.

Class VI extreme and exploratory: These runs have almost never been attempted and exemplify the extremes of difficulty, unpredictability, and danger. The consequences of an error are very severe and rescue may be impossible. These runs are for teams of experts only, at favorable water levels, after close personal inspection and taking all precautions. After a class VI rapid has been run many times, its rating may be changed.

DISTANCE: The distance of each run is given in miles, from the put-in to the take-out. This information has been obtained from computer-assisted measurement of topographic maps.

TIME: This is an estimate of the time, in hours, required to paddle the section described. Extra time should be added for lunch stops, side trips, playing the river, and for larger groups. When paddling a new river, add extra time as a safety margin.

SCENERY: The scenic appeal along each run is graded on the following scale, which puts a premium on natural beauty and solitude.

AA: Very beautiful and remote wilderness with no signs of civilization. These sections represent the terrain of the region as it was in the early 1800s.

A: Some signs of civilization but generally free from human habitation.

B: Some communities or resort areas along the stream, but still very scenic, with no visible signs of pollution.

C: Developed areas with signs of pollution, factories, and industry nearby.

WATER QUALITY: The clarity of each stream section is given using the scale below. Note, however, that bacteria are present even in sediment- and pollution-free water; to avoid illness, filter stream water before drinking it.

Excellent: Crystal-clear water.

Good: Clean water with a small amount of sediment but no pollution.

Fair: Muddy water with no signs of pollution.

Poor: Signs of pollution from industrial waste, heavy sediment.

GAUGE: The gauge for each stream section is listed in the sidebar. Additional information follows the descriptive passage.

LEVEL: This is the minimum level, in feet, needed to paddle the stream and is listed in the data sidebar.

GRADIENT: The average drop, in feet per mile, is given from the put-in to the take-out. If a section has a severe gradient, it will be listed in parenthesis. For example, 25 (1 mile @ 75).

GPS LOCATION (latitude and longitude): The final line in the sidebar lists the GPS coordinates for the put-in of the run. This section was added to help readers find some of the more difficult put-ins. Newer GPS units can be programmed to direct users to a set of coordinates. When combined with a laptop or in-vehicle directional system, this allows paddlers to set the directions and go right to the location of the put-in.

DESCRIPTION: This prose section describes the actual run so that paddlers will know what to expect. Possible routes to take and hazards to avoid are given for the more difficult obstacles, but some things are left unmentioned to gratify the exploratory nature in all of us. Special scenic areas are also mentioned.

SHUTTLE: Detailed directions to the put-in and the take-out are given. If there are numerous sections described for a stream, the first put-in and take-out are listed in the first section and then just the take-out, to avoid redundancy in subsequent sections.

GAUGE: Finally, each run profile concludes with detailed gauge information, including Internet addresses, when applicable. Water-level guidelines are given in feet, using the following touchstones:

Minimum: This is the lowest level for an enjoyable paddle.

Optimum: This is the ideal level for paddling the section.

Dangerous: This is the level at which the stream is too high for a safe paddle.

These water-level guidelines are given in section A for all rivers. The same levels apply to subsequent sections except in cases where additional touchstones are listed.

River Hydrology

Hydrology is the study of water and its circulation—something that paddlers spend a great deal of time doing if they live any distance from the rivers they run. Many of the Ozark streams in the Salem and Springfield Plateaus are fed by large springs that make them floatable year-round, but the steep gradient whitewater streams found in the Boston, Ouachita, and St. Francois Mountains are almost entirely dependent on runoff from rain. Every veteran paddler has experienced the disappointment of arriving at a favorite whitewater run only to find the stream reduced to a trickle. The following information is intended to help alleviate that disappointment by providing paddlers with the means to estimate reasonable water levels. Please keep in mind that there is no way to provide information that is 100 percent reliable, but the more you are armed with, the better your chances of having the type of trip you planned.

Each stream section in this book concludes with gauge information, including minimum, optimum, and dangerous levels and where to find the current water level. This is the level at which a paddler looks to determine what type of trip to expect on a particular day.

Online Sources for Gauge Information

The Internet has made available a plethora of information that one can use to determine the best river to run when planning an outing up to a week in advance.

The United States Geological Survey (USGS) keeps detailed information on most rivers described in this book. Information is available from numerous outfitters' Web sites, as well as, the National Weather Service, National Oceanic and Atmospheric Administration (NOAA), and local news organizations. These Web sites offer information on weather forecasts, current precipitation, and recent precipitation. This information can be used to plan an upcoming trip or a last-minute run. Listed below are some of the best sites for planning your Ozarks paddling trip and a brief explanation of each.

USGS Real Time Data for Arkansas Stream Flow
http://waterdata.usgs.gov/ar/nwis/current/?type=flow

This is one of the best sites for determining past and current levels, as well as predicting future levels for each river with a USGS gauge. Sister sites for rivers in Missouri and Oklahoma are accessed by replacing "ar" in the above URL with "mo" or "ok." The basic information for a river includes the most recent gauge height and the flow in cubic feet per second. Rivers are listed by

county, and clicking the number assigned to each produces a graph of the past 7–31 days' gauge readings and, when available, flow. Selecting "Recent daily" from the "Available data for this site" options atop the page allows you to review gauge information for the past 1–730 days. You can also tailor your graph to show just the information that you need (you may select from the discharge maximum, minimum, and mean and the gauge height maximum, minimum, and mean). In the example, the graph shows gauge height information for the Cossatot River for the period from April 30 to July 29, 2003. From this you can determine when the river crested and predict how long it will remain high enough to paddle. This is very useful if you plan to paddle on Saturday and the crest is on the Tuesday before. After determining the level on Tuesday, find a similar crest pattern and use that information to predict the level on Saturday.

National Weather Service Radar Image for Western Arkansas—Fort Smith
www.srh.noaa.gov/radar/latest/DS.78ohp/si.ksrx.shtml

This is one of the best sites for viewing real-time rainfall. Some of the data options are animated map loops showing rainfall over the past hour and animated loops showing storm totals for the past hour.

You can see exactly where and how much precipitation has fallen in a specific area. This information is very useful for plan-

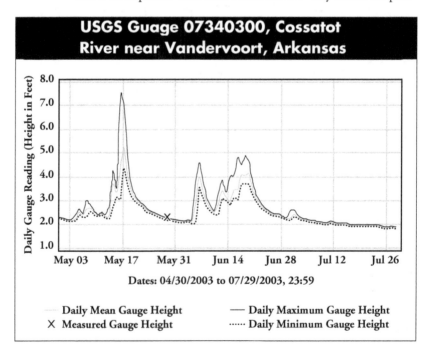

USGS Guage 07340300, Cossatot River near Vandervoort, Arkansas

Dates: 04/30/2003 to 07/29/2003, 23:59

Daily Gauge Reading (Height in Feet)

— Daily Mean Gauge Height
X Measured Gauge Height
— Daily Maximum Gauge Height
······ Daily Minimum Gauge Height

ning quick trips to your favorite creek or river. From the above URL, you can link to similar pages for adjacent geographic regions.

Intellicast.com
www.intellicast.com/Local/USLocalStd.asp?loc=ktul&seg=Local Weather&prodgrp=HistoricWeather&product= Precipitation&prodnav=none

Intellicast's Web page for Tulsa, Oklahoma, provides 24-hour Doppler radar rainfall estimate. This is an excellent site for determining precipitation in the Ozarks over a 24-hour period. Armed with this information you can make reasonable predictions on stream flow within hours of precipitation, as well as in the foreseeable future.

Ozark Creek Information Summary
www.ozarkpages.com/cgi-bin/stages.pl

Bill "Fish" Herring's comprehensive Web site features a table that lists in excess of 70 rivers, creeks, and playspots. For each there is a direct link to a real-time gauge, a description of the stream, photos, and a great dynamic color-coded system for water levels. Bill is on the cutting edge of creek boating, and you can bet he will keep adding information as it becomes available. This is a must bookmark!

In conclusion, when evaluating data from the Web sites above, remember that several factors affect the rate at which the water level drops on any river. The condition of the water table is very important. In wet years the river will fall much slower than in dry years. Heavy rainfall when a river is low results in a much quicker return to the minimum water level than does rainfall when the river is at an optimum level. The rate of drop is also more dramatic in the first few days after rainfall. The time of year is also important. In the winter and spring, there is little foliage to soak up the water and more runs into the rivers, but in the summer months, more precipitation is consumed by plant life in the watershed and never makes it to the river.

Telephone Sources for Gauge Information

The Waterline Service of the USGS is a 24-hour message service that has information for most of the USGS gauges listed in this book. Gauges are updated approximately every four hours. This is a good way to get river levels when you do not have access to the Internet. The Waterline Boater's Edition includes site and sponsors of interest to paddlers and floaters. Call (800) 452-1737 and enter the six-digit code for the river gauge listed in Appendix E (page 226).

Safety

Safety is one of the most important issues in paddling today. In recent decades, paddlers have placed an increasing emphasis on equipment and rescue techniques, making the sport both safer and more enjoyable. There are now books devoted to safety education and river rescue. If a high-profile accident occurs, experts analyze the circumstances to better understand how to prevent similar occurrences. Take the time to read some of the sport's excellent safety publications in order to have a more worry-free canoeing or kayaking experience. The *Whitewater Rescue Manual* by Charlie Walbridge and Wayne Sundmacher is one of the best books on safety and rescue available. In addition, Ozark-area clubs offer basic and advanced swift-water rescue courses. Investing your time in these courses will help you to become a safer and more responsible paddler.

> *Due to advances in boat designs and materials, high-tech paddling gear, and lighter, warmer apparel, boaters are not only making more difficult river trips but are doing so year-round. More frequency on more difficult streams that carry greater risks only highlights the need for safety and rescue awareness. To meet this need, there are concerted efforts by local paddling clubs to provide more rescue training to their membership. Mutual understanding within a paddling group of friends of how to respond in emergency situations will greatly lessen any accident potential.*
>
> *—Jim Simmons*

The Safety Code of American Whitewater (revised in 1998) offers several tips on personal, group, and equipment preparedness that will help to assure your paddling experience is both safe and enjoyable. The code is the combined effort of American Whitewater and more than 100 whitewater paddlers who share a concern for the dynamic safety issues associated with their sport. A summary of the code is listed below. The detailed version is available at the following Web site: http://www.americanwhite water.org/archive/safety/safety.html.

Personal Preparedness:

1. **Never boat alone.** Three boats is the preferred minimum. The logic behind this holds that if there is an accident, one boat can go for help and one boat can stay with the victim.

2. **Be a competent swimmer.** It is very important to have good swimming skills, because even the best paddler has been in the unfortunate situation of having to swim, and a calm, relaxed attitude prevents most dangerous situations. The ability to handle yourself underwater is a must.

3. Wear your life jacket. Good canoeists wear their life jackets just as good drivers wear their seat belts. You do not need a life jacket until it is too late to put on, so get into the habit of putting it on before you get into your boat. A snugly fitting vest-type life preserver offers back and shoulder protection as well as the flotation needed to swim safely in whitewater.

4. Wear a solid, correctly fitted helmet. This is essential in kayaks or decked canoes and recommended for open canoeists using thigh straps and rafters running steep drops.

5. Do not boat out of control. Your skills should be sufficient to stop or reach shore before reaching danger. Do not enter a rapid unless you are reasonably sure that you can run it safely and swim it without injury.

6. Know your ability. Do not attempt to run rivers that exceed your paddling skills. This mistake often occurs among novice paddlers who overestimate their ability. If there is any question, ask an experienced paddler or do not attempt the rapid or river.

7. Know the river. Many rivers look very innocent at the put-in and take-out but turn out to be very difficult class III–IV rivers just downstream. Whitewater rivers contain many hazards, which are not always easily recognized. The following are the most frequent threats: high water, cold water and weather, dams, wiers, ledges, reversals, holes, hydraulics, strainers, and broaching. Before paddling a river for the first time, talk to someone who has, or get topographic maps and study them.

8. Be practiced in self-rescue, including escape from an overturned craft. Proficiency at the Eskimo roll is strongly recommended for decked boaters who run rapids class IV or greater or who paddle in cold environmental conditions.

9. Be trained to help others. Obtain training in rescue skills, CPR, and first aid with a special emphasis on the recognizing and treating hypothermia. It may save your friend's life.

10. Carry equipment needed for unexpected emergencies. This includes footwear to protect your feet when walking to safety, a throw rope, a knife, a whistle, and waterproof matches. If you wear eyeglasses, tie them on and carry a spare pair on long trips.

11. Individuals must accept responsibility. Despite the mutually supportive group structure described in this code, individual paddlers are ultimately responsible for their own safety and must assume sole responsibility for the following decisions:

   a. The decision to participate on any trip.

   b. The selection of appropriate equipment.

   c. The decision to scout any rapid.

   d. The decision to pass up any walk-out or take-out opportunity.

All trip participants should consistently evaluate their own and their group's safety, voicing their concerns when appropriate and following what they believe to be the best course of action. You are encouraged to speak with anyone whose actions on the water are dangerous, whether they are a part of your group or not.

Group Preparedness and Responsibility:

1. Be organized. Participants share responsibility for the planning and outcome of a trip.

2. Scout the river conditions. The group should have a reasonable knowledge of the difficulty of the run before beginning.

3. Group equipment should be suited to the difficulty of the river. Cart throw lines, carabineers, prusiks, and first-aid kits.

4. Keep the group compact. Each boater should be able to see the boat in front and behind at all times. Maintain safe spacing.

5. Develop a float plan. The group's plans should be communicated to the appropriate authorities or individuals.

6. Avoid drugs. The use of alcohol or mind-altering drugs before or during river trips is not recommended.

7. Inform paddlers. Every participant on an instructional or commercially guided trip must realize and assume the risks associated with the serious hazards of whitewater paddling.

Boat and Equipment Preparedness:

1. Test new and different equipment. Do so before venturing into new and unfamiliar territory.

2. Maintain your equipment. Be sure your boat and gear are in good repair.

3. Install flotation bags in kayaks and canoes. This will prevent a craft from sinking should it capsize.

4. Have strong, properly sized paddles or oars.

5. Outfit your boat safely. Carry everything you need and secure it properly.

6. Provide ropes. This step will permit you to hold on to your craft so that it may be rescued.

7. Know your craft's carrying capacity.

8. Install car-top racks properly. Racks must be strong and fully attached to the vehicle.

Conservation and the Law

The natural splendor along Ozark waterways should be sufficient inspiration for sound environmental stewardship. And although a majority of paddlers take pains to protect the wilderness they enjoy, pollution remains an unfortunate, even dangerous reality. The author and publisher strongly recommend that paddlers make every effort to minimize their impact on the natural areas they transit and to support organizations devoted to preserving the natural state of the nation's waterways.

The intent of this passage, however, is to insure your compliance with the law. Since the last edition of this guide was published, the Arkansas legislature took measures to encourage responsible boating and prevent accidental littering. A new litter law that affects the users of The Natural State's waterways is now on the books.

The law bans the possession and use of glass containers, except for those containing prescription medicines, aboard easily overturned vessels. The law also establishes additional requirements if food and beverages are being transported. They are:

a. All coolers, ice chests, and other storage containers must be sealed or locked to prevent them from emptying into the water.

b. A mesh trash bag that can be tightly sealed must be securely affixed to the vessel.

c. All trash must be transported to a place where it can be legally discarded.

d. All beverages not in storage containers must be attached to or held within floating holders or other devices capable of preventing them from sinking if the craft is overturned.

Violating any of the law's provisions is a misdemeanor and carries a fine of up to $500 for each offense, and violations of several provisions may be considered separate offenses. Exempt from the law are houseboats, party barges, johnboats, runabouts, ski boats, bass boats, and "similar craft not easily susceptible to swamping, tipping, or rolling."

Legal Rights of Canoeists

The legal rights of canoeists in Arkansas were defined more clearly with the 1980 decision of the Arkansas Supreme Court in State v. McIlroy. Attorney Scott May summarized this important decision as follows:

> *In State v. McIlroy (Ark 595 S.W.2d 659), the Supreme Court of the State of Arkansas expanded the definition of "navigability" on the Mulberry River, from Wolf Pen to the Arkansas River, to include the public's right to use a stream which has a recreational value but lacks commercial adaptability in the traditional sense. The Court found that their old definition of navigability was a remnant of the steamboat era.*
>
> *In Arkansas a navigable stream belongs to the state and is held as a "public Trust" for those who wish to use the stream for all legitimate purposes, be they commercial, transportational, or recreational; therefore, members of the public have the right to navigate and exercise the incidence of navigation in a lawful manner at any point below the high-water mark on any navigable stream in the state, whether navigation is by oar or by motor-propelled small craft.*

This decision was a major victory for the many paddlers who use the streams in Arkansas and it should be a landmark decision when similar situations arise in Arkansas and other states.

There are some important things to remember if you encounter a landowner who wants to deny you access to a particular stream:

a. Do not try to discuss the legalities of the situation with an upset landowner, especially if he or she is armed. Just leave and notify the proper authorities.

b. If you must traverse privately owned land to access a public stream, try to get the landowner's permission to cross the land in question. Most of the time, a landowner will be glad to let you do so.

c. Treat the landowner's property with the utmost respect and practice the policy of "Leave No Trace." The most common complaint of landowners is the lack of respect for their property by others. Do not leave trash, harm plants, or leave gates open. This will insure future use for yourself and others who may follow.

part One

THE EASTERN OZARKS

ARCHEY CREEK

Archey Creek rises on the east side of AR 16 north of Nogo in Pope County and flows to the southeast through some of the more rugged country in Arkansas, similar to the terrain found on the Middle Fork of the Little Red River. Access is very limited, even on county roads, and an extremely long paddle is required. Plan on putting-in very early, or you will end up on the river after dark.

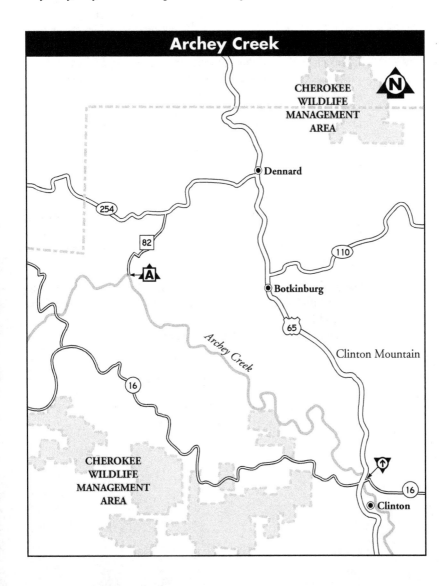

Water quality is very good along Archey Creek, its tree-lined banks thick with oak, pecan, and elm. The terrain is rugged. A paddler has the feeling of being in a virgin forest, as there are no signs of civilization. The gradient of the stream ensures a good current at optimum levels and an abundance of sporty rapids.

MAPS: Alread, Botkinburg, Clinton (USGS); Pope, Van Buren (County)

CASTLEBERRY CREEK TO THE US 65 BRIDGE

difficulty	II (II+)
distance	16.2
time	8
gauge	Middle Fork Little Red (USGS)
level	8.5
scenery	AA
water	Good
gradient	17
latitude	35 42.474N
longitude	92 36.264W

DESCRIPTION: Expect numerous class II rapids with an occasional class II+. Willow jungles are numerous and can be the most dangerous aspect on any Ozark stream. Hartsugg Creek enters on river left about 6 miles below Castleberry Creek. This confluence can be used as an alternate access, shortening the trip by approximately 6 miles.

SHUTTLE: The put-in is reached by going north on US 65 12.6 miles to Denard and turning west on AR 254 for about 4.5 miles to the first gravel road on the left (south) and following the right fork to a small ford over Castleberry Creek. Put-in and paddle a very short distance to Archey's Creek. To put-in on Hartsugg Creek, go north on US 65 for 7 miles. Turn left and proceed 3 miles west to Hartsugg Creek. The take-out is reached via the road on the southeast side of the US 65 bridge.

GAUGE: USGS Middle Fork of the Little Red at Shirley, Arkansas. Online at http://waterdata.usgs.gov/nwis/uv/?site_no= 07075000.

Minimum: 8.5 *Optimum:* 9.0–11.0 *Dangerous:* 12.0

BIG CREEK

Big Creek, located in Cleburne County, begins as a tiny stream near the town of Banner on AR 87. Big Creek twists through the Ozark foothills for approximately 38 miles to its confluence with the Little Red River near Pangburn, Arkansas. The best section to paddle is from Low-Water Bridge Three to the Old Iron Bridge just east of AR 110. Do not confuse this Big Creek with the Big Creek in Missouri, described in Part Six: "The St. Francois Mountains."

Big Creek is very scenic and remote due to limited access points. The area abounds with plants and wildlife, and the run is rife with deep green pools separated by fast rocky chutes that require the paddler to use backferrying skills to negotiate the course successfully. Hardwood forests and rock bluffs line the creek and protect the deer, squirrels, and wild turkey that paddlers often sight.

MAPS: Greers Ferry Dam, Floral, Pangburn (USGS); Cleburne (County)

LOW-WATER BRIDGE THREE TO THE OLD IRON BRIDGE

difficulty	I–II
distance	12
time	6
gauge	None
level	Local Inquiry
scenery	A
water	Good
gradient	11.3
latitude	35 30.882N
longitude	91 49.620W

DESCRIPTION: Paddlers will encounter no real difficulties on Big Creek, but they need to be familiar with basic river skills as taught by the American Canoe Association.

Approximately 3 miles above the take-out are the remains of the old Pangburn Dam site. In 1926, a little struggling company, Big Creek Power and Light, completed a dam to harness electrical power for the town of Pangburn. The spring rains of 1927 proved too much for the dam, and all that remains is a pile of rubble and the foundation of the hydroelectric plant. It is worth stopping to view the remains and to climb the bluff for a spectacular view.

Just below the dam site is a rapid that can generate moderate waves at optimum levels. Big Creek enters a canyon near the community of Hiram. There are several class II drops in this section that should be scouted at higher levels.

Take-out on the river-left, downstream side of the Old Iron Bridge.

SHUTTLE: Take AR 110 north out of Pangburn for 1.4 miles and turn right on McJester. Follow McJester Road for a mile to the Old Iron Bridge. The take-out is at the Old Iron Bridge on river left downstream of the bridge. To reach the put-in, go north on McJester Road 3.4 miles and then turn left on Bottorff Road. Go north approximately 1 mile and bear left onto Warren Mountain

Road. Go northwest 3.6 miles on Warren Mountain Road to the put-in.

GAUGE: Unfortunately, there is no gauge on Big Creek, so one must estimate the water level by the amount of water funneling through the culverts at Low-Water Bridge Three. At the absolute minimum level, water fills one third of the culverts; the optimum level ranges from two-thirds full to a foot of water running over the bridge. When a series of contoured waves is the only evidence of the low-water bridge, do not put-in!

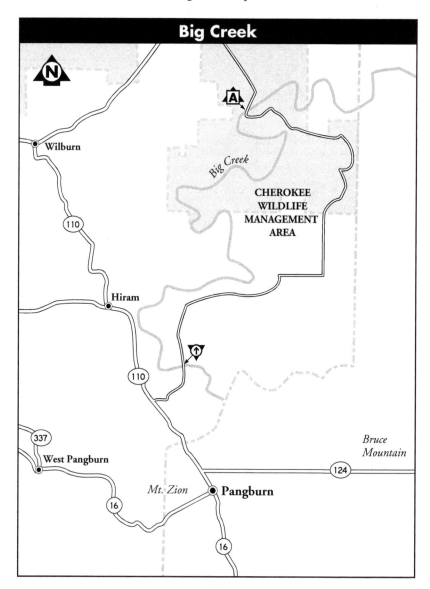

CADRON CREEK

Just east of Pearson, between AR 25 and AR 5, Cadron Creek begins, flowing southwest to its confluence with the Arkansas River near Conway. Many enjoyable miles of water await paddlers on Cadron, but the best runs are from Pinnacle Springs to AR 285.

Cadron Creek is very exciting, with many shoals, willow jungles, and spectacular bluffs. Expect an intermediate run that will keep novice paddlers on their toes at every turn. Hardwood forests enclose Cadron Creek in the upper section, and bluffs become more numerous below AR 65. This is an excellent winter run, with many large ice formations on the bluffs on the colder days of the year.

MAPS: Quitman, Morgantown, Guy, Damascus, Menifee (USGS); Faulkner, Cleburne (County)

PINNACLE SPRINGS TO US 65 BRIDGE

difficulty	I—II+
distance	4
time	2
gauge	Cadron USGS
level	1.75
scenery	A
water	Good
gradient	13
latitude	35 19.880N
longitude	92 23.061W

DESCRIPTION: The access at Pinnacle Springs is closed as of publication in early 2004. The only good alternative is to get permission from Cadron Creek Outfitters to use their access. When you make it to the put-in, you will find that the creek is full of willow runs and shoals that require precise boat control.

Approximately halfway to the US 65 bridge, you will encounter a rapid that is class III at optimum levels. The rapid is steep and requires maneuvering to avoid rocks in the channel.

The take-out point is the Arkansas Game and Fish Commission Access near the US 65 bridge. To reach the access, take the first right north of the bridge on Ozark Drive and go 1 mile. There is adequate parking under the bridge and a good ramp to the creek. There is also a road on the southeast side of the US 65 bridge, but there is no place to park.

SHUTTLE: From the Arkansas Game and Fish Commission Access, go northwest 1 mile to US 65. Go east (right) 2.5 miles, turn right on Old Highway 65, and go a short distance to Pinnacle Springs Road. Turn right and go east 1.5 miles to Cadron Creek Bridge. Continue east up the hill and take a left on Cargile Lane. Follow the signs to Cadron Creek Outfitters. They have a road that leads to the creek at their campground. Donations are accepted at a small box at the gate to help maintain the road. They can also help with shuttles and up-to-the-minute information about the creek; visit www.cadroncreekoutfitters.com.

GAUGE: USGS Cadron Creek near Guy, Arkansas. Online at http://waterdata.usgs.gov/nwis/uv/?site_no=07261000. *Minimum: 1.75 Optimum: 2.75–4.0 Dangerous: >6.0*

difficulty	I–II
distance	10
time	4.5
gauge	Cadron USGS
level	1.75
scenery	A+
water	Good
gradient	11.6
latitude	35 17.967N
longitude	92 24.179W

B

US 65 BRIDGE TO AR 285

DESCRIPTION: Bluffs and waterfalls, plus interesting rapids, make this a run worth doing anytime, but in the winter the scenery is spectacular!

Two-and-a-half miles below the US 65 bridge, paddlers encounter a very exciting class II rapid, followed by an excellent rest or lunch stop on river right.

Just below, as the creek turns northward, you will find a rapid with a house-sized boulder in midstream. Draw hard to the right to avoid this obstacle, or backferry into the eddy on river left above the boulder then drop through the narrow chute left of the rock.

The creek continues with willow runs and occasional shoals to the AR 285 bridge.

SHUTTLE: From the US 65 bridge, go north on US 65 for 5.9 miles to Damascus, Arkansas, and turn left on AR 124. Continue 4.3 miles and turn left on AR 285. Go 3.5 miles to Cadron Creek and park at the Arkansas Game and Fish Commission

Photo by Mike Coogan

Access (GPS: 35 17.114N, 92 28.355W) across the bridge on the right. There is ample parking well above the creek and a ramp to the creek's edge.

GAUGE: USGS Cadron Creek near Guy, Arkansas.
Minimum: 1.75 *Optimum:* 2.75–4.0 *Dangerous:* >6.0

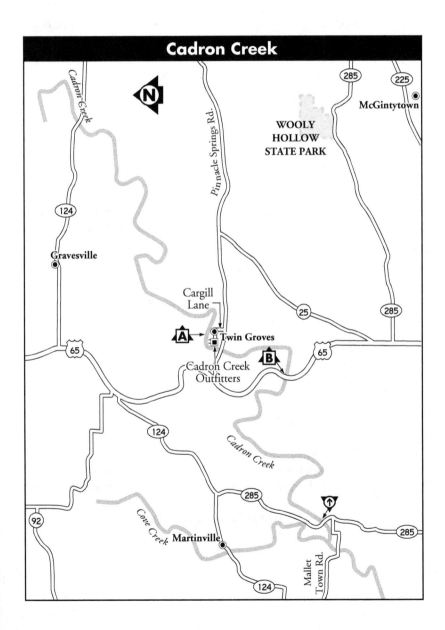

Cadron Creek

COVE CREEK

Cove Creek begins near Bee Branch, Arkansas, and flows southwest to its confluence with Cadron Creek just downstream of the Arkansas Game and Fish Commission Access at AR 285. The creek has a small watershed but is a good run when Cadron is high. The gradient of the creek is not too steep, but its remoteness offers good scenery. Cove Creek is an excellent choice when the Cadron gauge is over 4 feet.

MAPS: Springfield, Damascus (USGS); Conway, Faulkner (County)

MARTINVILLE TO MALLET TOWN

difficulty	II–II+
distance	5
time	3
gauge	Cadron USGS
level	4
scenery	A
water	Good
gradient	6
latitude	35 19.280N
longitude	92 29.110W

DESCRIPTION: There are few real difficulties on Cove Creek, but downed trees are always a potential danger for paddlers.

Cove Mountain constricts the creek about 1.5 miles below the put-in, and the scenery and bluffs are stunning.

Cove Creek flows into Cadron Creek 4.5 miles from the put-in. The take-out is 0.5 miles downstream at the Mallet Town Bridge over Cadron Creek.

SHUTTLE: From Damascus, Arkansas, go southwest on AR 124 for 6.5 miles to the bridge on the west side of Martinville, Arkansas. There is a dirt road on the southeast side of the bridge that leads to the creek. To reach the take-out, go east on AR 124 for 1.8 miles and turn south on AR 285. Go 3.8 miles south on AR 285 and turn right (west) on Mallet Town Road. Go 1.8 miles to the bridge over Cove Creek. You can reach the creek via a dirt road on the southeast side of the bridge (GPS: 35 16.762N, 92 29.102W).

GAUGE: USGS Cadron Creek near Guy, Arkansas. Online at http://waterdata.usgs.gov/nwis/uv/?site_no=07261000. The gauge is not located on Cove Creek, but is close and should be a good indicator of the correct level. Cadron Creek Outfitters can help with additional information; visit www.cadroncreekoutfitters.com.

Minimum: 4.0 Optimum: 4.5–7.0 Dangerous: 8.0

Cove Creek

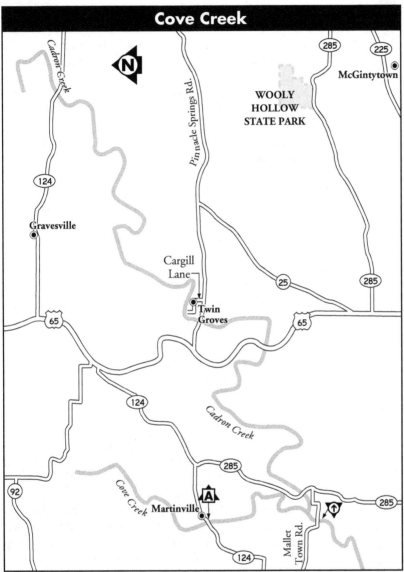

MIDDLE FORK OF THE LITTLE RED RIVER

The Middle Fork of the Little Red River rises near AR 254 several miles to the west of Denard, Arkansas, and flows southeast to Greer's Ferry Lake. The river cuts a path through some of the wildest and most rugged land in the state.

The shuttles required to reach the river are also among the most interesting in the state. The shuttle road that follows the river is on the old L&N Railroad grade, which is not maintained by the state. Each trip presents a new challenge, and major rains make the dirt road virtually impassable. Several gates with "No Trespassing" signs further complicate matters. Get permission from landowners or talk to the sheriff at Shirley, Arkansas, before venturing into this area.

The river is a pool-drop river, with class II rapids and standing waves as its most common obstacles. Willow jungles seem to be more intense than on most Ozark streams and can cause serious problems for paddlers who lack proficient boat control. Clear water and dense hardwood forests enhance the experience.

MAPS: Canaan, Leslie, Oxley, Old Lexington, Shirley, Fox, Parma (USGS); Van Buren, Stone (County)

ELBA TO ALBERG

difficulty	II—II+
distance	9.8
time	5
gauge	Middle Fork Little Red (USGS)
level	8.5
scenery	AA
water	Good
gradient	15.6
latitude	35 46.156N
longitude	92 26.780W

DESCRIPTION: Willow jungles, seemingly at every bend, characterize this river. Rapids are numerous along the run but limited to class II, with the exception of a class III rapid approximately 5 miles downstream of the put-in.

The Walter Diggs Rapid was named after a family that graciously invited many groups over the years to eat lunch at their cabin overlooking the rapid. Willows on river left and a steep bluff on river right form a narrow channel, approximately 16 feet wide, that is dotted with large boulders and drops for 200 yards. Complete control of one's boat is an absolute must before attempting this rapid. Scout it from the road on river right.

Class II rapids follow, with standing waves and willow jungles, for 4 miles until paddlers are faced with a class II+ rapid. An island splits the river, leaving paddlers two choices. River right offers a drop over a rock ledge that can be very difficult at low and moderate water levels. River left offers the easier route but requires the ability to backferry.

SHUTTLE: From the small community of Old Lexington on AR 110, go west for a short distance and take the first dirt road north for 2.7 miles to the community of Alberg, where a low-water bridge is the take-out. The put-in is reached by going 3 miles northwest on AR 110 and turning right on CR 85. Go 2.8 miles north on CR 85 to the community of Elba. Put in northeast of Elba at numerous points along CR 85.

GAUGE: USGS Middle Fork of the Little Red at Shirley, Arkansas. Online at http://waterdata.usgs.gov/nwis/uv/?site_no= 07075000.
    Minimum: 8.5 *Optimum:* 8.75–10.0 *Dangerous:* >11.0

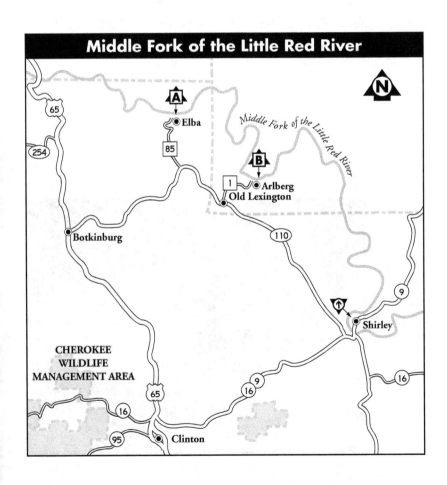

Middle Fork of the Little Red River

ALBERG TO SHIRLEY

difficulty	I—II
distance	14.5
time	7
gauge	Middle Fork Little Red (USGS)
level	8.5
scenery	A
water	Good
gradient	9.65
latitude	35 44.080N
longitude	92 23.384W

DESCRIPTION: Fast-moving water and willow jungles are characteristic in this section of the river. The shoals are less frequent but are still exciting.

There is a low-water bridge about 5 miles below Alberg that should be approached with caution and portaged.

This is a long section to paddle, so be prepared to spend most of the day on the river.

SHUTTLE: From Shirley, Arkansas, go south on AR 9 for 1 mile and turn right onto AR 110. Go 7.7 miles to CR 1 and turn right. Proceed 2.6 miles to the low-water bridge in Alberg. Take out at the bridge on River Road (CR 125) just north of Shirley.

GAUGE: USGS Middle Fork of the Little Red at Shirley, Arkansas.

Photo by Mike Coogan

NORTH SYLAMORE CREEK

South Fork and Cole Fork Creeks merge to form North Sylamore Creek at Barkshed Recreation Area in the Ozark National Forest north of Mountain View, Arkansas. The entire 20-mile creek is protected by the National Forest and it is under consideration for protection under the Wild and Scenic Rivers Act.

Paddlers will find a small, tight stream with a relatively small watershed that makes it runnable only when most area streams are too high to paddle. Hardwoods along its entire length protect the creek, and the water quality is excellent due to the creek's location far from civilization in the Ozark National Forest. Vegetation and wildlife abound, and don't be surprised if you spot a deer at the creek's edge!

MAPS: Norfolk SE, Calico Rock, Fifty Six, Sylamore (USGS); Baxter, Stone (County)

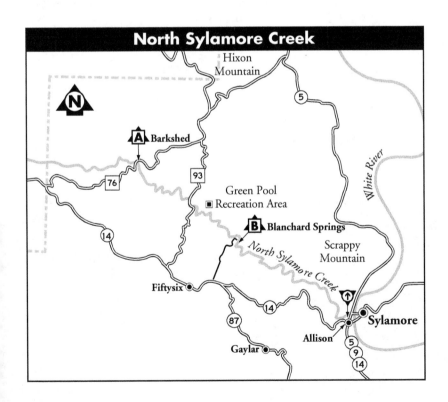

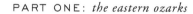

difficulty	I—II+
distance	8.4
time	3.5
gauge	N. Sylamore (USGS)
level	2.5
scenery	AA
water	Excellent
gradient	15
latitude	36 1.116 N
longitude	92 15.012W

BARKSHED TO BLANCHARD SPRINGS

DESCRIPTION: There are no major difficulties on this run, but be aware of fallen trees and brush piles. A blessing for paddlers, this normally shallow stream is only runnable when many of the other streams are in flood and unrunnable.

SHUTTLE: To reach the put-in from Mountain View, take AR 5 north for 5.8 miles to AR 14. Turn left and go northwest on AR 14 for 12 miles. Turn right to proceed northeast on CR 1115 (Cartwright Road) for 2 miles. Turn left and go northwest for 0.3 mile on Ridge Road and then go straight on CR 1102 for 1.4 miles to the creek. From Mountain View, reach the take-out by taking AR 5 north for 5.8 miles to AR 14. Turn left and go northwest on AR 14 for 5.7 miles. Turn north (right) on a Forest Service road and go 3 miles to Blanchard Springs Recreation Area.

GAUGE: USGS North Sylamore Creek near Fifty Six, Arkansas. Online at http://waterdata.usgs.gov/ar/nwis/uv/?site_no=07060 710&PARAmeter_cd=00065,00060.
Minimum: 2.5 Optimum: 3.5 Dangerous: >4.5

difficulty	I—II
distance	4.9
time	2.5
gauge	N. Sylamore (USGS)
level	2.5
scenery	AA
water	Excellent
gradient	13.7
latitude	35 59.102N
longitude	92 10.333W

BLANCHARD SPRINGS TO ALLISON (AR 5)

DESCRIPTION: Enjoy the rustic quality of this stream, but watch for fallen trees and strainers, a constant threat on the smaller creeks in the Ozarks.

SHUTTLE: The take-out is reached by going 5.8 miles north of Mountain View on AR 5 to Allison. Turn west on AR 14 and take a small road that leads to the creek.

GAUGE: USGS North Sylamore Creek near Fifty-Six, Arkansas.
Minimum: 2.5 Optimum: 3.5 Dangerous: >4.5

SALADO CREEK

Three small creeks combine just north of Floral, Arkansas, to form Salado Creek. The three creeks form a fast-flowing stream that takes a northeasterly route to its confluence with the White River near the town of Salado.

Salado Creek flows through a rugged gorge that is inaccessible below Girl Scout Camp Tahkodah to US 167. If you catch the creek at a good level, you will be blessed with spectacular scenery and many class II rapids. Beware of low water, as your trip could become a canoe hike. The Salado is a favorite among Memphis-area paddlers; it is the closest whitewater to Memphis, 87 miles away. The current is swift at optimum levels, and the water quality is good. The banks are lined with trees along most of the creek, restricting views of the adjacent farmland. The final mile is a major willow jungle with deadfalls in the current—so be careful!

The best section to paddle is from Camp Tahkodah to the US 167 bridge, a distance of 11 miles. One must obtain permission to put-in at Camp Tahkodah by calling (501) 252-1289. A nominal fee is usually charged to help with road maintenance within the camp.

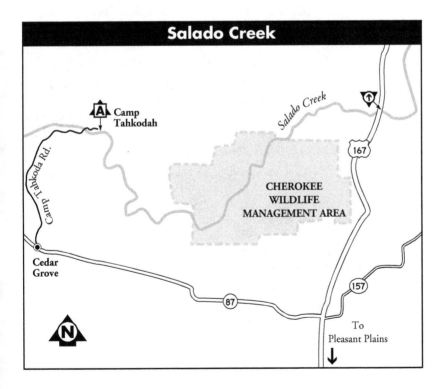

MAPS: Pleasant Plains, Salado, Newark (USGS); Independence (County)

difficulty	II—II+
distance	10
time	5—6
gauge	Visual
level	9 stones
scenery	A+
water	Good
gradient	17.6
latitude	35 36.450N
longitude	91 42.121W

CAMP TAHKODAH TO THE US 167 BRIDGE

DESCRIPTION: Just below Girl Scout Camp Tahkodah, paddlers encounter a rapid with a very good gradient. At lower levels, paddlers must approach the rapid on river right through a rock garden and proceed to the river-left chute midway down this run. At higher levels, you may choose to stay right or run left through good standing waves.

Two miles below the Girl Scout camp is the best rapid on the creek. At optimum levels, it approaches class III in difficulty. Paddlers face a narrow channel with a tight dogleg turn to the left. A large boulder directly in the center of the channel makes the turn even more difficult.

The next 4.5 miles are dotted with sporty class II rapids separated by quiet pools that enable paddlers to enjoy Salado Creek's beautiful scenery.

Half a mile above the take-out is the worst willow jungle I have encountered on any Ozark river. The creek seems to disappear into the trees. The best route is to the left, but be prepared to drag and pull your boat over downed trees and logs.

SHUTTLE: From the US 167 bridge, go south 4.4 miles and turn west on AR 87. Go 6.2 miles west to Cedar Grove, then turn north for 3.6 miles to Camp Tahkodah. The take-out is on river right on the upstream side of the US 167 bridge. Cars can drive down to the creek at this point.

GAUGE: There is no gauge on Salado Creek, so one must estimate the water level. A minimum can be determined using the old stone bridge at US 167. Nine visible stones is a minimum; if ten stones are visible, do not attempt to run the creek or you will drag your boat. The people at Camp Tahkodah can also provide helpful information about the amount of rainfall that has occurred recently.

SOUTH FORK OF THE SPRING RIVER

The South Fork of the Spring River begins as a series of small creeks near the community of South Fork, Missouri, and flows southeast to its confluence with the Spring River at Hardy, Arkansas.

The upper section of the South Fork is generally remote and wild with few signs of civilization. The riverside alternates between pastures and forests for most of the way, but more signs of civilization are apparent as the paddler approaches Cherokee Village. These are not overpowering. Sharp bends and rocky shoals characterize the river, with very few difficult spots to negotiate. The water quality is very

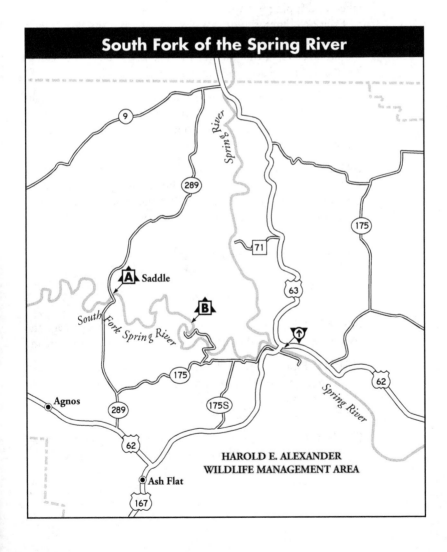

good and the river moves at good pace until it nears its junction with the Spring River, where it slows in the long pools.

MAPS: Agnos, Stewart, Hardy (USGS); Fulton, Sharp (County)

difficulty	I–II
distance	14
time	5
gauge	None
level	See text
scenery	A
water	Good
gradient	6
latitude	36 21.157N
longitude	91 38.063W

SADDLE TO CHEROKEE CAMP

DESCRIPTION: There are no difficult rapids, but give some thought to the air and water temperatures in comparison to your paddling skills before attempting this run. You don't want to take-out dripping wet with your teeth chattering.

Exciting chutes, standing waves, and sharp turns at optimum levels are in store for the experienced paddler in this section. Care should be taken at the low-water bridge at the Boy Scout camp, Kia Kima, Slick Rock, and Cherokee Village Golf Course.

SHUTTLE: From Hardy, go 10.3 miles on AR 175 and turn right on US 62. Go 2.37 miles and turn right on AR 289, go 7 miles to the AR 289 bridge. The take-out is at the bridge at Cherokee Camp on the right bank.

GAUGE: There is no gauge available, but a good way to estimate the water level is in comparison to the old bridge piers at Cherokee Camp. The minimum level is 12 inches below the piers. The optimum is from 5 inches below to level with the piers.

difficulty	I
distance	5
time	3
gauge	None
level	See text
scenery	B
water	Good
gradient	6
latitude	36 19.337N
longitude	91 32.035W

CHEROKEE CAMP TO HARDY

DESCRIPTION: This easy run requires that paddlers portage the low-water bridge on the right bank 1.35 miles below the put-in.

SHUTTLE: From Cherokee Camp, go 1 mile on Cherokee Road and turn left on AR 175. Go 1.8 miles to US 62, turn left, follow US 62 for 1.3 miles to US 63, and turn right in Hardy. The take-out is at the Hardy Public Beach.

GAUGE: Again, no gauge is available. Reference the preceding section for information on how to estimate the water level.

SPRING RIVER

The Spring River begins as the Warm Fork of the Spring River north of Thayer, Missouri. Mammoth Spring, one of the largest springs in the state of Arkansas, adds tremendously to the volume of the water in the river. The crystal-clear, cold water that emerges from the spring is ideal for trout, and the Arkansas Game and Fish Commission stocks the river, making it an excellent trout-fishing stream from below Mammoth Spring to Many Islands Camp.

The Spring River is canoeable from the Dam 3 Access to the Black River, a distance of 61 miles. The scenery is good and the difficulty does not exceed class II. Add a constant flow of water from Mammoth Spring, and you have one of the most popular canoeing streams in the Ozarks.

The Spring River has distinctive characteristics not found on the other Ozark Rivers. Long pools are broken by waterfalls that range 1–5 feet in height. The paddler must pick the correct slot to successfully negotiate the drop, or prepare to drag or overturn. Along the run, gently sloping banks alternately border hardwood forests and farmland.

MAPS: Mammoth, Spring, Stuart, Hardy, Sitka, Ravenden, Imboden, Noland (USGS); Fulton, Sharp, Lawrence (County)

DAM 3 TO MANY ISLANDS CAMP

difficulty	I–II
distance	8
time	4
gauge	None
level	See below
scenery	A–B
water	Good
gradient	8.3
latitude	36 27.998N
longitude	91 31.767W

DESCRIPTION: This section is characterized by many small waterfalls that are negotiable by finding the correct slot in the ledge for your canoe or kayak. There are several fast riffles that can cause trouble for beginning paddlers. Sadler Falls, 5.3 miles from the put-in, is a double waterfall preceded by a series of fast chutes. Approach the chute staying to the inside (left) bank and dropping over the 2.5-foot falls. Continue to the left of the islands in preparation for Saddler Falls.

The first drop is 4 feet tall and should be entered to the middle left, dropping straight into the pool and lining up for the second drop of 3 feet, which is perpendicular to the first drop. The second drop is sometimes tricky, as the water tends to flow through the chute towards a small flat boulder in the pool below. For those wishing to portage the second drop, do so on the river-left bank.

English Creek enters on river right just downstream of Saddler Falls.

Approximately one-half mile downstream is Horseshoe Falls, a drop of 5 feet. The best slot is in the middle of the falls with more difficult drops to either side. The sneak route is a chute 50 yards above the falls on river left. A word of caution to those who do not know how to cross a fast jet of water: Prepare to get wet!

Many Island Camp is 1.5 miles downstream on river left.

SHUTTLE: From Hardy, Arkansas, go north on US 63 for 14.4 miles and turn left onto SR 342. Proceed 0.8 mile to the put-in at Dam 3 Access. To get to Many Island Camp from Hardy, go

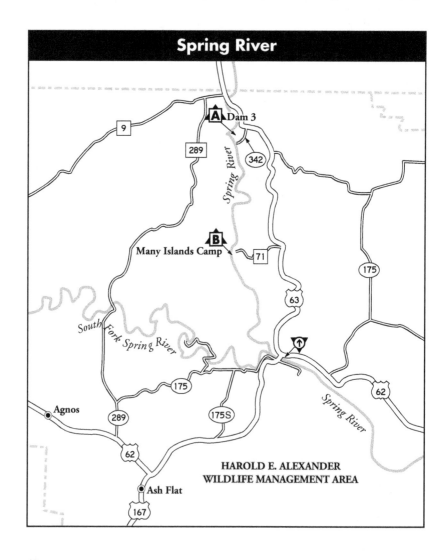

north on US 63 for 7.2 miles and turn left at the sign for Many Islands Camp. Proceed 3.5 miles to the camp.

GAUGE: None, but the river is floatable year-round.

MANY ISLANDS CAMP TO HARDY

difficulty	I–II
distance	8
time	4
gauge	None
level	See below
scenery	A–B
water	Good
gradient	5
latitude	36 23.331N
longitude	91 31.866W

DESCRIPTION: This section of the river does not have as many waterfalls and fast chutes as the upper section, but the waterfall drops tend to be larger.

The first drop of any difficulty is the Devil's Shoot. The river is constricted to half its normal size as it drops over a 3-foot falls, creating moderate standing waves and a very fast jet of water with good eddies on both sides. This is a good place to practice ferrying and eddy turns.

One-half mile downstream is Humphries Ford, a low-water bridge that must be portaged. Take-out well above the bridge on river right and carry your boat around it. The bridge can be dangerous at any level, and at lower levels could trap an overturned canoe or individual. At higher levels a hydraulic forms on the downstream side of the bridge and can easily hold canoes, paddles, or bodies. Be careful!

Paddlers encounter several more good drops before arriving at High Falls, a drop of 6 feet at the confluence of the Spring River and the South Fork of the Spring River. High Falls can be run by dropping through the slot on river left. Upsets are numerous, but the river is forgiving, with a long recovery pool below.

Take-out below US 62 at Hardy Beach.

SHUTTLE: Hardy Beach is located near US 62 in the town of Hardy, Arkansas. To get to the put-in from Hardy, go north on US 63 for 7.2 miles and turn left at the sign for Many Islands Camp. Proceed 3.5 miles to the camp.

GAUGE: None, but the river is floatable year-round.

STRAWBERRY RIVER

The Strawberry River begins in Fulton County, west of Salem, Arkansas, and flows southeast through farmland to its confluence with the Black River north of Newport, Arkansas. Area residents have waged several battles to keep it from being dammed. The most notable concerned the Bell Foley Dam Project, which was defeated with the help of the Ozark Society. Paddlers can expect a relatively easy but remote stream that combines a leisurely float with good scenery.

The Strawberry River cuts through the rolling foothills of the Ozarks. Hardwood forests of oak, pecan, and elm trees line the banks, blocking all but an occasional view of the abundant farmland. The water exhibits the familiar green tint found on many Ozark streams. It flows at a leisurely pace that affords paddlers time to enjoy the peaceful sounds of wildlife and the beautiful scenery.

MAPS: Bryon, Oxford, Franklin, Myron, Sidney, Evening Shade, Poughkeepsie, Smithville, Strawberry, Stranger's Home (USGS); Fulton, Izard, Sharp, Lawrence, Independence (County)

A

difficulty	I–II
distance	10.7
time	5
gauge	None
level	NA
scenery	A
water	Good
gradient	6.5
latitude	36 5.922N
longitude	91 36.525W

US 167 TO LOW-WATER BRIDGE 3 MILES EAST OF EVENING SHADE

DESCRIPTION: Do not confuse the first bridge north of Evening Shade with the Strawberry River Bridge, which traverses Piney Fork Creek. It does flow into the Strawberry River above the take-out, however, so it won't be a total disaster if you mistake it for the Strawberry. The actual put-in is 2 miles north of Evening Shade, Arkansas, on US 167.

This run presents no real difficulties for the experienced paddler, but watch out for obstructions caused by downed trees and water that sweeps into such obstructions.

Piney Fork enters on river right 6.5 miles below the put-in and adds considerable volume to the river.

Less than a mile downstream of the confluence with Piney Fork, the river makes a wide horseshoe bend as you pass two houses on river right. The road is less than 0.1 mile away, but the river continues for over 2 miles to the take-out.

SHUTTLE: The put-in is on US 167 2.5 miles north of Evening Shade. To reach the take-out, go 2.5 miles south on US 167 to Evening Shade. Turn left (east) on AR 56, go 3.5 miles to CR 9, and turn left (northeast). Go 1.8 miles on CR 9 to the take-out.

GAUGE: None; visual inspection is required.

LOW-WATER BRIDGE 3 MILES EAST OF EVENING SHADE
TO AR 58 IN POUGHKEEPSIE

difficulty	I–II
distance	10
time	6
gauge	None
level	NA
scenery	A
water	Good
gradient	4.1
latitude	36 4.684N
longitude	91 32.296W

DESCRIPTION: Watch for downed trees and willow snags. Be careful! These obstacles can cause serious accidents for the unsuspecting paddler.

The river divides around an island about 7 miles below the put-in. Take either route.

Be cautious at the low-water bridge 1.5 miles below the island. You must portage your vessel and may use either side of the river.

North Big Creek enters on river left 1.5 miles below the low-water bridge.

SHUTTLE: To reach the take-out from the put-in, go southwest 1.8 miles on CR 9 to Arkansas 56. Go east (left) on AR 56 for 4.8 miles and turn northeast (left) on AR 58. Go 3.3 miles to the Strawberry River.

GAUGE: None; visual inspection is required.

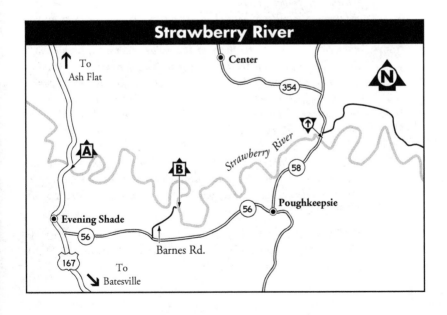

Photo by Mike Coogan

WHITE RIVER

White River ran free until the U.S. Army Corps of Engineers built a series of dams in the late 1950s. The impoundment of the river produced both negative and positive results for paddlers. The dams rendered sections of the White River unrunnable, but below Bull Shoals Lake it is almost always floatable due to the daily water releases for power generation. The canoeing is good for 79 miles to Sylamore. The White River has also become one of the most famous trout streams in the nation, and anglers in guided johnboats are its most common users. Be wary of the guides on the river, especially if you happen to stop on the same gravel bar for lunch or camping. They will tell some of the biggest fish tales that you will ever hear!

The White River is wider than most Ozark streams, but the crystal-clear water flows at a good pace. In most places, the river bottom is visible even in deep holes where the big trout like to hide. The fishing guides claim that the biggest trout stay in the same holes for life, never moving more than a few hundred yards. The banks are lined with trees, bluffs, and fishing camps. If you are looking for a pure wilderness experience, you will not find it on this part of the White River.

MAPS: Cotter, Mountain Home West, Buffalo City, Norfork, Norfork Dam South, Calico Rock, Boswell, Sylamore (USGS); Marion, Stone, Izard (County)

BULL SHOALS TO COTTER

difficulty	I
distance	16.5
time	7–8
gauge	Visual
level	NA
scenery	A–B
water	Good
gradient	9.8
latitude	36 21.789N
longitude	92 34.965W

DESCRIPTION: There are numerous guide services clustered on river left just downstream of Bull Shoals Recreation Area. Their numbers attest to the popularity of the White River as a trout stream.

Remember that most of the guide services are located on private property, so get permission before using an establishment as an access point.

Wildcat Shoals is approximately 12 miles below the put-in. The take-out is at public-access area in Cotter.

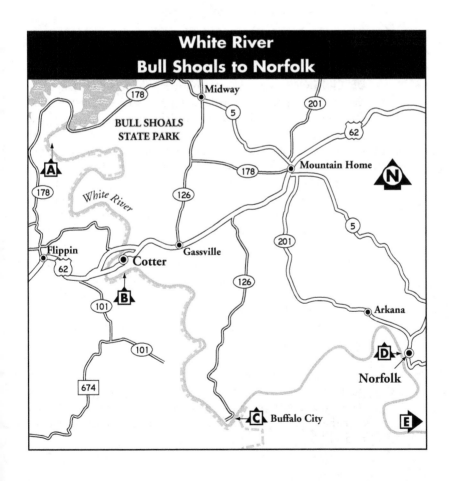

White River
Bull Shoals to Norfolk

SHUTTLE: To reach the put-in from Mountain Home, Arkansas, go west 5.1 miles on AR 178 to AR 126. Turn north (right) on AR 126 and go 3.2 miles to Midway, Arkansas. Go west (left) 7.7 miles on AR 178 to Bull Shoals State Park. To reach the take-out from Bull Shoals State Park, go 2.8 miles to AR 178. Proceed across the dam and go south 10.7 miles to US 62/412. Go east (left) on US 62/412 for 4.2 miles to Cotter, Arkansas, and turn right on AR 345. Go 1.4 miles to the city's pubic-access point.

GAUGE: USGS White River, at Calico Rock, Arkansas. Online at http://waterdata.usgs.gov/ar/nwis/uv/?site_no=07060500&PARAmeter_cd=00065,00060. Flows average 4–7 feet. Swift currents at higher flows are the greatest danger to paddlers. Check locally for flood conditions and stay off the river if it is flooded. There should always be sufficient water to float a canoe.

B

COTTER TO BUFFALO CITY

difficulty	I
distance	12.4
time	7
gauge	Visual
level	NA
scenery	A–B
water	Good
gradient	3
latitude	36 16.145N
longitude	92 31.259W

DESCRIPTION: Many people consider this upper section to be the best for canoeing and trout fishing. If you have never fished for trout, this is the place to try it. Make sure you have a current fishing license and a trout stamp. The state has made it easy, and you can now purchase your fishing license and trout stamp online at http://www.ark.org/agfc/license/index.php.

Just below the access in Cotter, there is a long hole that contains some of the best trout on the river. We have caught our limit here many times. Rim Shoals, just above Crooked Creek, is another great spot for trout fishing.

Crooked Creek enters on river right approximately 5 miles below Cotter. There is a gravel bar at the mouth of Crooked Creek that's great for camping or lunch. This spot is also the sight of the infamous Whitewater real-estate deal, which plagued the Clinton White House.

One mile above the mouth of the Buffalo National River, there is a series of rapids known as Buffalo Shoals. The best route is on river left.

A large bluff on river right separates the White River and the Buffalo National River. One guide who grew up in the area claims that a very profitable moonshine operation once thrived over the ridge on the bluff, because it was almost impossible to find.

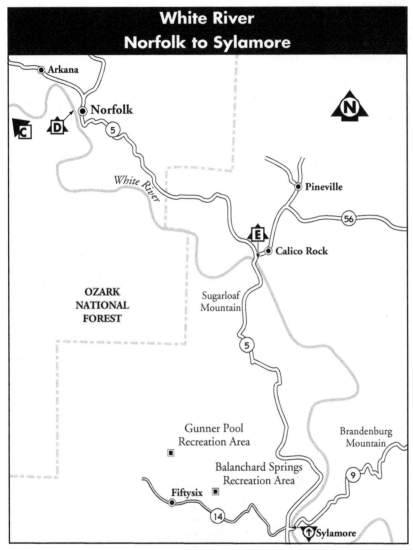

SHUTTLE: To reach the take-out from Cotter, Arkansas, go 3.1 miles to Gassville, Arkansas, turn right on Bueford Road, and go 2.3 miles to CR 4. Turn right and continue 0.9 mile to CR 3, then bear left for 1.3 miles to CR 624. Go 1.4 miles on CR 624 and turn right (south) on AR 126. Go 6.8 miles on AR 126 to Buffalo City, Arkansas.

GAUGE: USGS White River, at Calico Rock, Arkansas. See notes in the section A above.

difficulty	I
distance	11.3
time	5
gauge	Visual
level	NA
scenery	A
water	Good
gradient	2.7
latitude	36 9.456N
longitude	92 26.121W

BUFFALO CITY TO NORFORK

DESCRIPTION: The Buffalo National River enters on river right just downstream of the access point. Be careful of the shoal on river left at the confluence. A man-made dam has been built to divert the water and can be dangerous in high water.

A very long gravel bar, an excellent camping spot, is just downstream.

Remember that water levels fluctuate with power generation, so set your camp well above the water line. This area is very susceptible to flash floods from the Buffalo.

SHUTTLE: To reach the take-out at Norfolk, Arkansas, from Buffalo City, Arkansas, go 0.8 mile on CR 641 to AR 126. Head north 7.1 miles on AR 126 to turn east (right) on CR 57. Go 3.4 miles to AR 201, then go 6.5 miles on AR 201 to AR 5. Go 0.6 mile on AR 5 to Norfolk River Road, then continue 0.3 mile to the Norfolk Access.

GAUGE: USGS White River, at Calico Rock, Arkansas. See notes in the section A above.

difficulty	I
distance	17.2
time	9
gauge	Visual
level	NA
scenery	A–B
water	Good
gradient	2.5
latitude	36 12.576N
longitude	92 17.384W

NORFOLK TO CALICO ROCK

DESCRIPTION: Rapid Shoals is approximately 2 miles below the access.

Otherwise, this section begins to slow and the trout fishing is not as good as in the upper sections.

SHUTTLE: From the put-in at Norfolk, the take-out at Calico Rock is 13.4 miles southeast via AR 5.

GAUGE: USGS White River, at Calico Rock, Arkansas. See notes in the section A above.

CALICO ROCK TO SYLAMORE

DESCRIPTION: This section is used mainly by fishermen, but the scenery is good.

SHUTTLE: From the put-in at Calico Rock, the take-out is reached by going south 16.7 miles on AR 5 to turn left on AR 335. The access is 0.3 mile down the road in Sylamore, Arkansas.

GAUGE: USGS White River, at Calico Rock, Arkansas. See notes in the section A above.

difficulty	I
distance	17
time	8
gauge	Visual
level	NA
scenery	A–B
water	Good
gradient	1
latitude	36 6.966N
longitude	92 8.599W

part**Two**

THE CENTRAL OZARKS

BIG PINEY CREEK

Big Piney Creek rises in the Boston Mountains near the small town of Fallsville, Arkansas, and flows generally southward to its confluence with Lake Dardanelle, a distance of approximately 67 miles. The headwaters of both the Buffalo and the Mulberry Rivers are within a few miles. Big Piney Creek is one of the more challenging streams in the state of Arkansas, offering paddlers rapids up to class III at optimum levels. Expect a pool-drop type of stream with a good current in the short pools and exciting rapids with large standing waves and occasional boulders in the main current. These rapids appear every quarter-mile at minimum and more often in many places.

Paddlers are blessed with a panorama of remote and wild scenery, from the limestone bluffs that constrict the creek to one-third it normal size to the varied wildlife thriving in the natural refuge along the banks of Big Piney Creek. The water quality is good, and at normal levels the water flows the milky green color that is unique to Ozark streams. In addition, Longpool Campground is among the most beautiful campsites in the state of Arkansas. It's worth the effort to make Longpool your base camp while paddling Big Piney Creek.

MAPS: Fallsville, Swain, Rosetta, Fort Douglas, Treat, Lee Mountain, Knoxville (USGS); Newton, Johnson, Pope (County)

difficulty	II–III
distance	5.75
time	3
gauge	Big Piney (USGS)
level	5
scenery	A
water	Excellent
gradient	33.6
latitude	35 47.311N
longitude	93 21.660W

WALNUT CREEK TO LIMESTONE

DESCRIPTION: Put-in at the low-water bridge at Walnut Creek and paddle one-third mile on Walnut Creek to the Big Piney.

Big Piney drops very quickly over class II+ and III rapids in this section. The remoteness of this run increases the degree of difficulty, especially if you encounter problems. Do not attempt this run unless you are a competent class III boater and you have plenty of support.

Take-out at the low-water bridge at Limestone.

SHUTTLE: To reach the put-in from Edward's Junction, go 0.8 mile southeast on AR 16 and turn south (right) on CR 64. Proceed 2.8 miles and bear southwest on CR 64 for 1.9 miles to the low-water bridge over Walnut Creek. To reach the take-out

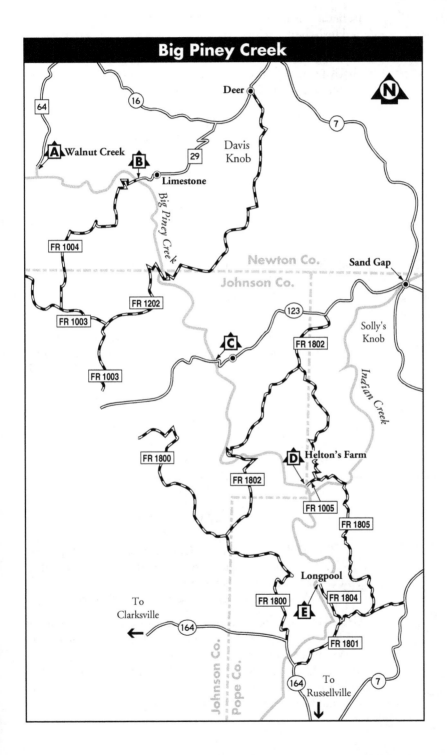

Big Piney Creek

from the put-in, backtrack to AR 16 and go east (right) 4.5 miles and turn south (right) on CR 27. Go south 4.9 miles to the town of Limestone.

GAUGE: USGS Big Piney at AR 164 near Dover. Online at http://waterdata.usgs.gov/nwis/uv/?site_no=07257006. This gauge was moved by the USGS several years ago and reads approximately half a foot lower than the old USGS gauge at Longpool. A visual gauge remains at Longpool, however.
    Minimum: 5.0 *Optimum:* 5.5–6.5 *Dangerous:* >8.0

difficulty	II—II+
distance	10.37
time	6
gauge	Big Piney (USGS)
level	3.5
scenery	AA
water	Excellent
gradient	15.5
latitude	35 46.894N
longitude	93 17.443W

LIMESTONE TO FORT DOUGLAS

DESCRIPTION: The greatest thing this section has going for it is the remoteness of the run. The shuttle is not very easy, but it's worth it, especially if you combine it with the lower sections to make an overnight trip.

SHUTTLE: From the put-in at Limestone, backtrack to AR 16 and turn east (right) to reach the take-out. Go 6.9 miles northeast and bear right at AR 7. Go south 13.2 miles on AR 7 to AR 123 and turn west (right). Go 12 miles to the bridge over the Big Piney.

GAUGE: USGS Big Piney at AR 164 near Dover.
    Minimum: 3.5 *Optimum:* 4.0–5.5 *Dangerous:* >7.0

difficulty	II
distance	8.66
time	5
gauge	Big Piney (USGS)
level	2.5
scenery	A
water	Good
gradient	12.25
latitude	35 40.637N
longitude	93 14.114W

FORT DOUGLAS (AR 123 BRIDGE) TO HELTON'S FARM

DESCRIPTION: This is another remote section of the Big Piney that is seldom paddled but deserves your attention. The shuttle is a bit easier from here but still very long.
    This section is known as a canoe-camping destination.

SHUTTLE: From the put-in at Fort Douglas, the take-out is reached by going east 6.5 miles on AR 123 and turning south (right) on FR 1802. Go south 3.2 miles on FR 1802 and bear south (left) on FR 1805. Go 5.7 miles on FR 1805 to FR 1005 and turn west (right). Go 0.7 mile to Helton's Farm. Be sure to stop and make a small donation for passage to the river.

GAUGE: USGS Big Piney at AR 164 near Dover.
Minimum: 3.0 *Optimum:* 3.5–5.0 *Dangerous:* >6.0

HELTON'S FARM TO LONGPOOL CAMPGROUND

difficulty	II—II+ (III)
distance	10.5
time	5
gauge	Big Piney (USGS)
level	2
scenery	AA
water	Good
gradient	10.6
latitude	35 37.074N
longitude	93 11.059W

DESCRIPTION: The first few hundred yards below the put-in are tight and twist through a narrow passage. It is common for trees to block your route, so be careful and scout if you are not sure.

Below Indian Creek, The Ledge extends across the channel. At levels of 3.75 feet and above, beware of hydraulics that form along parts of the ledge. Experienced paddlers can surf this ledge on river left.

There are several class II rapids in the next 1.5 miles before the creek turns to the right into a calm pool. Notice the house-sized boulders on river left; they mark the approach to Birthday, or 1-2-3 Surprise Rapid. The creek is constricted to one-third its normal size by willows on the right and a bluff on river left, creating an extremely swift current with high, irregular waves. Near the bottom of the rapid, strong crosscurrents tend to push the unsuspecting paddler into very dangerous willow trees. Many boats have been pinned here.

A short pool follows, then the creek is constricted again. Several boulders dot the channel in this short-but-fun section. Holes form behind the boulders at higher levels, creating many

interesting play spots. There are several additional class II rapids in the next 1.5 miles before paddlers encounter the Roller Coaster, a class III rapid. The standing waves, which can approach 4 feet provided the river level exceeds that, can be fun to run if you have adequate floatation, but they can be disastrous if you do not. Open and decked boats can surf the waves again and again by using the eddy on river left to return to the top of the rapid.

Surfing Rapid, a class II rapid 2 miles below the Roller Coaster, is an excellent place to "play the hole." The hydraulic that forms will hold both open and decked boats and is good for pop-ups.

Immediately upon leaving Surfing Rapid, one can see a large bluff on river left with a formation known as the Turtlehead. There actually appears to be a huge stone sculpture of a turtle's head in the bluff. This marks the approach to the Cascades of Extinction, also know as the Devil's Elbow and the Mother.

The Cascades of Extinction is a long class III rapid that you should scout before running. Approach on the inside of the bend on river right. Immediately after rounding the bend, the rock known as the Little Mother comes into view. Paddlers must decide to go right or left of the Little Mother. The right route is a straight run, requiring only control of the boat. The left route requires that you drop over a ledge and make a quick right turn to avoid the Big Mother, a house-sized boulder in the current. Eddy right or left immediately to avoid having to negotiate the Sisters, three boulders in mid-stream, with a boat full of water.

The remainder of the run to Longpool is class II, with one bad willow jungle to negotiate. The Forest Service has provided an excellent take-out on river left near the Longpool picnic area. There are also changing rooms with hot showers. There is a nominal day-use fee that you need to pay. If you don't, you will get a ticket!

SHUTTLE: From Russellville, Arkansas, to reach Longpool Campground go north on AR 7 for 6.9 miles to Dover, Arkansas. Continue north on AR 7 for 5.5 miles to AR 164. Turn left (west) on proceed 3.5 miles to Old AR 7 Highway and turn right (north). Go north 2.7 miles and bear left on Longpool Road. Proceed 2 miles to Longpool Campground.

To reach the put-in at Helton's farm from Longpool Campground, go southeast on Longpool Road 2.2 miles to FR 1805. Go north (left) 9.6 miles on FR 1805 and turn west (left) on FR 1005. Go west 1.3 miles to Helton's Farm. Put-in via the pasture road after paying a nominal access fee at the farmhouse.

GAUGE: USGS Big Piney at AR 164 near Dover.
Minimum: 2.0 Optimum: 2.5–4.5 Dangerous: >5.0

LONGPOOL CAMPGROUND TO TWIN BRIDGES

difficulty	II
distance	4.5
time	3
gauge	Big Piney (USGS)
level	2.0
scenery	A
water	Good
gradient	10
latitude	35 33.024N
longitude	93 9.713W

DESCRIPTION: Big Piney Creek splits around an island below Longpool Campground. The left chute is a straight run with minimum difficulty. The right chute is boulder-strewn and requires the ability to use eddies effectively and backferry with confidence. Take the left chute if there is any question about your abilities!

There are many class II rapids in this section. Unfortunately, some of the best-named rapids have disappeared due to the changing streambed.

Two miles downstream of Longpool, paddlers encounter a sharp bend to river left at Leola's Roost. Strong currents can push an unsuspecting paddler into dangerous willows on the outside of the bend.

Below Leola's Roost 1.2 miles, paddlers encounter a willow jungle as the river turns right into a narrow passage. The currents are always unpredictable in this section, and downed trees are a constant problem. Use extreme caution in this section.

Take-out on river left just downstream of the AR 164 bridge at Moore Outdoors. They charge a nominal fee to park.

SHUTTLE: To reach the take-out from the put-in at Longpool, head southeast on Longpool Road 5.2 miles to AR 164 and turn west (right). Go west on AR 164 for 0.6 mile to the Moore Outdoors' take-out at the bridge over Big Piney. Make sure you stop at Moore Outdoors at the junction of FR 1805 and AR 164 and pay a nominal fee to use their take-out at the AR 164 bridge. Moore Outdoors can be very helpful with river levels and information about the area. Visit http://www.mooreoutdoors.com or call (479) 331-3606.

GAUGE: USGS Big Piney at AR 164 near Dover.
Minimum: 2.0 Optimum: 2.5–4.5 Dangerous: >5.0

BUFFALO NATIONAL RIVER

The Buffalo River begins as a tiny stream in the Boston Mountains on the north side of AR 16 near Fallsville, Arkansas, and flows approximately 140 miles to its confluence with the White River. Its entire length is protected by its own unique legislation, hence its name as the nation's only "National River." It is one of the most popular streams in the nation, and during the months of March through October, thousands of canoeists paddle the thrilling, fast water of the upper stretches and the placid pools of the middle and lower Buffalo River.

The river is surrounded by some of the most awe-inspiring bluffs in the country and by hardwood forests, which obscure the surrounding farmland. This gives the paddler a feeling of remoteness more intense than on most other rivers in the area. The milky green water that is unique to the Ozarks characterizes the Buffalo's entire length.

The Buffalo and the adjoining property are administered by the National Park Service (NPS). Along its length, the Park Service has developed and maintains facilities and improvements that enhance the experience of paddling the river: convenient access points, camping facilities, well-maintained gravel access roads, and well-marked hiking trails.

Canoeing begins at the AR 74 low-water bridge in Ponca, except in periods of high runoff when paddlers may put-in 6 miles upriver at Boxley.

The upper stretches—from Boxley to Kyle's Landing—are very sensitive to water levels and contain rapids of class II difficulty at optimum levels. These sections should be attempted only by paddlers familiar with basic river-canoeing skills.

MAPS: Fallsville, Boxley, Osage SW, Ponca, Jasper, Hasty, Mt. Judea, Western Grove, Eula, Snowball, Marshall, Maumee, Cozahome, Rhea Valley, Big Flat, Buffalo City (USGS); Newton, Searcy, Marion (County)

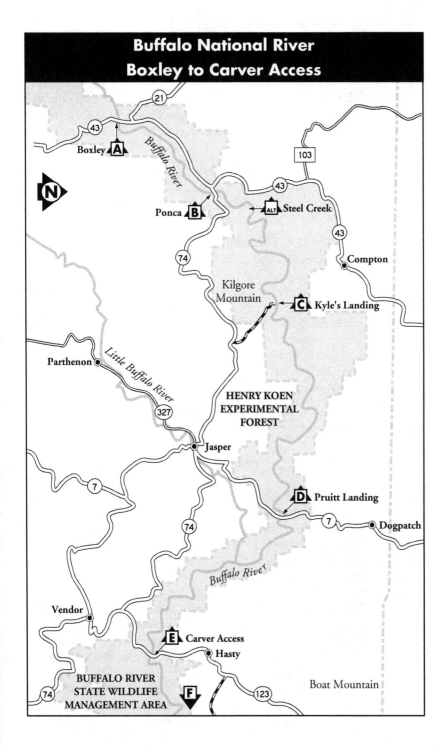

Buffalo National River
Boxley to Carver Access

difficulty	I–II
distance	6
time	2.5
gauge	Buffalo (USGS)
level	5.6
scenery	AA
water	Good
gradient	13
latitude	35 57.655N
longitude	93 24,27 4W

BOXLEY TO PONCA

DESCRIPTION: Paddlers can expect to find many sharp turns and willow jungles that will tax their ferrying skills. This section is generally class II, but approaches class III difficulty at very high levels.

SHUTTLE: Put-in at the Boxley Bridge on AR 21. The take-out is reached by taking AR 21 northeast for 0.3 mile to the intersection with AR 43. Go 4.5 miles right (northeast) on AR 43 and turn right on the small gravel road that leads to the Ponca access.

GAUGE: USGS Buffalo near Boxley, Arkansas. Online at http://waterdata.usgs.gov/nwis/uv/?site_no=07055646. Or the Buffalo National River Hydrologic System; online at www. buffaloriverandrain.com. The latter is an excellent web resource maintained by the Park Service. It includes information on river levels, recent rainfall, and recommended floating levels. Explore the many resources on this site before planning your trip. There are four distinct gauges that are used for water levels and each is completely independent of the other.

Minimum: 3.5 Optimum: 4.0–6.0 Dangerous: >7.0

difficulty	I–II
distance	10.1
time	5
gauge	Buffalo (USGS)
level	2.5
scenery	AA+
water	Good
gradient	12.6
latitude	36 1.276N
longitude	93 21.281W

PONCA TO KYLE'S LANDING

DESCRIPTION: About 2.5 river miles below Ponca, the NPS has added a new campground and access point at Steel Creek. The Park Service encourages paddlers to start their upper-river trips here to ease some of the congestion at Ponca. A good compromise is to camp at Steel Creek and put-in at Ponca. The logistics are a little more difficult, but it's worth the effort.

The Buffalo is most famous for its towering multicolored bluffs. After departing from Ponca, paddlers are rewarded almost immediately with Roark Bluff, and 2 miles below Steel Creek is Big Bluff, which rises 500 feet above the river. The Goat Trail along the face of Big Bluff is an exciting side trip hike for the more adventuresome.

Five miles from Steel Creek is Hemmed-in-Hollow, a box canyon with a spectacular 200-foot waterfall—a side trip of less than a mile that is a must for all paddlers.

A short distance above Kyle's Landing, the river bends left from a quiet pool and enters the 150-yard Grey Rock Shoals. High standing waves at optimum water levels and shoal water in the troughs may have you scraping bottom. Be careful. The shoals terminate at Grey Rock, protruding from river left with most of the current crashing into it. It is easy to avoid Grey Rock by staying to the right (a good backferry will help). Ignore the false instructions being shouted by the crowds gathered there hoping to encourage upsets.

SHUTTLE: To reach Steele Creek from the put-in at Ponca, take AR 74 northeast for 1.2 miles and turn north (left) on Steele Creek Road. Go 1.4 miles to the camping and river access. From Ponca, to reach the take-out at Kyle's Landing follow AR 74 9.3 miles to Kyle's Landing Road and turn north (left). Go 2.3 miles to the access at Kyle's Landing. The road conditions can be difficult when the weather is inclement.

GAUGE: USGS Buffalo near Boxley.
Minimum: 2.5 Optimum: 3.0–5.5 Dangerous: >6.0

KYLE'S LANDING TO PRUITT

difficulty	I–II
distance	13.5
time	6.5
gauge	Buffalo (USGS)
level	2.5
scenery	AA+
water	Good
gradient	8.1
latitude	36 3.255N
longitude	93 17.107W

DESCRIPTION: Erbie Ford is about 5.2 miles below Kyle's Landing. It should be approached and run with caution due to variations in water flow. Although there is an access here, the NPS in 1986–1987 completed a larger, newer access and campground about a mile downstream. In sight of and immediately above this access on river right is what may be the world's greatest lunch stop for paddlers. Besides a huge flat rock to spread edibles, there is also a super-playable chute that even has surfing possibilities at optimum levels.

Paddlers have a choice of take-outs. The first is on river right at Ozark, a fine camping area 1 mile above Pruitt. The second is on river left, just below the AR 7 bridge at Pruitt. A Park Service information center is located above the bridge, on river right, at Pruitt.

SHUTTLE: To reach the take-out at Ozark from the put-in, go southeast on Kyle's Landing Road for 2.3 miles and turn left on AR 74. Go east for 5 miles on AR 74 and turn northeast (left) on AR 7. Go 3.9 miles to the Ozark turnoff, turn left, and continue 1.6 miles to the campground and access. To reach Pruitt, follow

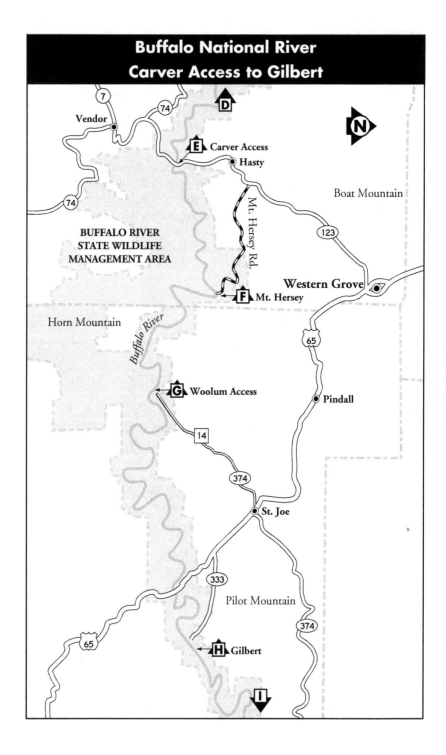

Buffalo National River
Carver Access to Gilbert

Vendor

Carver Access

Hasty

Boat Mountain

Mt. Hersey Rd.

BUFFALO RIVER
STATE WILDLIFE
MANAGEMENT AREA

Western Grove

Mt. Hersey

Horn Mountain

Buffalo River

Woolum Access

Pindall

St. Joe

Pilot Mountain

Gilbert

the same directions but continue for 1.6 miles beyond the Ozark turn to Pruitt. Follow the signs to the campground and landing.

GAUGE: USGS Buffalo near Boxley.
Minimum: 2.5 Optimum: 3.5–5.5 Dangerous: >6.0

PRUITT (AR 7) TO CARVER

DESCRIPTION: Paddlers can expect to find pools separated by shoals and willow runs on this stretch of the Buffalo. There are also several nice bluffs along this section of the river.

Approximately 4 miles below Pruitt, the Little Buffalo River enters on river right. Seven miles below the Pruitt Bridge Riggs, Bluff appears on river left. As you approach, look carefully up the wooded hill at the upper end of the bluff. About 200 feet from the river is Chimney Hole, a natural bridge that rewards a short walk with some fine photography possibilities.

John Eddings Cave is on river right just above the take-out at AR 123. Unfortunately, the cave is closed to the public.

difficulty	I–II
distance	11.3
time	6
gauge	Buffalo (USGS)
level	1
scenery	AA
water	Good
gradient	3.3
latitude	36 3.668N
longitude	93 8.273W

SHUTTLE: From the put-in at Pruitt, go 5.6 miles southwest on AR 7 to Jasper. Turn southeast (left) on AR 74 and go 9.9 miles to AR 123. Turn left and continue 2.5 miles to the Carver access.

GAUGE: Buffalo National River Hydrologic System, Pruitt Gauge. See section A above.
Minimum: 1.0 Optimum: 1.5–2.75 Dangerous: >3.0

CARVER TO MT. HERSEY

DESCRIPTION: There are no major difficulties along this stretch, but wildlife and good scenery abound.

SHUTTLE: To reach the take-out at Mt. Hersey from Carver, head north on AR 123 4 miles to Mt. Hersey Road. Turn east (right) and go 5.8 miles, then turn right again at the Mt. Hersey access.

difficulty	I
distance	7
time	4
gauge	Pruitt (BNRHS)
level	1
scenery	A
water	Good
gradient	4
latitude	35 59.019N
longitude	93 2.605W

GAUGE: Buffalo National River Hydrologic System, Pruitt Gauge. See section A above.
Minimum: 1.0 Optimum: 1.5–2.75 Dangerous: >3.0

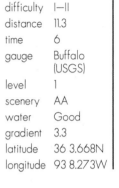

difficulty	I
distance	10.5
time	5
gauge	Pruitt (BNRHS)
level	1
scenery	AA
water	Good
gradient	5.8
latitude	36 0.542N
longitude	921 57.158W

MT. HERSEY TO WOOLUM

DESCRIPTION: The Nars (Narrows) is approximately 8 miles from Mount Hersey. This unusual bluff was formed by Richland Creek and the Buffalo River, which wore away the rock over millions of years but never quite destroyed the last saddle-backed, 4-foot wide dividing bluff. A long gravel bar provides an excellent place to camp and explore the Nars. If you hike the trail that extends up the backbone of the bluff, you will be treated to spectacular views of the Buffalo River and Richland Valley.

Skull Bluff is just downstream of the Nars. This bluff has several cavities at water level that make it look like a skull. At low to moderate water levels, one can paddle into the skull.

SHUTTLE: To reach the take-out at Woolrum from the put-in at Mt. Hersey, head 1.3 miles northeast on Mt. Hersey Road to CR 21. Take CR 21 for 3.8 miles north (left) to US 65. Go east (right) on US 65 for 8.4 miles to CR 18. Turn southwest (right) on CR 18, go 1.4 miles, and turn right on CR 14. Go 6 miles on CR 14 to Woolum.

GAUGE: Buffalo National River Hydrologic System, Pruitt Gauge. See section A above.
Minimum: 1.0 *Optimum:* 1.5–2.75 *Dangerous:* >3.0

difficulty	I
distance	20.7
time	11
gauge	Pruitt (BNRHS)
level	1
scenery	A
water	Good
gradient	2.7
latitude	35 58.210N
longitude	92 53.226W

WOOLUM TO GILBERT

DESCRIPTION: The late Jim Raymond of the Bluff City Canoe Club claimed that one of the best camping spots on the Buffalo lies just downstream of the Woolum access on river left. The campsite is sheltered under a group of trees where the river takes a sharp bend to the left—providing a great place to bodysurf the rapid. He was probably right.

There is a take-out used by outfitters at Baker Creek Ford, approximately 11 miles from Woolum. The Park Service maintains an information board at the access but does not list it in any NPS literature. It is a good place to camp with relatively easy access from St. Joe via AR 374. When the road turns from gravel

to blacktop after you leave US 65, go one-quarter mile, turn left on a gravel road, and proceed to the river. You will pass through two cattle gates. Always close these gates behind you.

The US 65 access can be used to shorten this trip by approximately 4 miles. Below US 65, the river makes a large bend to the north and you will encounter some beautiful scenery on the river.

A must stop is at Baker General store near the take-out at Gilbert. The general store has a little of everything, including some very interesting antiques. Gilbert is also famous for registering Arkansas's coldest temperatures during the winter. If the folks at the store have time, ask to see their photographs of the 1982 flood. You may not believe what you see!

SHUTTLE: To reach Gilbert starting at St. Joe, Arkansas, go 3.2 miles southeast on US 65 and turn left on SR 333. Go 3.5 miles on SR 333 to the Gilbert access.

GAUGE: Buffalo National River Hydrologic System, Pruitt Gauge. See section A above.
   Minimum: 1.0 *Optimum:* 1.5–2.5 *Dangerous:* >3.0

GILBERT TO BUFFALO POINT

difficulty	I
distance	23
time	12
gauge	US 65 (BNRHS)
level	3.5
scenery	A
water	Good
gradient	4.2
latitude	35 59.335N
longitude	92 42.784W

DESCRIPTION: To shorten the length of this section by approximately half (or to extend its predecessor), use the South Maumee access, on river right, 12 miles downriver from Gilbert. To get there, take AR 27 north from Marshall for 3.5 miles to Morning Star, Arkansas. Turn left and proceed 6 miles to the river.

AR14 crosses the Buffalo River just above Buffalo Point and can be used as an access. This is a nice place for someone who would like to try canoeing on the short 1.5-mile float to Buffalo Point.

SHUTTLE: To reach the take-out from Marshall, go east on AR 27 for 10.8 miles to Harriet, Arkansas, and turn northwest on AR 14. Go northwest for 9.5 miles, then turn east on SR 268. Go east on SR 268 for 2.3 miles to Buffalo River State Park.

GAUGE: Buffalo National River Hydrologic System, US 65 gauge.
   Minimum: 3.0 *Optimum:* 5.0–10.0 *Dangerous:* >12.0

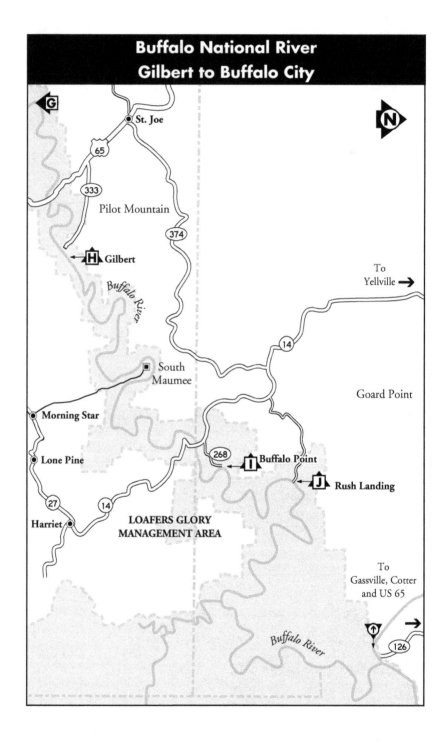

Buffalo National River
Gilbert to Buffalo City

G

St. Joe

65

333

Pilot Mountain

374

H Gilbert

To
Yellville →

Buffalo River

14

South
Maumee

Goard Point

Morning Star

Lone Pine

268 I Buffalo Point

J Rush Landing

27

14

Harriet

LOAFERS GLORY
MANAGEMENT AREA

To
Gassville, Cotter
and US 65

Buffalo River

126

N

BUFFALO POINT TO RUSH LANDING

difficulty	I
distance	7.5
time	4
gauge	Buffalo Point (BNRHS)
level	3.5
scenery	A
water	Good
gradient	2
latitude	36 4.680N
longitude	92 33.599W

DESCRIPTION: This long flatwater section has some of the most spectacular scenery to be found along the Buffalo River.

SHUTTLE: To reach the take-out at Rush Landing from Buffalo River State Park, go 2.4 miles west on SR 268 to AR 14 and turn north (right). Go 2.7 miles on AR 14 and turn east (right) on CR 26. Continue 8.5 miles to Rush Landing.

GAUGE: Buffalo National River Hydrologic System, AR 14 bridge, Buffalo Point. See section A above.
Minimum: 3.0 *Optimum:* 5.0–9.0 *Dangerous:* >10.0

RUSH LANDING TO BUFFALO CITY

difficulty	I
distance	23
time	12
gauge	Buffalo Point (BNRHS)
level	3.5
scenery	AA
water	Good
gradient	2
latitude	36 7.518N
longitude	92 32.891W

DESCRIPTION: This stretch should be considered a two-day trip because of the distance involved.

The Buffalo River ends its long free-flowing course in Buffalo City, where it flows into the White River. The Buffalo City take-out is on the opposite bank of the White River and boaters must paddle upstream for a short distance to reach the take-out. This can be a serious workout when the White River is running high, as it frequently is due to power generation at Bull Shoals Dam.

SHUTTLE: To reach the take-out at Buffalo City from the Rush Landing put-in, go 1.9 miles west on CR 26 to AR 14 and turn north (right). Go north on AR 14 for 11.7 to Yellville, Arkansas. Turn east (right) on US 62/412 and go east 14.2 miles to Gassville, Arkansas. Turn right on Bueford Road, go 2.3 miles to CR 4, and turn right. Go 0.9 mile to CR 3 to then bear left for 1.3 miles to CR 624. After 1.4 miles on CR 624, turn south (right) on AR 126. Go 6.8 miles on AR 126 to Buffalo City.

GAUGE: Buffalo National River Hydrologic System, AR 14 Bridge, Buffalo Point.
Minimum: 3.0 *Optimum:* 5.0–9.0 *Dangerous:* >10.0

CROOKED CREEK

Crooked Creek rises south of Harrison, Arkansas, and runs alongside AR 7, flowing through Harrison before heading east. It then parallels AR 62 until it flows into the Buffalo National River. It lives up to its name, twisting and turning constantly along its course. Crooked Creek is known more for smallmouth-bass fishing than for canoeing, but canoeists can combine fishing and paddling for a very scenic trip through the Ozarks.

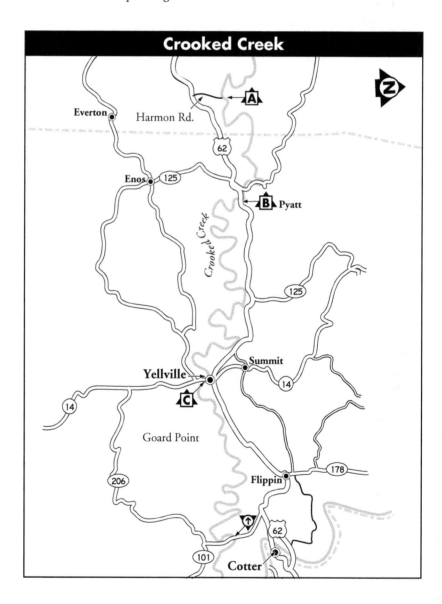

Paddlers can expect a mild stream protected by tree-lined banks—studded in oak, pecan, and elm—that make the stream seem secluded. Water quality is good upstream of Harrison but declines downstream from Harrison due to small amounts of pollution that enter the stream from the city.

MAPS: Harrison, Bergman, Zinc, Everton, Pyatt, Bruno, Yellville, Rea Valley, Buffalo City (USGS); Boone, Marion (County)

HARMAN TO PYATT

difficulty	I (II)
distance	9.6
time	4–5
gauge	Crooked Creek (USGS)
level	3.5
scenery	A-B
water	Good
gradient	11
latitude	36 14.026N
longitude	92 55.335W

DESCRIPTION: There are no major difficulties along this stream, but be careful of willows and downed trees.

SHUTTLE: To reach the put-in from Harrison, go east on US 62 11.1 miles to Harman, Arkansas. Turn north (left) on Harmon Road and go 1.8 miles to Crooked Creek. To reach the take-out, backtrack 1.8 miles on Harmon Road to US 62 and go east (left) 5.9 miles to the US 62 bridge at Pyatt, Arkansas.

GAUGE: USGS Crooked Creek, near Yellville, Arkansas. On-line at http://waterdata.usgs.gov/ar/nwis/uv/?site_no=07055608&PARAmeter_cd=00065,00060.
Minimum: 3.5 Optimum: 4.0–5.0 Dangerous: >6.0

Photo by Mike Coogan

difficulty	I
distance	22
time	14
gauge	Crooked Creek (USGS)
level	3.5
scenery	A
water	Good
gradient	7.7
latitude	36 14.757N
longitude	92 50.096W

PYATT TO YELLVILLE

DESCRIPTION: Because of the distance involved in this section, plan an overnight trip with all the requisite gear. There are no public access points between the put-in and the take-out.

You should be aware that Crooked Creek can rise rapidly from flash floods or prolonged rain and can be very dangerous. Choose a campsite well above the high-water line.

SHUTTLE: The take-out is 10.3 miles east of the put-in on US 62, then south on AR 14 for 0.8 mile.

GAUGE: USGS Crooked Creek, near Yellville, Arkansas. *Minimum: 3.5 Optimum: 4.0–5.0 Dangerous: >6.0*

difficulty	I
distance	16.6
time	9
gauge	Crooked Creek (USGS)
level	3.5
scenery	A
water	Good
gradient	5.3
latitude	36 13.381N
longitude	92 40.796W

YELLVILLE TO AR 101

DESCRIPTION: AR 101 is the last take-out before Crooked Creek enters the White River. When the creek is up, many fishermen motor up Crooked Creek in pursuit of the smallmouth bass for which it is famous. If you miss the take-out, your next chance is Buffalo City on the White River.

SHUTTLE: The take-out is 8.9 miles east on US 62 and 2.3 miles south (right) on AR 101 to Crooked Creek.

GAUGE: USGS Crooked Creek, near Yellville, Arkansas. *Minimum: 3.5 Optimum: 4.0–5.0 Dangerous: >6.0*

EAST FORK OF THE ILLINOIS BAYOU

The headwaters of the East Fork of the Illinois Bayou are south of AR 16 on the southern slope of Walker Mountain. The stream flows through the East Fork Wilderness Area, which was established by Congress in 1984. The 10,688-acre wilderness protects the East Fork of the Illinois Bayou from development and ensures pristine stream quality. Wilderness areas like the East Fork play an important role in achieving the Forest Service's stated mission: "to secure for the American people of present and future generations the benefits of an enduring resource of wilderness." The Forest Service requires everyone to practice "leave no trace" principles when enjoying the East Fork Wilderness.

Paddlers can expect a class II–II+ stream with rocky shoals, willow jungles, and scenic bluffs. The main hazard is downed trees that block your passage. Remember to scout ahead if your route is not clear.

MAPS: Lost Corner, Solo (USGS); Pope (County)

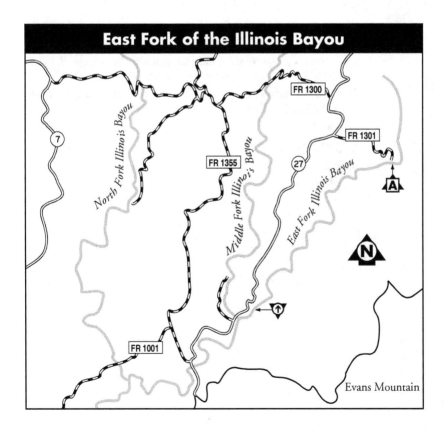

East Fork of the Illinois Bayou

difficulty	II—II+
distance	10
time	5-6
gauge	Illinois Bayou (USGS)
level	6.5
scenery	A
water	Good
gradient	28
latitude	35 36.395N
longitude	92 50.352W

FR1301 to Lindsey Mountain Way Road

DESCRIPTION: This is a long, isolated stretch without access between the put-in and take-out. The isolation and difficulty of rescue always add to the classification of a stream. Plan ahead and make sure you have the proper number of boats for safety.

Good gradient, willows, and rocky shoals characterize this stream. Higher water levels increase the size of waves in its rapids and the danger presented by willow jungles. Water quality is excellent due to the East Fork Wilderness's protected status.

Few paddlers run this section due to the popularity of the Middle Fork of the Illinois Bayou, just west on AR 27, but give it a try when you are in the area.

The take-out is just upstream from the confluence of the Middle and East Fork of the Illinois Bayou. Camping is available at the Forest Service's Bayou Bluff Campground.

SHUTTLE: To reach the put-in from Hector, Arkansas, go north 15.7 miles on AR 27 and turn east (right) on White Oak Mountain Road. Continue southeast 4.6 miles to the access. To reach the take-out from Hector, go north 6.9 miles on AR 27 to the first road (Lindsey Mountain Way) on the right past the bridge over the Middle Fork of the Illinois Bayou. Follow it 0.4 mile east to the access.

GAUGE: USGS Illinois Bayou near Scottsville, Arkansas. Online at http://waterdata.usgs.gov/nwis/uv/?site_no=07257500
Minimum: 6.5 *Optimum:* 7.0–9.0 *Dangerous:* >10.0

FALLING WATER CREEK

Falling Water Creek originates on the north side of Raspberry Mountain just north of AR 16 and flows approximately 11 miles to its confluence with Richland Creek at Richland Creek Campground. Forest Roads 1313 and 1205 parallel the creek for most of the way, pro-viding numerous access points. The narrow creek is runnable only during periods of high runoff, and a visual inspection is usually necessary. The run itself is very tight and technical and more suited to smaller boats.

Falling Water Creek is a very swift stream that races through the Ozark National Forest, with tree-lined banks on one side and FR 1205 on the other. Several tight turns that take paddlers under overhanging trees can be particularly difficult. Water quality is very good due to the protected status of Ozark National Forest and the remoteness of the area. Access becomes a little more difficult along the last 3 miles, when the road veers slightly away from the creek. On one particular trip, a group of paddlers from the Bluff City Canoe Club challenged the creek in the snow and returned to report that it was like paddling through their own private winter wonderland. Another group of paddlers from the Arkansas Canoe Club had less appreciative things to say when a snowstorm stranded them in the valley overnight until four-wheel-drive vehicles could be dispatched. Road and weather conditions are indeed a significant factor when planning a trip to Falling Water Creek.

MAPS: Smyrna, Moore (USGS); Pope, Searcy (County)

FR 1205 TO RICHLAND CREEK CAMPGROUND

difficulty	II–III+
distance	6.67
time	3.5
gauge	Richland (USGS)
level	4
scenery	AA
water	Excellent
gradient	46
latitude	35 43.336N
longitude	92 56.955W

DESCRIPTION: Put-in just below Falling Water Falls unless you want the excitement of running the falls, a drop of at least 10 feet. The falls are usually runnable in the middle, but watch out for the tree directly below the recovery pool. Expect a very narrow course for the first 3 miles of the run, with numerous technical rapids. Strainers are a constant concern in this section.

The creek crosses FR 1205 about 3 miles from the put-in and enters Richland Creek Wilderness Area. The road is very inconspicuous but never more than one-quarter mile away on river right. The difficulty of the creek increases from the bridge to Richland Creek Campground due to the distance from the road.

SHUTTLE: To reach the put-in from AR 16, take FR 1205 south for 6.75 to Falling Water Falls. Put-in below the falls. The take-

out is located at Richland Creek Campground, just downstream of the confluence of Falling Water and Richland Creeks on river right at the parking access.

GAUGE: USGS Richland Creek near Witt Springs, Arkansas. Online at http://waterdata.usgs.gov/nwis/uv/?site_no=07055875
Minimum: 4.0 *Optimum:* 5.0 *Dangerous:* >6.5

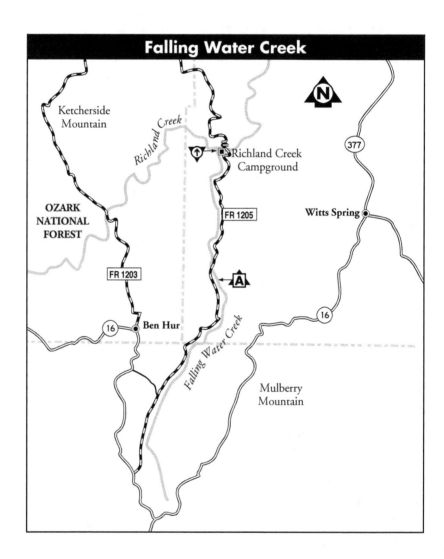

Falling Water Creek

Ketcherside Mountain

Richland Creek

Richland Creek Campground

377

OZARK NATIONAL FOREST

FR 1205

Witts Spring

FR 1203

A

16

16   Ben Hur

Falling Water Creek

Mulberry Mountain

HAILSTONE RIVER

Hailstone River is a code name for the upper 16 miles of the Buffalo River above Boxley, Arkansas. Many years ago it was considered too difficult for most paddlers, and the name Hailstone was devised to protect the identity of this class III+ jewel. The headwaters of the Buffalo are formed by the combination of Reeves Fork and Big Buffalo Creek near Fallsville, Arkansas, at an elevation of 1,640 feet. This area is currently under consideration for protection under the Wild and Scenic Rivers Act and certainly is a prime candidate due to the remoteness and beauty of the surrounding area. The river drops an average of 38.5 feet per mile, with some sections approaching 45 feet per mile. This is not a river for novice paddlers. One should be a competent class III boater paddling a canoe filled with flotation or decked because of the difficulty of rescue in this section of the river.

The ride down the shuttle road lets you know that this is no ordinary river. At the bottom, you are in one of the most remote wilderness gorges in the United States. Civilization is nonexistent for the next 14 miles. This run places you alone with nature at its best. The swift current takes you through short pools separated by steep drops that leave little time to enjoy the hardwood-lined canyon walls. Waterfalls cascade to the canyon floor, keeping the many native plants well nourished. Be sure to stop and enjoy this incredible beauty.

MAPS: Fallsville, Boxley (USGS); Newton (County)

FR 1463 TO BOXLEY

difficulty	III—III+(IV)
distance	13.34
time	7
gauge	Buffalo (USGS)
level	10" airspace
scenery	AA+
water	Excellent
gradient	41
latitude	35 49.374N
longitude	93 27.825W

DESCRIPTION: Paddlers are introduced to this small, pristine stream by many class II rapids in its first 2 miles.

Approximately 2 miles below the put-in, paddlers encounter Double Drop, an exciting class III rapid. The first drop is constricted by a large boulder that blocks the entire channel except for a small slot on river left. Drop through the slot and turn 90° over a second drop into a recovery pool below.

Class II and III rapids follow for about 2 miles to the confluence with Terrapin Branch on river right.

Approximately 3.5 miles below Terrapin Branch, Whitaker Hollow is on river left. Bluffs 700 feet high constrict the river valley on both sides. Here the intense rapids begin.

Keyhole Rapid (class III) is one-half mile below Whitaker Hollow. Rocks push the river to the left through a slot and into the left bank.

Numerous pool-drop rapids follow for the next few miles before paddlers encounter Deliverance Falls, a blind drop through boulders on river left. Class III rapids follow until the river is again blocked by a boulder with a route on river left.

The river valley begins to widen and the rapids become less numerous as you near the take-out at Boxley.

SHUTTLE: From Fallsville, the put-in is reached by going east on AR 16 for approximately 1.4 miles to FR 1463, which is just beyond Sullivan Cemetery on the north side of the road. Follow FR 1463 north for 3 miles to the river. From Fallsville, the take-out is reached by going northeast for 8.7 miles to AR 21 and turning left (north). Go 10.8 miles on AR 21 to the Boxley Bridge.

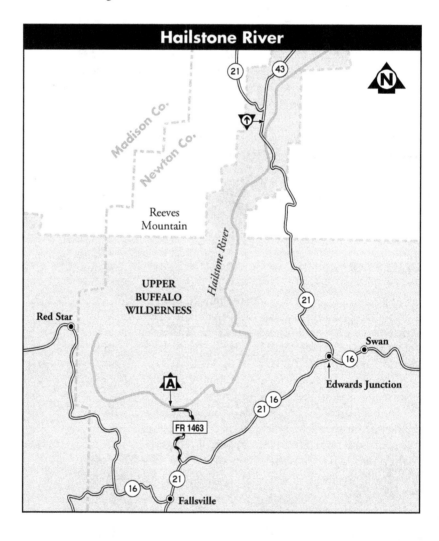

GAUGE: USGS Buffalo near Boxley, Arkansas. Online at http://waterdata.usgs.gov/nwis/uv/?site_no=07055646.

Minimum: 4.8 *Optimum:* 5.0–5.8 *Dangerous:* >6.0

The low-water bridge at Ponca is also used to determine water levels. Judging the amount of airspace below the bridge is the method of measurement.

Minimum: 10" *Optimum:* 0"–5" *Dangerous:* 12"

The Buffalo Outdoor Center at Ponca, which can provide helpful information on water levels, can be reached by calling (800) 221-5514. Buffalo River gauges are online at http://www.ozarkpages.com/whitewater/nps_buf_rain.html.

HURRICANE CREEK

Hurricane Creek begins near the community of Deer, Arkansas, and flows southwest for 18.5 miles to its confluence with Big Piney Creek just north of Fort Douglas. The creek flows through the Hurricane Creek Wilderness, and there is no access below Chancel. The scenery along the creek is some of the best in the state. Paddlers can expect a stream that is a step up from the Big Piney but not as challenging as Richland Creek. Willow jungles and strainers must be contended with, so competent boat control is a prerequisite for running Hurricane Creek. If you have any doubts about your ability to catch eddies and backferry, do not attempt this creek.

MAPS: Chancel, Fort Douglas (USGS); Newton, Pope (County)

difficulty	II–III+
distance	10.2
time	5
gauge	Big Piney (USGS), Deer rain guage
gauge level	5
scenery	AA
water	Good
gradient	33.33
latitude	35 46.082N
longitude	95 8.727W

CHANCEL TO FORT DOUGLAS

DESCRIPTION: Put-in on Cub Creek and paddle approximately 500 feet to its confluence with Hurricane Creek. In the first 4.5 miles, paddlers encounter sporty class II–II+ rapids and some of the best scenery to be found in Arkansas. Umbrella magnolia trees stand amongst the other hardwoods, and pines dot the banks in this section. Downed trees present an ever-changing problem in this section. Make sure your route is clear and scout blind turns.

The next 3.5 miles of the creek are the canyon section of this run. There are eight major rapids in this section. Two rapids approach class IV, five rapids are class III, and the remainder are class II–III in difficulty.

Entrance Rapid marks the beginning of the canyon stretch. This class II drop makes a dogleg turn to the left with a large boulder on river right.

Boulder Garden, a long class III rapid is just downstream as the creek turns to the right. Large boulders line the creek on river left, and steep banks on river right constrict the creek and increase the flow. At moderate levels, there are many eddies in this rapid, but the course is pretty straight. Midway through this run is a house-sized boulder on river left.

Double Drop is next as the creek flows over two drops very quickly. Higher levels tend to make this one long rapid with huge waves.

A short pool below Double Drop allows paddlers to prepare for the next set of exciting rapids. When you see a pyramid-shaped rock in midstream, take the right route through Pyramid Rapid. The course is hard to see until you have dropped into this

rapid and are committed to the run. Huge boulders on both river left and right constrict the creek to less than 15 feet near the bottom of this run. At high flows, Pyramid Rapid approaches class IV in difficulty.

"Uh Oh" Rapid, just below, is a sporty class II drop. Huge boulders dot the entire creek. Approach "Uh Oh" in the center of the creek, drop over the first small ledge, and follow the current to the left between boulders and then slightly right, away from the waves piling up on boulders to the left.

The Squeeze is just below "Uh Oh." Huge boulders completely block the creek except on river left. The entire creek is squeezed to one-third its normal width.

Drop Baby Drop is not far below. The creek drops 8 feet in a span of less than 90 feet, and a huge rock outcropping on river right constricts the creek at the bottom of this drop.

The Roller Coaster is the last major rapid before the take-out. At medium to high levels, the waves are reminiscent of Table Saw Rapid on the Ocoee.

The final 2.2 miles offer more class II rapids and great scenery. Take-out just before the confluence with Big Piney Creek on river left where the road fords the creek.

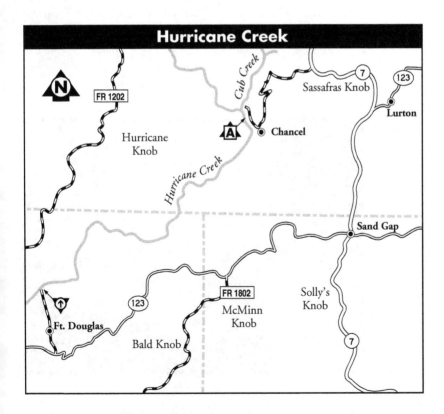

SHUTTLE: To reach the put-in from Pelsor, Arkansas, go north on AR 7 for 6 miles to Hurricane Trail Road (GPS: latitude 34 46.994N, longitude 93 6.779W). Turn west onto Hurricane Trail just before the "Who'd a Thought It" gift shop. Proceed 500 feet and bear right on Hurricane Trail Road 3.27 miles from the highway. Bear right along the creek, and put-in at the low-water bridge on Cub Creek. To reach the take-out from Pelsor, Arkansas, go west on AR 123 for 10.7 miles to the bridge at Big Piney Creek. Take the gravel road on the east side of the bridge north (right) for 1.8 miles, then park at the pull-out on the left just before Hurricane Creek.

GAUGE: USGS Big Piney Creek at AR 164 near Dover. Online at http://waterdata.usgs.gov/nwis/uv/?site_no=07257006.

   Minimum: 5.0 *Optimum:* 5.5–7.0 *Dangerous:* >7.5

   USGS, Richland Creek. Online at http://waterdata.usgs.gov/nwis/uv/?site_no=07055875.

   Buffalo National River Hydrologic System, Deer gauge. Online at http://www.ozarkpages.com/whitewater/nps_buf_rain. html.

   Each of the above gauges is helpful in determining a good level. Look for a minimum of 3 feet on the Richland Creek gauge, as opposed to 5 feet on the Big Piney. The headwaters of Hurricane Creek are near Deer, and 1.5 inches of rain on the gauge at Deer is a good indicator.

ILLINOIS BAYOU

The Illinois Bayou begins on the eastern slopes of Divide Mountain near the small town of Tilly, Arkansas. The name bayou is deceptive, as this is truly a whitewater stream that flows southward to the backwaters of Lake Dardenelle near Russellville, Arkansas.

The river flows through many willow jungles and over rock ledges, presenting paddlers with a very interesting run, and its isolated shoreline offers a good refuge to wildlife. Gently sloping banks of hardwood forests block the view of surrounding farmland, thereby adding to the wilderness experience, and help protect the water quality. The stream widens and slows after it passes Scottsville. The moderate gradient creates some class II rapids, especially in the upper sections and near the Hector Bridge.

MAPS: Smyrna SW, Hector, Dover, Lee Mountain (USGS); Pope (County)

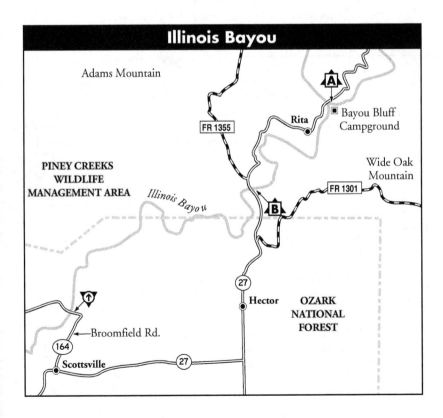

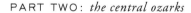

difficulty	II—II+ (III)
distance	4.3
time	3
gauge	Illinois Bayou (USGS)
level	6
scenery	A
water	Good
gradient	16
latitude	35 31.698N
longitude	92 56.486W

AR 27 (BAYOU BLUFF CAMPGROUND) TO HECTOR BRIDGE

DESCRIPTION: There are several nice shoals in the area of Bayou Bluff Campground that can be surfed in a canoe or a kayak.

Two miles above the take-out, the river enters a remote section with several class II rapids. Just above the take-out, paddlers encounter Hector Rapid. This class II+ rapid approaches class III difficulty at optimum water levels.

SHUTTLE: From Hector, Arkansas, the put-in is 6.5 miles north on AR 27. The take-out is 3.2 miles north on AR 27 on the upstream (river-right) side of Hector Bridge. Cars may drive down a dirt road that accessed from AR 27 on the north side of Hector Bridge.

GAUGE: USGS Illinois Bayou near Scottsville, Arkansas. Online at http://waterdata.usgs.gov/nwis/uv/?site_no=07257500. *Minimum: 5.5 Optimum: 6.0–7.0 Dangerous: >7.5*

difficulty	II
distance	7.6
time	4.5
gauge	Illinois Bayou (USGS)
level	5.5
scenery	A—B
water	Good
gradient	13.6
latitude	35 30.135N
longitude	92 58.304W

HECTOR BRIDGE (AR 27) TO SCOTTSVILLE (AR 164)

DESCRIPTION: A very difficult rapid with downed trees to avoid is approximately one-half mile below the put-in. Approach this obstacle with extreme caution.

The remainder of the run is characterized by class II rapids and willow runs that require paddlers to utilize basic boat control. Just above the take-out bridge, a series of ledges forms a natural slalom course for paddlers. Hydraulics form at these ledges at higher levels, so pay close attention. One should be mindful of the river level in this section.

SHUTTLE: To reach the take-out from Hector, Arkansas, head 5.4 miles south on AR 27 and turn north (right) on AR 164. Proceed 1.6 miles to the bridge over the Illinois Bayou.

GAUGE: USGS Illinois Bayou near Scottsville, Arkansas. *Minimum: 5.5 Optimum: 6.0–7.0 Dangerous: >7.5*

LITTLE PINEY CREEK

Little Piney Creek rises just east of AR 21 near Devil's Knob at an elevation of 2,335 feet and flows to the southeast past Hagarville, Arkansas, and into Lake Dardenelle. The whitewater is not as noteworthy as that on Big Piney Creek, but paddlers are treated to a very remote area of the Ozark National Forest. Fast, milky green water flows over rocky shoals and through tree-lined banks. Willow jungles and brush piles constitute the most significant obstacles. Some of the willow jungles should be scouted due to the lack of a definite course.

MAPS: Ozone, Rosetta, Hagarville (USGS); Johnson (County)

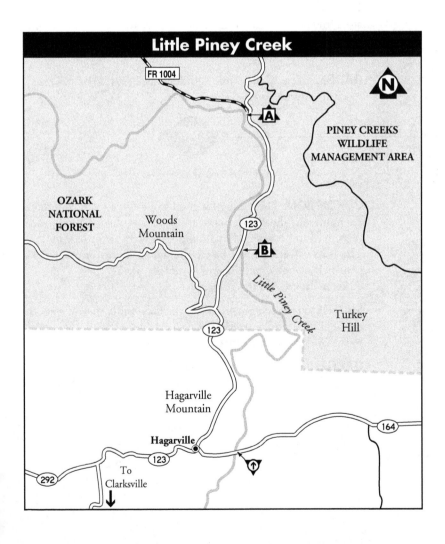

difficulty	II (II+)
distance	4.36
time	2
gauge	Telephone
level	See text
scenery	A
water	Good
gradient	22.7
latitude	35 37.825N
longitude	93 18.034W

Mt. Levi (AR 123 and FR 1004 Junction) to AR 123 Bridge

DESCRIPTION: There are numerous willow jungles and brush piles to contend with on this run but no major rapids. Most of the river passes through private property, so remember to respect the rights of landowners. Approximately 1 mile below the put-in is a good class II run visible from the highway.

SHUTTLE: To reach the put-in from Hagarville, go north on AR 123 9.4 miles and turn northwest (left) on FR 1004. Put-in along the road. To reach the take-out, backtrack on AR 123 4.2 miles to the AR 123 bridge. Take the access road on the northeast side of the creek.

GAUGE: None. Call Moore Outdoors at (479) 331-3606; they can help provide river levels.

difficulty	II (II+)
distance	7.8
time	3.5
gauge	Telephone
level	See text
scenery	A
water	Good
gradient	17.7
latitude	35 35.040N
longitude	93 18.239W

AR 123 Bridge to Hagarville

DESCRIPTION: The gradient is good along this stretch, and there are numerous shoals just below the put-in. At higher levels, paddlers need to be aware of hydraulics that form at the ledges. The Narrows are 6 miles below the put-in. Bluffs on river right constrict the creek and the area is very scenic. Take-out at the AR 164 bridge.

SHUTTLE: From the put-in, reach the take-out by heading south on AR 123 5.6 miles to AR 164. Go east (left) on AR 164 1 mile to the bridge over the creek.

GAUGE: None. See section A above.

MIDDLE FORK OF THE ILLINOIS BAYOU

The Middle Fork of the Illinois Bayou begins south of AR 16 near Witt Springs and flows south to join the East Fork of the Illinois Bayou near AR 27, forming the Illinois Bayou. The 25-mile section contains some of the most remote areas in the state. Access is almost nonexistent for the first 15 miles, except for one low-water bridge on FR 1300 An ongoing legal controversy involving an uncooperative landowner in the area of the Nogo access recalls the State vs. McElroy case regarding the Mulberry River (see "Legal Rights of Canoeists," page 14). The landowner claims that owning land on both sides of the river renders it a private river. The U.S. Forest Service holds that the river is navigable and that access cannot be denied. While the case plays out, the best advice for paddlers is to put-in quickly on the low-water bridge and not to leave vehicles in the area. As always, do not try to reason with an irate landowner.

The hassles required to access the upper 10-mile section of the Middle Fork of the Illinois Bayou are worth it. Paddlers are rewarded with a stretch of class II–III whitewater that relatively few boaters have run. Water levels are critical, and the upper sections should not be attempted unless you are sure there is sufficient water for the trip.

For its entire length, the Middle Fork of the Illinois Bayou is a very swift and narrow stream that runs through boulder gardens and moderate drops that create large standing waves. There are also sections that constrict and push the stream through narrow, willow-lined passages less than half the width of a canoe or kayak. The banks are lined with hardwood forests and moderately high bluffs. Water quality is excellent due to the remoteness of the area.

MAPS: Smyrna, Solo (USGS); Pope (County)

NOGO TO SNOW CREEK

difficulty	II–III
distance	9.7
time	4
gauge	Illinois Bayou (USGS)
level	7
scenery	AA
water	Good
gradient	27.6
latitude	35 39.060N
longitude	92 55.167W

DESCRIPTION: A good class II rapid is just downstream of the put-in with a large boulder in the current. Run either side and eddy out behind the rock.

Three miles below the put-in, the river turns left and you will find a rapid known as Six Football Fields. The river seems to be as wide as a football field, and the standing waves and holes are continuous for over 600 yards.

Approximately 1 mile downstream, Meyer Branch enters on river left and there is a good class III rapid at the junction. Several willow jungles long the next few miles can be very tight.

One is so narrow that a kayak can barely fit through it.
A class III rapid with 200 yards of standing waves and boulders to negotiate is just above the take-out at Snow Creek.

SHUTTLE: To reach the put-in from the AR 27 bridge over the Middle Fork, go north on AR 27 for 11 miles and turn left (west) on FR 1300 at the small community of Nogo, Arkansas. Go west on FR 1300 for 3.9 miles to the low-water bridge. The take-out is reached from the AR 27 bridge by going south on AR 27 one-quarter mile and turning west (right). Follow FR 1312 3 miles to the take-out at Snow Creek.

GAUGE: USGS Illinois Bayou near Scottsville, Arkansas. Online at http://waterdata.usgs.gov/nwis/uv/?site_no=07257500
   Minimum: 7.0 *Optimum:* 7.5–9.0 *Dangerous:* >10.0

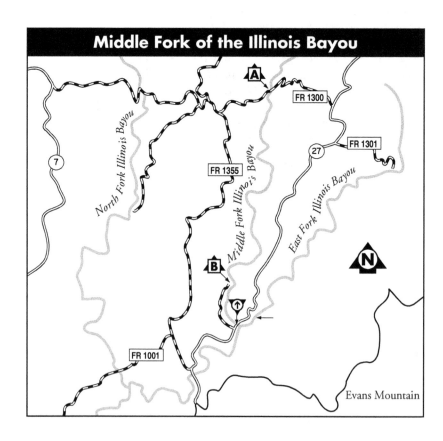

Middle Fork of the Illinois Bayou

SNOW CREEK TO AR 27 BRIDGE

difficulty	II—II+
distance	2.3
time	1.5
gauge	Illinois Bayou (USGS)
level	7
scenery	AA
water	Good
gradient	22.6
latitude	35 31.699N
longitude	92 56.988W

DESCRIPTION: The rapids in the first mile of this stretch are very tight and technical, and the lower the water, the more technical they become. At high water, the rapids tend to be standing waves and are almost continuous.

There is a very narrow section about 1 mile above the take-out where the creek is pushed into a boulder on river left. A good backferry will help overcome the obstacle.

SHUTTLE: Take-out on the downstream side of the AR 27 bridge over the Middle Fork.

GAUGE: USGS Illinois Bayou near Scottsville, Arkansas
Minimum: 7.0 Optimum: 7.5–9.0 Dangerous: >10.0

NORTH FORK OF THE ILLINOIS BAYOU

The North Fork of the Illinois Bayou begins near Ben Hur, Arkansas, and flows to the south for 23 miles before joining the Illinois Bayou near Hector, Arkansas. The entire length is protected by the Ozark National Forest and is under consideration for protection under the Wild and Scenic Rivers Act. The city of Russellville also has visions of using the North Fork of the Illinois Bayou as a future water supply and has applied for a permit from the Corps of Engineers for dam construction on the North Fork. Forest Service roads that cross and parallel the stream allow for easy access.

Paddlers can expect a relatively narrow stream that flows at a moderate pace over rocky shoals to form sporty rapids. Water quality is good due to the lack of civilization and the protected watershed. Hardwood forests enclose the stream and restrict views of the road.

MAPS: Lurton, Sandgap, Simpson, Dover (USGS); Pope (County)

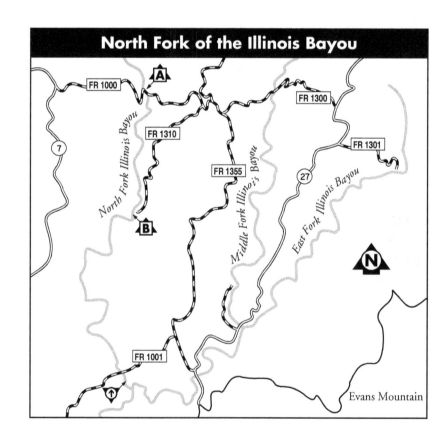

Victor (FR 1001) to FR 1310A

DESCRIPTION: Typical class II rapids are numerous, as are downed trees and the famous Ozark willow jungles.

Payne and Nolin Creeks enter on river right about 1 mile below the put-in and add to the volume of the stream.

Take-out at FR 1310A, reached via FR 1310.

SHUTTLE: From Dover, Arkansas, to reach the put-in go north 22 miles on AR 7 and turn east (right) on FR 1000. Go east 4.7 miles on FR 1000 to the access. To reach the take-out from the put-in at Victor, go east on FR 1000 and turn southwest (right) on FR 1310. Go 7.5 miles on FR 1310 and turn west (right) on FR 1310A. Proceed 0.25 miles to the stream.

GAUGE: USGS Illinois Bayou near Scottsville, Arkansas. Online at http://waterdata.usgs.gov/nwis/uv/?site_no=07257500.
Minimum: 6.0 *Optimum:* 6.5–7.5 *Dangerous:* >8.5

difficulty	II—II+ (III)
distance	5.5
time	3
gauge	Illinois Bayou (USGS)
level	6
scenery	AA
water	Excellent
gradient	30
latitude	35 39.040N
longitude	93 0.327W

FR 1310A to FR 1818

DESCRIPTION: Forest Road 1310A crosses the North Fork several times in this section. Watch for willow jungles.

Take-out at FR 1818. The West Fork of the Illinois Bayou joins the North Fork at FR 1818.

SHUTTLE: To reach the take-out from Dover, go northeast 6.3 miles on AR 27 and turn north (left) onto AR 164. Go 3 miles north on AR 164 to Granny Gap Road and turn northeast (right). Go 2 miles on Granny Gap Road to the access.

GAUGE: USGS Illinois Bayou near Scottsville, Arkansas.
Minimum: 6.0 *Optimum:* 6.5–7.5 *Dangerous:* >8.5

difficulty	II—II+
distance	8.5
time	4-5
gauge	Illinois Bayou (USGS)
level	6
scenery	AA
water	Excellent
gradient	20
latitude	35 35.232N
longitude	93 0.761W

RICHLAND CREEK

Richland Creek begins near the small community of Sandgap, located at the intersection of AR 7 and AR 16, and flows northeast for approximately 33 miles to its confluence with the Buffalo National River. The Ozark National Forest and the Richland Creek Wilderness Area protect the creek.

Richland Creek can be characterized as a very tight, technical stream that is very sensitive to water levels. It is normally floatable when other streams are in flood. The creek flows swiftly over moderate shoals in the first few miles, until it reaches the gorge section and the bottom drops out. Paddlers are treated to a class III–IV whitewater jewel. The banks close in and funnel the water though narrow drops and over waterfalls up to 7 feet in height. There is little time to enjoy the beauty of the area from the water, so stopping to do so is a must. The area is one of the most scenic in the Ozarks. The whitewater does not let up until you reach Richland Creek Campground, and then just briefly before the excitement begins again in the second section.

MAPS: Sandgap, Lurton, Moore, Euala (USGS); Newton, Searcy, (County)

A

Ben Hur to Richland Creek Campground

difficulty	III–IV
distance	6
time	4
gauge	Richland (USGS)
level	3
scenery	AA
water	Excellent
gradient	47.3
latitude	35 46.446N
longitude	92 59.293W

DESCRIPTION: Richland Creek drops almost 300 feet in 6 miles, creating numerous waterfalls and class III+–IV rapids. The remoteness of the area makes this a class IV+ run.

The first mile is fairly easy, but don't be fooled because the gorge begins just downstream with a series of ledges where the creek is constricted. Even in this first section, boaters need to be alert for new strainers, which appear from time to time and may require portaging.

After several class II rapids, paddlers will encounter several wide ledge drops, which offer good play opportunities at some levels. The river constricts again at Lunch Counter, one of the popular play spots on this run. Open boats and larger kayaks will find good surfing, and boaters in today's smaller rodeo kayaks are sometimes seen cartwheeling in the hole. Immediately downstream, the ledges grow taller and you must be cautious when choosing a route through the hydraulics that form at higher levels. As a tall bluff looms to your left, begin looking for Splat Rock, another popular play spot where almost the entire river flows directly into a sloped rock but pillows harmlessly off. Continuing downstream, paddlers encounter several more class II drops before coming to class III

Stolen Paddle (a.k.a., Rock Garden). Next you encounter Crack-in-the-Rock, where a giant boulder obstructs the channel creating a blind drop. The traditional route is to the right over a 5-foot drop with a recovery in the pool below. However, those attempting Richland in shorter kayaks should consider taking the river-left route, as the hydraulic at Crack-in-the-Rock is especially retentive of shorter boats. This hole looks very innocent, but has been the scene of numerous swims and at least one shoulder dislocation. The hole requires a good rope toss from the bank to facilitate swimmer exit at some levels.

Shortly below Crack-in-the-Rock, paddlers find another narrow drop at Green Rock, named after the sloping, moss-covered rock that can be sighted dead ahead as you approach the drop and line up for the slot. Be prepared to move quickly either left or right as soon as you reach the bottom of this slot in order to avoid being sucked into the too-narrow slot just to the left of Green Rock. After Green Rock, you will find S-turn, another fast class III rapid, and further downstream, Bloody Knuckles (a.k.a., Knuckle-buster), named for its potential to do serious damage to your hand if your low brace drags along the left side. Enter Bloody Knuckles just left of center, run down the left bank, and then work right at the bottom to avoid the sharp bedrock outcroppings on your left. After Bloody Knuckles, don't miss the fine surfing wave in the middle of the next rapid. Just below, a beautiful, high waterfall on your left signals the approach of Richland Falls, a 7-foot waterfall that extends across the entire creek. The traditional run is on river right approximately 10 feet from the bank, but many paddlers now choose to drop over about 10 feet out from the left bank. At high water, other routes are preferable, so either scout or consult with local paddlers to choose your best option. Below Richland Falls are several sporty class II rapids followed by a good class III rapid at the mouth of Devil's Fork Creek.

It is worth the time to stop and hike the quarter-mile to the confluence of Long Devil's Fork and Big Devil's Fork Creeks to see the spectacular Twin Devil's Falls. Although both Long Devil's and Big Devil's Creeks have been run by experienced creek boaters, do not attempt to run Twin Falls except at very high water levels, as you need both high water and a good launch to clear the shallow rock shelf hidden in the pool below.

More class II and III rapids follow before the paddler encounters the most difficult part of the run, consisting of five class III+ and IV rapids just above Falling Water Creek.

Cindy's Hole can be class III or IV depending on the water level. The horizon line hides a significant hydraulic; at low to medium levels a right-to-left run will allow you to punch the left side of the hole where it is weaker; as the levels get higher, you

might want to consider using the narrow sneak route that develops on river left.

Apple Pie is a long class III+ that has one danger spot, a boulder on river left at the very bottom of the rapid. At levels somewhere above 4 feet, some of the water begins going through a sieve under the left side of this boulder. Several paddlers have reported near misses at this location, with experienced boaters requiring assistance to extricate themselves from the sieve. At high water, the safe route is center or right of center at the bottom of Apple Pie.

Upper Screw-up is a class III+ at the bottom. If your roll is solid, you can simply go over anywhere, flush out, and roll, but a more stylish run can be accomplished by running slightly left

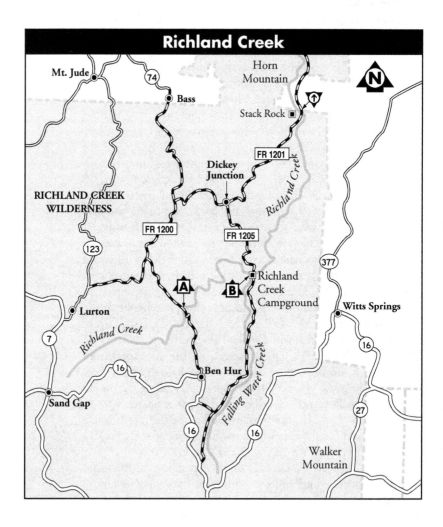

of center and using the padded shelf rock to boof out past the hydraulic. However, don't get too far left or you'll learn why some boaters call this drop "Wingard's Right" after an unfortunate miscommunication that had undesirable consequences.

Lower Screw-up (LSU) is a class IV rapid made very difficult because of a boulder that is severely undercut and dangerous in the traditional far-right channel, now known as Door #1. The second most common route, and a good low-water choice, is Door #2, the second channel out from river right. Be sure to hold your paddle parallel to your boat as you slip through Door #2, and be ready with a brace as soon as you land in the tricky cross-currents. Moving left across the river, Door #3 provides a relatively straight-forward route at high water, while Door #4, the far left channel, is rarely run. Shifting boulders in the run-out from LSU have pinned a number of paddlers and shown several the value of a good helmet. Also, stay right of center in the run-out to avoid ending up in the "Green Room," an overhanging and undercut house-sized boulder at the bottom of this drop. Scout LSU and be sure you are confident before running the drop or else portage! In fact, if you are going to portage one rapid on Upper Richland, it should be LSU.

The third rapid is class II with a ledge and hole, followed by the class III+ Maytag, a very steep drop with a large boulder that paddler David Smallwood claims "possesses terrific magnetic powers over ABS, fiberglass, wood, and metal." As water levels drop, it gets progressively harder to make it through Maytag without hitting one of the many smaller boulders hidden in the frothy water. At higher water, you can simply run the whole rapid on the right side, but be ready to brace quickly if needed.

The final rapid, a class II, is just above Richland Creek Campground. Take-out on river right or continue slightly further to the campground bridge in order to enjoy one more class III rapid hidden in the willow trees.

SHUTTLE: The put-in is 3.5 miles north of Ben Hur on FR 1203 at the low-water bridge. The take-out is at the Forest Service's Richland Creek Campground. From Ben Hur, go south 1.3 miles and turn northeast (left) on FR 1205. Proceed north 9.4 miles to Richland Creek Campground.

GAUGE: USGS Richland Creek, near Witt Springs, Arkansas. Online at http://waterdata.usgs.gov/nwis/uv/?site_no=07055875. Also, Buffalo National River Hydrologic System, Ben Hur rain gauge. Online at http://www.buffaloriverandrain.com/cgi-bin/sub map/rainmap?bh-324.
Minimum: 3.0 Optimum: 3.5–5.0 Dangerous: >5.5

difficulty	II—III (III+)
distance	8.44
time	5
gauge	Richland (USGS)
level	2.8
scenery	AA
water	Excellent
gradient	33.7
latitude	35 47.822N
longitude	92 55.716W

RICHLAND CREEK CAMPGROUND TO STACK ROCK

DESCRIPTION: This section is not as difficult as the upper section, but it has an average gradient of 34 feet per mile and several fun sections.

The first few miles are very exciting, with almost constant class II+ rapids. The creek then swings to the left into a gorge section with three class III+ rapids. The first is a course through a boulder field that requires good control of your boat.

Just downstream is a rapid named Lou's the Pinball. It is named after Lou Ingram, who was bounced like a pinball when attempting to negotiate this rapid. It is a boulder-strewn course with no easy, straight route.

A short distance downstream is a class III+ 5-foot drop that should be scouted. Like many rapids on Richland, this one has the potential to catch large trees and create new hazards, some of which cannot be identified in advance.

Richland Creek begins to flatten out from this point to the take-out as it approaches its confluence with the Buffalo National River, but watch out for willow thickets and blind turns.

SHUTTLE: To reach the take-out at Stack Rock, go north from Richland Creek Campground on FR 1205 5.6 miles and turn northeast on FR 1201 at Dickey Junction. Go 5.9 miles to the access at Stack Rock (GPS: 35 53.352N, 92 53.764W).

GAUGE: USGS Richland Creek, near Witt Springs, Arkansas, Buffalo National River Hydrologic System, Ben Hur rain gauge. *Minimum: 2.8 Optimum: 3.2–4.7 Dangerous: >5.2*

SHOAL CREEK

Shoal Creek begins on Mount Magazine and tumbles 18 miles to Lake Dardenelle. The creek is runnable only when most other area streams are in flood. The watershed is extremely limited and requires a very large or continued rain to be runnable. Shoal Creek is extremely tight and technical, with a severe gradient that drops an average of 61 feet per mile.

The moment you see Shoal Creek, it is apparent you're in for a very fast run on a narrow runoff stream. What is not apparent is the spectacular gorge that is a short distance downstream of the put-in. Steep walls enclose the creek and make rescue very difficult if not impossible. Steep tree-lined banks and excellent water quality enhance the pristine atmosphere of the gorge stretch of the creek.

MAPS: Scranton, Mt. Magazine NE (USGS); Logan (County)

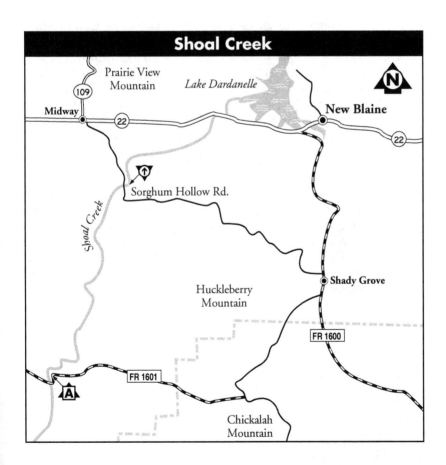

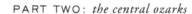

difficulty	III
distance	6.75
time	4-5
gauge	None
level	12" over
bridge	
scenery	AA
water	Excellent
gradient	61
latitude	35 11.697N
longitude	93 32.648W

ROCKY FORD (FR 1601) TO SORGHUM HOLLOW ROAD (FR 1614)

DESCRIPTION: On Shoal Creek, paddlers will encounter a very fast, tight run with one of the steeper gradients in the state. Downed trees present the greatest danger, and paddlers must be cautious when approaching any blind turns.

The canyon section has some of the best drops, reaching class IV in difficulty.

Below Brushy Creek, willow jungles are more common and sometimes present the paddler with several routes to consider. Scout ahead if you have any doubts! The remoteness of this region, coupled with the creek's distance from the road, adds considerable risk if difficulty is encountered.

SHUTTLE: To reach the take-out from Midway, Arkansas, go 0.6 mile east on AR 22 and turn south (right) on Sorghum Hollow Road. Go 2.4 miles to the low-water bridge over Shoal Creek. Do not attempt to cross this bridge if more than 6 inches of water flows over it. Instead, go back to AR 22 and turn east. Continue 5.5 miles and turn right onto Spring Lake Road. Follow it 15 miles to the put-in. To reach the put-in, continue from the take-out on Sorghum Hollow Road for 6.9 miles to Spring Lake Road. Turn right on Spring Lake Road and go 10.3 miles to the bridge over Shoal Creek. Vehicles can be parked on the west side of the bridge.

GAUGE: The low-water bridge at the take-out provides the only accurate method of gauging the creek level. Water must be running over the bridge before you can paddle Shoal Creek.

Minimum: 1" *Optimum:* 24"–36" *Dangerous:* >48"

The low-water bridge of Sorghum Hollow Road also acts as a gauge in that you cannot successfully run the river unless the bridge is submerged at least 6 inches.

SPADRA CREEK

Spadra Creek begins south of AR 215 and west of AR 21 and flows to the south through Clarksville, Arkansas, before it empties into Lake Dardenelle.

Spadra Creek is a small, narrow stream with good rapids up to class III in difficulty and numerous willow jungles to thread your way through.

The creek is seldom paddled, but it is a run worth doing if you are in the area.

MAPS: Oak, Harmony, Ludwig, Clarksville (USGS); Johnson (County)

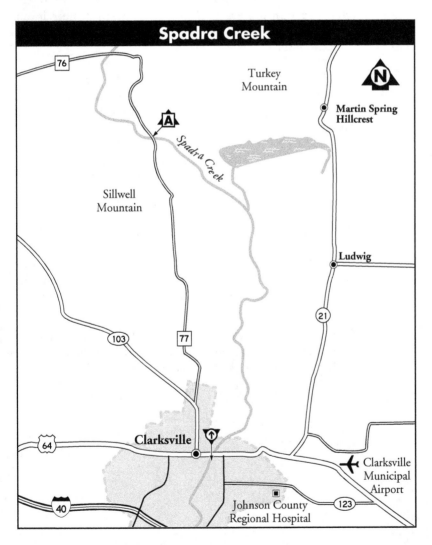

difficulty	II–III
distance	6.8
time	3.5
gauge	Spadra (USGS)
level	4
scenery	A-B
water	Good
gradient	23
latitude	35 32.325N
longitude	93 28.682W

CR 77 TO CLARKSVILLE

DESCRIPTION: The creek is a tight, willow-infested run for the first few miles and requires a paddler to pick the correct course.

One mile below the put-in is a small ford. About a mile below, Dick's Branch enters on river left. At optimum water levels, there is significant flow from Lake Ludwig.

One of the more difficult willow jungles is just below. Turn left at the rusted car with a tree growing from the hood and stay left at each turn and you will make it through. Remember, if you cannot see a clear path, scout or portage any obstructions, which occur from time to time in this area.

A short distance downstream, there are several barbed-wire fences with which to contend. These should be portaged.

The Clarksville Water Plant is 5.9 miles below the put-in. Make sure you take the right chute to avoid the dam and the killer hydraulic that forms below it.

The class III Waterworks Rapid is just below. It is a great double drop with several places to surf.

Take-out downstream of the US 64 bridge on river right.

SHUTTLE: To reach the put-in from the intersection of US 64 and AR 103, go north on AR 103 0.7 mile to College Street. Bear north (right) on College Street for 1.5 miles to CR 77. Continue north on CR 77 3.2 miles to the bridge over Spadra Creek. To reach the take-out from the intersection of AR 103 and US 64, go 0.3 mile east on US 64 and turn south (right) on the road just before the US 64 bridge. Go a very short distance to the take-out.

GAUGE: USGS Spadra Creek at Clarksville, Arkansas. Online at http://waterdata.usgs.gov/nwis/uv/?site_no=07256500.
Minimum: 4.0 Optimum: 4.5–6.5 Dangerous: >7.5

part**Three**

CEDAR CREEK AND WEST CEDAR CREEK

Cedar Creek begins just east of Cedarville, Arkansas, at the confluence of West Cedar Creek and East Cedar Creek. West Cedar Creek begins near Kimes Mountain and flows southwest towards Cedarville. East Cedar Creek begins approximately 4.5 miles west of Chester, Arkansas, and flows southwest towards Cedarville. Both forks of Cedar Creek are runnable at periods of heavy rainfall, although the route described below begins on West Cedar Creek. The USGS Frog Bayou gauge at Rudy, Arkansas, is a good indicator of water levels on Cedar Creek and its tributaries.

Paddlers should expect a very tight run on all three creeks. Expect steep gradients, approaching 50 feet per mile on the branches and 20 feet per mile on Cedar Creek. The terrain is steep, the run is tight and technical, and the location is remote. Before attempting these runs, you should at minimum be an advanced-intermediate open boater or kayaker. You should feel comfortable with tight eddy turns and should have extremely good boat control. Downed trees are a common hazard on Cedar Creek. If you cannot see the route by eddy scouting, stop and scout from the shore.

MAPS: Rudy (USGS); Crawford (County)

AR 162 TO RUDY

difficulty	II–III
distance	9.35
time	5
gauge	Rudy (USGS)
level	6
scenery	A
water	Good
gradient	29
latitude	35 34.255N
longitude	94 20.745W

DESCRIPTION: West Cedar Creek drops at a rate of 47 feet per mile in the first 1.6 miles before its confluence with East Cedar Creek and averages 25 feet per mile for the next 8.35 miles. Continuous class II and III rapids characterize Cedar Creek.

One notable rapid just past the AR 162 bridge drops through a tight boulder field that requires precision moves and perfect timing. The rapid can be run on the river-right or river-left chutes. The left chute is more difficult and drops into a hole that can be a boat eater at higher levels. The right chute requires an approach from middle river left to river right in preparation for a quick left-then-right maneuver to run this rapid successfully.

Class II rapids continue nonstop for approximately one-quarter mile and then paddlers encounter a class II+ slide ledge that takes them under a large rock shelf with no danger. It is just spectacular! Note the waterfall on the right side of the creek.

The creek swings to the left (east) and drops over a 4-foot

waterfall that should be run on river left. There are several good surfing holes here.

Paddlers encounter a low-water bridge less than a quarter mile from the falls. Pull-out on river left and portage to avoid the culverts in the bridge. This low-water bridge is an alternate put-in (GPS: 35 33.469N, 94 20.868W) for this section that can be used to shorten the trip by approximately 1 mile.

The creek continues with sporty class II rapids for a short distance, then East Cedar Creek enters on river left as paddlers pass the remaining abutments of old wagon bridge. The low-water bridge upstream on East Cedar Creek is also a put-in that can be used when water levels are questionable.

Just below the confluence with East Cedar Creek, paddlers encounter a class II+ run that is very exciting. A 4-foot horseshoe waterfall is a short distance downstream. Just below the waterfall, the creek splits. Take the left channel and prepare for a very tight, fast run. Always be on the lookout for fallen trees.

Just downstream, a small creek enters on river right as Cedar Creek turns left. Eddy out and surf the waves here.

Just downstream is a low-water ford. River left is the safe route; hydraulics form from the middle to the right. The creek

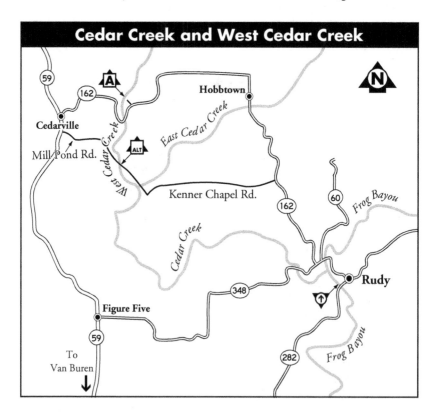

Cedar Creek and West Cedar Creek

slows its rate of drop for the next 2 miles, but the current still moves steadily and very few pools are encountered.

Acceleration Rapid awaits where the creek narrows; take the channel on river left. There is a small downed tree at the top of the drop, but it is easily avoided. The current is swift and the waves increase in size for 700 feet, ending with waves and holes large enough to swamp an open boat. The total drop is approximately 6 feet in a span of 150 feet.

One-quarter mile downstream, willows constrict the creek and there is no clear channel. Boulders in midstream complicate the situation. Paddlers can slip through near mid-channel. If there is any doubt, portage.

Jim's Jump is a 4-foot drop that can be run on river right.

A short distance downstream, paddlers encounter a very bad blockage. The creek turns left, and the view is obstructed. The creek then turns right and is blocked by two very large and dangerous trees. There is an eddy on river right that must be caught, or the results could be disastrous.

Just above and in sight of the AR 348 bridge is a ledge of 3–4 feet that should be run on river left. The surfing opportunities are numerous at this ledge.

Below the bridge are two very exciting rapids with numerous holes, surfing waves, and eddies. This short section from the AR 348 bridge to Rudy is so good that you may elect to put-in at the AR 348 bridge and play this section if you have too little time to make a long run.

Paddle to the confluence of Frog Bayou and then a short distance to the take-out at Rudy.

SHUTTLE: To reach the put-in, take AR 282 west from Rudy. Cross Frog Bayou and turn right on AR 60 and go north a short distance. Turn left (west) on AR 348 and turn north on Hobbtown Road after less than a quarter mile. Follow Hobbtown Road for approximately 3.5 miles and bear left onto AR 162. Follow AR 162 for approximately 2.5 miles to Creekway Road. Creekway Road is located on the right side of the highway just before the bridge over West Cedar Creek. Follow Creekway Road down to West Cedar Creek and put-in anywhere along the creek. Be respectful of the landowner at this put-in and try to leave the area better than you found it. Do not block the roads at the put-in because the landowner needs to use them. The take-out is located in Rudy, Arkansas (GPS: 35 31.552N, 94 16.310W). Rudy is 2.75 miles west of I-540 via the AR 282 exit.

GAUGE: USGS Frog Bayou at Rudy. Online at http://waterdata.usgs.gov/nwis/uv/?site_no=07251500.

   Minimum: 6.0 *Optimum:* 6.5–7.5 *Dangerous:* >8.5

CLEAR CREEK

Clear Creek begins just south of Winslow, Arkansas, and makes a mad dash southward to its confluence with Frog Bayou near Mountainburg, Arkansas, a distance of only 14 miles. Clear Creek's watershed is small, but when it is up, it delights paddlers with a tight, technical class III run in the upper stretches and a great class II+ run on the lower section.

Railroad tracks follow the creek for almost it entire length. In fact, this creek was the only route the railroad could find over the rugged Boston Mountains to Fayetteville years ago. The community of Schaberg was a resort that could only be reached by the railroad in the 1930s and 1940s. It is now a small community of private homes, so respect the owners' rights while in the area.

The upper section is remote, with no signs of civilization until paddlers are well past the recently constructed bridge for I-540. The only signs of civilization are the railroad and interstate, which crosses the creek four times. Water quality that was degraded during the construction of the interstate is now returning to normal.

MAPS: Winslow, Mountainburg, Mountainburg SW (USGS); Washington, Crawford (County)

SCHABERG TO CHESTER

difficulty	II–III
distance	5
time	3
gauge	Rudy (USGS)
level	7.5
scenery	AA
water	Good
gradient	41
latitude	35 43.589N
longitude	94 10.175W

DESCRIPTION: Clear Creek greets paddlers with a very tight and technical run. Class II and III drops are numerous, and downed trees and brush piles are a constant and ever-changing problem.

Riley Creek enters on river right 1.65 miles below the put-in and adds more volume to the creek.

Approximately 1.25 miles below Riley Creek there is a low-water bridge that can be dangerous. Portage if you are not sure you can safely paddle under it.

Moccasin Branch enters on river right just above the bridge over Clear Creek in Chester.

Take-out just below the bridge on river right at the church parking lot.

SHUTTLE: To reach the put-in from Mountainburg, go 8 miles north on US 71 and turn west (left) on Schaberg Road. Go west on Schaberg Road for 2.4 miles. To reach the take-out from Mountainburg, go north on US 71 for 2.6 miles to AR 282. Turn west (left) on AR 282 and go 1.8 miles to Chester,

Arkansas. Turn left on CR 29, go 0.2 mile, cross the creek, and turn left again into the Chester Community Church parking area.

GAUGE: USGS Frog Bayou at Rudy. Online at http://water-data.usgs.gov/nwis/uv/?site_no=07251500.
   Minimum: 7.5 *Optimum:* 8.0–10.0 *Dangerous:* >11.0

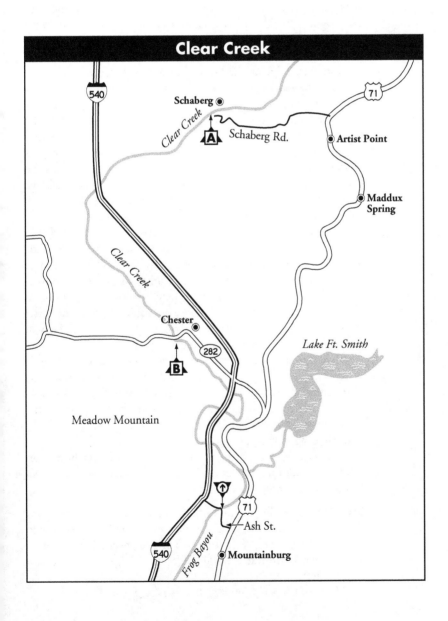

B

CHESTER TO MOUNTAINBURG

difficulty	II–II+
distance	4.5
time	2.5
gauge	Rudy (USGS)
level	5.5
scenery	A–B
water	Good
gradient	30
latitude	35 40.785N
longitude	94 10.749W

DESCRIPTION: Horseshoe Falls, a 2.5-foot drop, is just below the put-in. Be careful of the hole that develops in higher water.

Three hundred yards downstream, there is a good class II drop that should be approached from river left. Then move to river right to avoid the diagonal hole at the bottom of the drop.

One-quarter mile downstream the creek turns sharply to the right. The rapid is not very difficult, but the creek is pushed into an undercut ledge at the bottom of a hard-left turn. Backferry through the left turn or catch the eddy on river right, then forward ferry through the turn.

Clear Creek Canyon is approximately 1.65 miles below the put-in. This area is below the first of three I-540 bridges that you will see in this second stream section. Canyon Rapids begins as the creek makes a hard turn to the right. Stay away from the downed trees that tend to lay on the outside of the curve. Large waves continue for approximately 150 yards with many chances to catch eddies behind large boulders in the creek.

You will pass under another interstate bridge, followed closely by two very good class II rapids with boulders that should be avoided. Although the interstate is nearby, you will hardly notice it in this section. The third interstate bridge is just a mile downstream of the second, and immediately below it is a railroad bridge. A very good class II rapid begins as you paddle under the bridge. The bedrock makes the current squirrelly, and diagonal waves form with numerous surfing and play spots.

Clear Creek flows into the Frog Bayou not far downstream. If water is flowing from the dam, the volume increases considerably. Large standing waves are numerous from here to the take-out.

The river splits around an island a short distance below the confluence. Take the left channel unless the level is really high; you will drag in the right channel.

Take-out on the upstream side of the Ash Street bridge on river left. Caution: Do not attempt to paddle under the Ash Street bridge for any reason!

SHUTTLE: From the junction of AR 282 and US 71 on the south side of Mountainburg, go north on US 71 for 1.3 miles to Ash Street and turn west (left) to reach the take-out. Go 0.5 miles across the railroad track to the Ash Street bridge. Park upstream on river left.

Minimum: 5.5 Optimum: 6.0–8.0 Dangerous: >9.0

COVE CREEK

Cove Creek begins in Washington County near the small community of Hubbard, Arkansas, and flows southeast to its confluence with Lee Creek just below Lee Creek Community. The total length of the creek is approximately 25 miles. The upper stretches are close to a road and lack the wildness of the final 12 miles, which are protected by the Ozark National Forest. This creek is a good run when Lee Creek is high.

MAPS: Prairie Grove, Strickler, Evansville, Natural Dam, Rudy NE (USGS); Washington, Crawford (County)

BARKER GAP ROAD TO CREEK FORD ROAD

difficulty	II–II+
distance	5.3
time	3
gauge	Lee Creek (USGS)
level	6.5
scenery	A
water	Good
gradient	20
latitude	34 43.297N
longitude	94 24.859W

DESCRIPTION: The gradient and the action are good along this run. Paddlers need to be aware of hazards created by downed trees.

The take-out low-water bridge presents a very significant hazard. The landowner, in an attempt to control his cattle, has strung an electric wire about 8 feet in the air along the upstream side of the low-water bridge. Dangling from that wire is barbed wire entwined with electric wire. Unsuspecting paddlers could get a good shock if they were to brush against the dangling wires.

SHUTTLE: To get to the put-in from Natural Dam, go north on AR 59 for 1.1 miles and turn right on Liberty Hill Road. Go north for 4.1 miles on Liberty Hill Road and turn right on Barker Gap Road. Go 1.5 miles northeast on Barker Gap Road and bear right at the intersection just before the bridge over Cove Creek. There is a small road that goes to the creek on the downstream (east) side of the bridge. To reach the take-out from the put-in, backtrack to AR 59 and turn right. Take Liberty Hill Road for 1.6 miles to Peaceful Way Road. Turn right and go 1.2 miles to Peaceful Home Road. Turn right and go 0.2 mile on Peaceful Home Road to Creek Ford Road. Turn left and continue 1.3 miles to the low-water bridge. Parking is limited.

GAUGE: USGS Lee Creek near Short, Oklahoma. Online at http://waterdata.usgs.gov/ar/nwis/uv/?site_no=07249800&PARAmeter_cd=00065,00060.
  Minimum: 6.5 *Optimum:* 7.0–9.0 *Dangerous:* 10.0

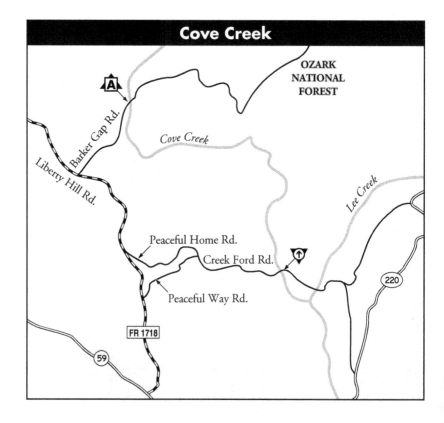

FROG BAYOU

The headwaters of Frog Bayou are on the north slope of Shepherd Mountain in Crawford County, Arkansas. The stream flows generally west until it reaches the impoundment of Lake Fort Smith, a part of the Fort Smith municipal water supply. The present dam is being raised 100 feet to increase the water supply. The new dam will have a negative effect on the flow of Frog Bayou downstream. The headwaters for boating begin below the dam near the junction of Clear Creek and Frog Bayou. Water flowing over the spillway is a real plus for paddling, but at times Clear Creek alone supplies enough water for a good float.

Frog Bayou is an exciting class II stream with nice drops, willow jungles, and rock gardens. Steep, forested ridges protect the stream, giving paddlers a sense of wilderness even though the highway is close by in many places. The water quality is good, including the Ozarks' famous greenish water. The popularity of Frog Bayou has grown over the years. Paddlers throughout the region now enjoy the Frog, especially boaters from the Fort Smith area, who can be on the stream only a half-hour after leaving home.

MAPS: Mountainburg, Mountainburg SW, Rudy (USGS); Crawford (County)

MOUNTAINBURG (ASH STREET LOW-WATER BRIDGE) TO AR 282 (SILVER BRIDGE)

difficulty	I—II
distance	2.2
time	1
gauge	Rudy (USGS)
level	3.5
scenery	A—B
water	Good
gradient	21
latitude	35 38.728N
longitude	94 49.620W

DESCRIPTION: On Frog Bayou, paddlers encounter numerous class II rapids created by willow jungles and small drops. One noteworthy rapid is less than one-third mile from the put-in. The stream turns to river left creating nice waves and several large holes. Scouting is always an option.

SHUTTLE: The put-in is in the town of Mountainburg. From US 71, go west on Ash Street across the railroad tracks for a short distance to the low-water bridge. Parking is available on river left above the bridge or on river right across the bridge. To reach the take-out, head south 1.3 miles on US 71 and turn west (right) on AR 282. Follow AR 282 for 0.2 mile and turn right onto Silver Bridge Road just before the Conoco truck stop. Go 1.1 miles on Silver Bridge Road to the bridge and park at the gravel bar.

GAUGE: USGS Frog Bayou at Rudy. Online at http://ar.water data.usgs.gov/nwis/uv?site_no=07251500.
Minimum: 3.5 Optimum: 4.5–6.5 Dangerous: 8.0

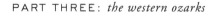

difficulty	I—II
distance	4.31
time	2.5
gauge	Rudy (USGS)
level	3.5
scenery	A
water	Good
gradient	11
latitude	35 37 073N
longitude	94 11.055W

AR 282 (Silver Bridge) to Grotto (AR 282 Low-Water Bridge).

DESCRIPTION: This section is not as active as the first but has the typical willow jungles that always require attention.

Approximately 1 mile above the take-out, there is a very difficult willow jungle where the creek turns to the left and splits through many channels. Scout the obstacle to determine the best route.

There is a good rapid at the railroad trestle near the take-out with several nice places to surf.

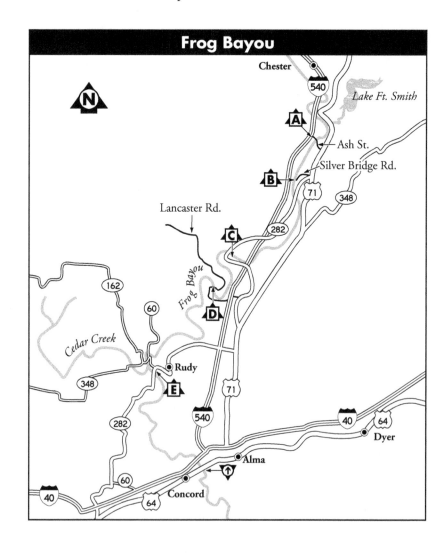

SHUTTLE: To reach the take-out from the put-in at Silver Bridge, go 0.6 mile to AR 282. Turn south (right) and go 4.9 miles to the low-water bridge over Frog Bayou. Park on the south side of the river near the railroad trestle.

GAUGE: USGS Frog Bayou at Rudy.
Minimum: 3.5 Optimum: 4.0–6.0 Dangerous: 8.0

GROTTO (AR 282 LOW-WATER BRIDGE) TO LANCASTER

difficulty	I–II
distance	4.31
time	2.5
gauge	Rudy (USGS)
level	3.5
scenery	A
water	Good
gradient	11
latitude	35 37 073N
longitude	94 11.055W

DESCRIPTION: There is a nice class II rapid 1 mile above the take-out with good standing waves and a strong eddy on river left. Avoid the overhanging trees on river right.

A short distance downstream, as the river turns to the right, is another class II rapid that should be run in the middle to avoid the rock garden. At higher flows, this rapid has some excellent surfing spots and good eddies.

SHUTTLE: To reach the take-out is from the put-in, go south on AR 282 for 1.9 miles and turn west (right) on Lancaster Road. Go 1.8 miles to the river and park across the bridge on the upstream side.

GAUGE: USGS Frog Bayou at Rudy.
Minimum: 3.5 Optimum: 4.0–6.0 Dangerous: 8.0

LANCASTER TO RUDY

difficulty	I–II+
distance	7.25
time	3.5
gauge	Rudy (USGS)
level	3
scenery	A–B
water	Good
gradient	14.6
latitude	35 35.190N
longitude	94 13.413W

DESCRIPTION: This is the classic run on the Frog. The fun begins just below the railroad trestle at the put-in. A small ledge forms a nice hole on river left.

Half a mile below the ledge, a sporty class II rapid begins as the creek narrows and then turns to river left. The Falls Drop, named after the beautiful waterfall on river right, has eddies on both river left and right. Be sure to eddy on the right to see the waterfall. Peel out and catch the eddies behind the boulders in midstream and on river right. Watch for the tree on river left reaching out over the creek and boulders below on the left.

Dog Leg Left is 1.6 miles below the Falls Drop. The creek narrows and makes a hard turn to the left. A large flat rock shelf constricts the creek even more, creating large waves and violent eddies on river right.

Pourover Rapid is within sight of Dog Leg Left. The Creek is again constricted by a boulder on river right that creates squir-relly currents and ender opportunities at levels between 3.5 and 4 feet and again at 6 feet.

A short distance downstream, paddlers pass under the second railroad trestle. The creeks splits, but take the river-left chute and surf the waves below the trestle.

The third railroad trestle is just over a mile downstream from the second. There are several nice play spots just above and below the third trestle.

Rapid Transit, one-quarter mile below the third trestle, is a class II+ drop with good waves and several rocks to avoid. Watch out for the large hole in the center of the drop. Approach from the center and run right of center to avoid the hole and the rock.

Canyon Falls Rapid (II+) is 2 miles below Rapid Transit where the creek makes a sharp bend to the left. There is a rock right of center about two-thirds of the way through Rapid Transit that creates an obstacle at lower levels and a hole at higher levels. The stream is obstructed on river right by a house-sized boulder at the bottom of the rapid. Good boat control is essential in order to successfully negotiate this rapid. A good backferry will save you at this rapid.

Take-out 1 mile downstream on river left on the upstream side of the bridge. You can drive you car down to this point.

SHUTTLE: To reach the take-out from the put-in, go 1.8 miles east on Lancaster Road to AR 282. Turn south (right) and go 1.2

Photo by Mike Coogan

miles to US 71, Head south (right) 0.7 mile to AR 282 and turn west (right). Go 3.8 miles on AR 282 to Rudy.

GAUGE: USGS Frog Bayou at Rudy.
Minimum: 3.0 *Optimum:* 4.0–6.0 *Dangerous:* 8.0

RUDY TO US 64

difficulty	I—II
distance	6.6
time	4
gauge	Rudy (USGS)
level	3
scenery	A—B
water	Good
gradient	12.1
latitude	35 31.557N
longitude	94 16.319W

DESCRIPTION: This final stream section is often overlooked, but is a good run, especially in the winter months. There are no major difficulties, but willows and downed trees are a danger.

Half a mile below the put-in, the river makes a sharp turn to the left and creates a nice class II rapid with several good eddies.

About halfway through the run, look for a series of smooth surfing waves created by a series of ledges in an otherwise flat stretch of the creek.

Take-out at the US 64 bridge on river right, the northwest side of the bridge, before going under the bridge.

SHUTTLE: To reach the take-out from the put-in at Rudy, cross the AR 282 bridge over Frog Bayou and go west a short distance before turning south (left) on AR 282. Go 6.5 miles to US 64 and turn east (left) onto US 64. Go 3.1 miles east on US 64. Cross the Frog Bayou and begin looking for a gravel road in the median where you can turn back west on the divided highway. Park on the small road on the upstream, northwest side of the bridge.

GAUGE: USGS Frog Bayou at Rudy.
Minimum: 3.0 *Optimum:* 3.5–5.5 *Dangerous:* 7.0

ILLINOIS RIVER

The Illinois River rises near Hogeye, Arkansas, and flows north to Benton County, then heads west through the Ozark National Forest along AR 68 before flowing into Oklahoma and Lake Francis. Expect a class I stream that has become very popular among novice canoeists and tubers. Several outfitters that rent canoes and provide shuttle service are located in the AR 68 area. Ken Smith's book, The Illinois River *(available from the Ozark Society), is an excellent in-depth look at the river and the surrounding area.*

The cool, deep-green water that courses over small rocky chutes in the Ozark National Forest attracts people from northwest Arkansas and eastern Oklahoma. Along most of the stream, paddlers find tree-lined banks with occasional bluffs that obscure the view of pastures and small hills. There are few signs of civilization except at bridges and access points.

MAPS: Strickler, Prairie Grove, West Fork, Wheeler, Robinson, Gallatin, Watts (USGS); Washington, Benton (County)

LAKE WEDDINGTON (AR 16) TO CHAMBERS SPRINGS ROAD

difficulty	I—II
distance	11.3
time	5
gauge	Illinois (USGS)
level	2.75
scenery	A
water	Good to Fair
gradient	5.8
latitude	36 6.182N
longitude	94 20.642W

DESCRIPTION: Paddlers should expect a class I stream with no major difficulties. However, brush piles and downed trees can be a problem in some bends in the river.

SHUTTLE: The put-in is west of Fayetteville, Arkansas, on AR 16. The take-out is reached by going west from the put-in 7.1 miles on AR 16 and turning north (right) on Chambers Springs Road. Go north 4.7 miles to the access at the Illinois River.

GAUGE: USGS Illinois River south of Siloam Springs, Arkansas. Online at http://waterdata.usgs.gov/ar/nwis/uv/?site_no=07195430&agency_cd=USGS.
  Minimum: 2.75 Optimum: 3.0–4.5 Dangerous: >5.0

CHAMBERS SPRINGS ROAD TO AR 59

difficulty	I
distance	10.9
time	6
gauge	Illinois (USGS)
level	2.75
scenery	A
water	Good to Fair
gradient	3.2
latitude	36 9.999N
longitude	94 26.022W

DESCRIPTION: This stream section is a class I run with good current and good water quality. This section is generally floatable even in the summer months.

There are some very scenic bluffs about 3.5 miles below the put-in.

Two miles below the AR 16 bridge, you come to Fisher's Ford. You can recognize it by the old iron bridge crossing the river. Not far downstream is a nice little drop. Not hard, but fun. Many locals drive to the bridge and use this spot to practice river skills.

SHUTTLE: From the put-in at Chambers Springs Road, reach the take-out by going north on Chambers Springs Road 0.2 mile to US 412 and turning west (left). Go west 5.2 miles and turn south (left) on AR 59. Continue 6.2 miles on AR 59 to the bridge over the Illinois River.

GAUGE: USGS Illinois River south of Siloam Springs.
Minimum: 2.75 *Optimum:* 3.0–4.5 *Dangerous:* >5.0

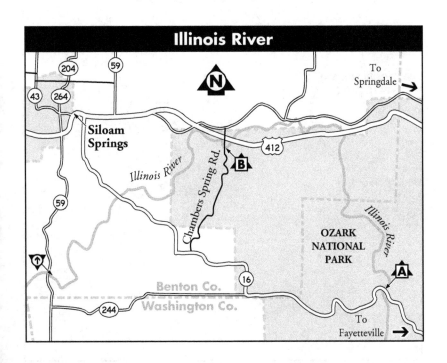

KING'S RIVER

King's River begins near Boston, Arkansas, and flows to the north before running into Table Rock Lake. Boston is the headwaters for two other notable streams, the Mulberry River on the south side of AR 16 and War Eagle Creek on the northwest side of town. The upper sections of the King's River are in the Boston Mountains and tend to have a greater drop per mile than the lower sections, which are in the Springfield and Salem Plateaus.

The river itself is not too difficult, with class II rapids the norm. Willow jungles and gravel shoals are the main difficulties in the floatable sections of the river. There are some larger drops near the headwaters, but these sections are floatable only a few times a year.

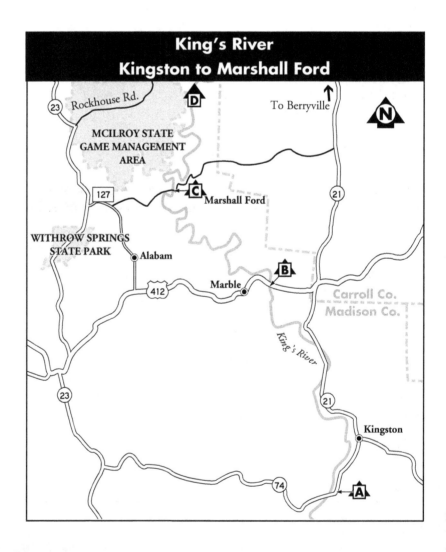

Hardwood forests and an occasional rocky bluff greet paddlers on King's River. Water quality is above average and exhibits the famous milky green tint found on rivers in the Ozarks. The wilderness experience is enhanced by a lack of river use relative to many of the rivers close by. Wildlife is abundant, offering paddlers the chance to see squirrels, beaver, deer, and many species of native plants. Spring is an especially good time to experience clear water conditions and many different flowers and plants in bloom.

MAPS: Boston, Weathers, Kingston, Marble, Forum, Rockhouse, Eureka Springs, Grandview (USGS); Madison, Carroll (County)

AR 74 to Marble (AR 412)

difficulty	I–II
distance	13.3
time	6
gauge	King's (USGS)
level	2.5
scenery	A–B
water	Good
gradient	8
latitude	36 1.119N
longitude	93 32.359W

DESCRIPTION: This section of the river has no major difficulties, but be on the lookout for downed trees and brush piles. The surrounding land is alluvial and the river is very dependent on rainfall.

SHUTTLE: The put-in is 2.7 miles west of Kingston, Arkansas, at the AR 74 bridge. To reach the take-out from the put in, go 2.7 miles northeast to AR 21 and turn north (left). Continue 7.5 miles on AR 21 and turn west (left) on AR 68/412. Go 2.5 miles northwest on AR 68/412 and turn north (right) on CR 271 in Marble. Go 0.6 mile to the low-water bridge.

GAUGE: USGS King's River near Berryville, Arkansas. Online at http://ar.waterdata.usgs.gov/nwis/uv/?site_no=07050500 &PARAmeter_cd=00065,00060. The USGS gauge is at Grandview and may not be indicative of water levels on the upper sections. Local inquiry is helpful if you plan to float sections above Trigger Gap. King's River Outfitters is located at Trigger Gap, and they can be very helpful with water levels. Call (479) 253-8954.

Minimum: 2.5 Optimum: 3.0–4.5 Dangerous: >5.0

difficulty	I—I+
distance	11.25
time	6
gauge	King's (USGS)
level	2.5
scenery	A
water	Good
gradient	5.3
latitude	36 8.612N
longitude	35.623W

MARBLE (AR 412) TO MARSHALL FORD

DESCRIPTION: The pace is a little faster on this stretch than in the previous section, and more bluffs begin to appear. This section is one of the better kept paddling secrets in Arkansas. The scenery rivals that of the Buffalo River without the crowds. Some of the bluffs in this section are just as spectacular as those on the upper Buffalo.

SHUTTLE: To reach the take-out, go east from the put-in on AR 412 for 6.2 miles and turn north (left) on AR 127. Go north 1.5 miles on AR 127 to Alabam, Arkansas, and turn northeast (right) and proceed 4 miles to Marshall Ford.

GAUGE: USGS King's River near Berryville.
Minimum: 2.5 Optimum: 3.0–4.5 Dangerous: >6.0

difficulty	I
distance	15.85
time	8
gauge	King's (USGS)
level	2.5
scenery	AA
water	Excellent
gradient	7.8
latitude	36 11.342N
longitude	93 39.104W

MARSHALL FORD TO ROCKHOUSE

DESCRIPTION: The pace is slow on this section, but the scenery may be the best on the King's River. This stretch is similar to the previous one, with bluffs comparable to what you expect to see on the Buffalo and no crowds.

The smallmouth bass fishing is great in the deep, cool pools that flow at a leisurely pace.

A winter overnight trip on this section is particularly special.

SHUTTLE: From the put-in at Marshall Ford, reach the take-out by going southwest 4 miles and turning south (left) on AR 127. Go 1.5 miles south to US 412 and turn west (right). Drive 3.8 miles southwest on US 412 and turn north (right) on AR 23. Go 17.4 miles north on AR 23 and turn east (right) on AR 221. Go east 5.8 miles on AR 221 and turn south (right) on old AR 221 at the sign to King's River Outfitters. Continue south 2.1 miles. Just past Rockhouse Cemetery on the left, there is a dirt road that bears left in front of an old white church. Follow the road to the access at Rockhouse.

GAUGE: USGS King's River near Berryville.
Minimum: 2.5 Optimum: 3.0–4.5 Dangerous: >6.0

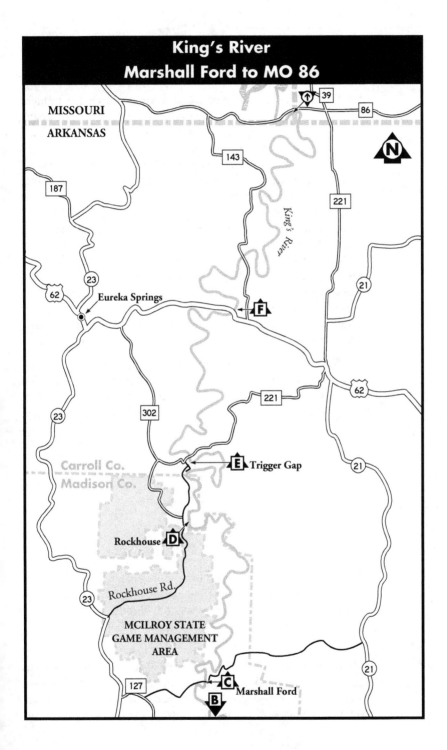

King's River
Marshall Ford to MO 86

difficulty	I
distance	7.5
time	4
gauge	King's (USGS)
level	2.5
scenery	AA
water	Excellent
gradient	4.5
latitude	36 16.91N
longitude	93 39.84W

ROCKHOUSE TO TRIGGER GAP

DESCRIPTION: This is the perfect day trip in winter or summer. In the summer, you will find crystal-clear pools of water that are perfect for swimming, fishing, or snorkeling. Eagle sightings are numerous in the winter months.

The river makes a large, sweeping bend, known as Mason's Bend, on this stretch. This bend makes the shuttle short allowing for maximum time on the river.

There is a great surfing and play hole at Trigger Gap. You will find deck boaters at this spot when the river is too high for a normal float trip.

King's River Outfitters owns the take-out at Trigger Gap, the sight of the old AR 221 bridge. They charge a nominal fee for access, but it is worth it, especially if you let them shuttle you. Your vehicle can be safely parked, and the short shuttle to Rockhouse allows you to spend a leisurely day on the river having fun and enjoying the scenery. Camping is also available at Trigger Gap.

SHUTTLE: From the put-in at Rockhouse, backtrack to the road that goes north just past the old white church. Go north 2 miles and turn right at the sign for King's River Outfitters. Proceed to Trigger Gap. There is a small fee for access. Make sure you stop at the store to pay.

GAUGE: USGS King's River near Berryville.
Minimum: 2.5 Optimum: 3.0–4.5 Dangerous: >6.0

difficulty	I
distance	12.75
time	7
gauge	King's (USGS)
level	2.5
scenery	A
water	Good
gradient	4.1
latitude	36 18.89lN
longitude	93 39.810W

TRIGGER GAP TO US 62

DESCRIPTION: Paddlers encounter more boaters on this section of the river than on any other section during the peak paddling months of spring. The scenery is good, and the river is not too difficult, making this the most popular section of the King's River.

SHUTTLE: From the put-in at Trigger Gap, reach the take-out by going north to AR 221 and turning east (right). Go northeast 11.7 miles to Berryville, Arkansas, and turn west (left) on US 62. Go northwest 4.9 miles on US 62, cross the bridge over the

King's River, and take the first right past the bridge. Follow the Arkansas Game and Fish Commission signs to the access.

GAUGE: USGS King's River near Berryville.
Minimum: 2.0 Optimum: 3.0–4.5 Dangerous: >6.0

US 62 TO MO 86

difficulty	I
distance	21.86
time	8
gauge	King's (USGS)
level	2.5
scenery	A–B
water	Good
gradient	4
latitude	36 23.687N
longitude	93 37.997W

DESCRIPTION: This stretch of river has good current, but the difficulty is minimal. This is a section for hardy fishermen. If you do this section, plan to spend at least one night on the river.

SHUTTLE: From the put-in at the Arkansas Game and Fish Access, return to US 62 and turn left. Go 1.1 miles southeast on US 62 and turn north (left) on AR 143. Go north 10.9 miles to MO 86 and turn east. Go east 3.2 miles to the access.

GAUGE: USGS King's River near Berryville.
Minimum: 2.0 Optimum: 3.0–4.5 Dangerous: >6.0

Photo by Mike Coogan

LEE CREEK

Lee Creek begins just south of West Fork, Arkansas, and flows southwest to the Arkansas River near Van Buren, Arkansas. Along the way, the tributaries of Blackburn Creek, Fall Creek, Cove Creek, and Mountain Fork Creek add to the flow of Lee Creek.

Lee Creek is a typical Ozark Mountains stream with willow jungles, rock gardens, and an occasional waterfall. Water quality is very good, and the milky green water characteristic of this area is at its best on Lee Creek. Hardwood forests line the steep banks along much of the creek. The autumn months bring out some of the most spectacular scenery in the Ozarks. Lee Creek tends to be less touched by civilization than many other streams due to its remoteness and protection in the Ozark National Forest. Access is very limited below AR 220, and local inquiry should be made about road conditions near Lee Creek Community.

MAPS: Winslow, Strickler, Rudy NE, Natural Dam (USGS); Washington, Crawford (County)

difficulty	II—II+
distance	6.85
time	4
gauge	Lee Creek (USGS)
level	6
scenery	AA
water	Good
gradient	24
latitude	35 45.837N
longitude	94 16.309W

DEVIL'S DEN STATE PARK TO AR 220

DESCRIPTION: This section requires very tight and technical paddling because of numerous willow jungles, downed trees, and strainers. Paddle this section only when accompanied by someone familiar with these hazards.

Blackburn Creek enters on river left 3 miles below the put-in, and just downstream are two nice ledges approximately 50 yards apart. Both ledges form creek-wide hydraulics. Exercise extreme caution at these ledges.

Fall Creek enters on river right 5 miles below the put-in. A short distance downstream, the creek drops abruptly out of a large pool into a narrow passage that flows through an S-curve from river right to left.

The old Silver Bridge at AR 220 was removed and replaced by a new concrete bridge. The access on river right just downstream has been blocked. The take-out is now on river left just upstream of the new bridge. The Arkansas Canoe Club and the Forest Service recently completed a new set of stone steps at the access.

SHUTTLE: From the take-out at the AR 220 bridge over Lee Creek, the put-in is reached by going north on AR 220 approximately 8 miles. Just below the entrance to Devil's Den State Park is a dirt road on the right that leads to the creek.

GAUGE: USGS Lee Creek near Short, Oklahoma. Online at http://waterdata.usgs.gov/nwis/uv/?site_no=07249800.
Minimum: 6.0 *Optimum:* 6.5–8.0 *Dangerous:* >8.5

AR 220 TO LEE CREEK COMMUNITY (COVE CITY)

difficulty	II–II+
distance	3
time	1.5
gauge	Lee Creek (USGS)
level	4.5
scenery	AA
water	Good
gradient	19
latitude	35 42.142N
longitude	94 19.672W

DESCRIPTION: Half a mile below the put-in is a nice class II drop that should be run on river left. Paddlers should be very cautious in low water because there are many rocks in the drop.

Downstream, Football Fields Rapid is over 100 yards of standing waves and surfing holes.

El Horendo follows closely. This rapid used to be a very tight and narrow drop on river right, but over the years floods have tamed this monster, which is now a wide rapid with a 3-foot drop on river right.

A short distance downstream, as the creek turns left, there is a small ledge that forms a good hydraulic. It's fun, but be careful because it's sticky.

Buck and Flush is a short distance downstream. This classic surfing hole was made famous by J. P. Bell's poster photograph commemorating the 25th anniversary of the Arkansas Canoe Club. Nice waves are formed by a rock outcropping on river left just downstream.

The new National Forest access is on river left just below the rock outcropping. Native stone steps lead to a parking lot and boat access (GPS: 35 42.229N, 94 20.485W). This is a great take-out for a short run from AR 220. C. B. Stotts recently completed, for his Eagle Scout project, a one-quarter mile gravel trail to Buck and Flush rapid complete with a bench that has a great view of the rapid.

There are several nice drops below this access point that require your attention, but take time to enjoy the good scenery in this stretch.

Take-out on river left at the ford at Lee Creek Community.

SHUTTLE: From the put-in, go 0.4 mile south on AR 220 and turn right on Lee Creek Road. Go 1.8 miles southwest to Creek Ford Road and turn right. Go 0.6 mile to the ford across the creek. Do not attempt to ford the creek when it is high enough to paddle!

GAUGE: USGS Lee Creek near Short, Oklahoma.
Minimum: 4.5 *Optimum:* 5.5–8.0 *Dangerous:* 8.0

difficulty	I—II
distance	5.5
time	3
gauge	Lee Creek (USGS)
level	4.5
scenery	A
water	Good
gradient	16
latitude	35 40.924N
longitude	94 21.413W

LEE CREEK COMMUNITY (COVE CITY) TO AR 59

DESCRIPTION: Two miles below the put-in, a barbed wire fence stretches across the creek at head level. The fence comes into view as paddlers pass through a willow jungle and turn downstream. Portage on river right.

Just below this point is the sight of the proposed Pine Mountain Dam. This was a dead issue, but has again been raised by some of the small communities in Crawford County.

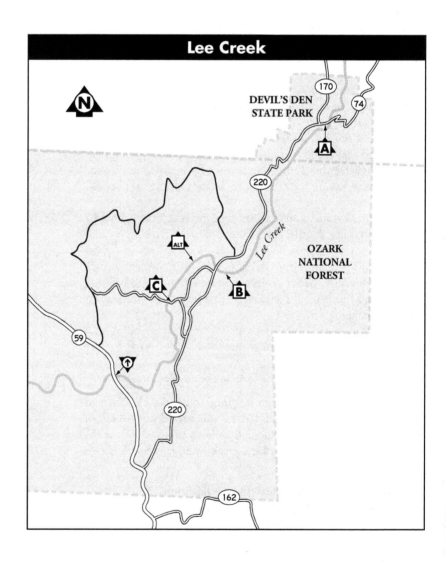

There is a good class II rapid just above the take-out at Natural Dam. Three-foot standing waves form as the stream is squeezed between two islands.

SHUTTLE: From the put-in at Lee Creek Community, go east on Creek Ford Road for 0.6 mile and turn right on Lee Creek Road. Go south on Lee Creek Road for 1.5 miles to AR 220. Turn right (southwest) on AR 220 for 6.1 miles to AR 59 and turn right. Go north on AR 59 for 4.2 miles to the bridge over Lee Creek. Take the dirt road on the upstream right side of the bridge.

GAUGE: USGS Lee Creek, near Short, Oklahoma.
Minimum: 4.5 *Optimum:* 5.0–8.0 *Dangerous:* 8.0

LITTLE MULBERRY CREEK

Little Mulberry Creek is a major tributary of the Mulberry River. The creek rises in Madison County, Arkansas, near the small community of Red Star at an elevation over 2,002 feet and tumbles 19 miles to its confluence with the Mulberry River. Some paddlers have run the 5 miles above Spoke Plant (the put-in as described here), but the access is tough and there is a potential for conflict with landowners.

Expect a narrow creek with willows and downed trees. Scouting all blind turns is highly recommended on this route. Good boat control and class III experience are prerequisites. Little Mulberry Creek sees few paddlers, but it is worth the effort to make the trip.

MAPS: Boston, Oark, Yale (USGS); Madison, Johnson (County)

difficulty	II–III
distance	6.5
time	4
gauge	Turner Bend (USGS)
level	4.5
scenery	A
water	Excellent
gradient	36
latitude	35 45.97N
longitude	93 35.37W

SPOKE PLANT TO OZARK HIGHLANDS TRAIL BRIDGE

DESCRIPTION: Screaming Left Turn is the first rapid that will get your attention. The creek is split by a small rock island with most of the current pushed into the left channel and forced hard left at the bottom of the drop by a large boulder.

Boulder Rapid is marked, appropriately, by a huge boulder in the center of the creek. Paddlers have the choice of river left, a tight but easy squeeze, or river right, a drop over a small hydraulic.

The Willow Jungle rapid poses major potential problems. The right channel takes paddlers through a narrow chute with willows and over-hanging trees. This chute is impassable at lower levels. The left chute is a blind curve with a major blockage of downed trees. This stretch is a must-scout. Below the blockage, the current is swift, and it continues to pick up speed as it flows over bedrock ledges to create several good surfing holes before ending in a nasty hydraulic.

The creek turns left and then abruptly right at Screaming Right Turn. The run is fun, and there is a good surfing wave at the bottom.

Friley's Ledge is just above the bridge at Friley. The ledge is a 3-foot drop that can be run in several places. The left-center drop has several hidden rocks at lower levels.

Just downstream of Friley Bridge is the Boulder Sieve. The creek is forced to river right by a boulder bar in the center of the

creek. The only passage is a narrow willow- and boulder-strewn chute on river right.

The final 2.5 miles are fun and free of major difficulties, but be careful of downed trees in the blind curves.

Take-out on river left upstream of the bridge, and drag your boat to the road.

SHUTTLE: To reach the put-in from Turner Bend, Arkansas, go north on AR 23 for 3.1 miles to AR 215 and turn east (right). Go east 11.1 miles to CR 33 (the first road past the Little Mulberry Bridge) and turn north (left). Go north 2.1 miles and bear right at CR 407. Continue north for 7.7 miles to the low-water bridge at Spoke Plant. To reach the take-out from Spoke Plant, go 5.6 miles south to the concrete bridge just south of the Ozark Highlands Trail crossing. Park upstream; the downstream area is private land.

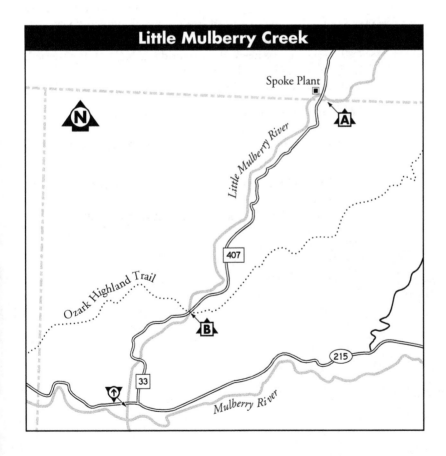

Little Mulberry Creek

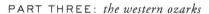

GAUGE: USGS Mulberry River above Mill Creek. Online at http://waterdata.usgs.gov/nwis/uv/?site_no=07252000. This gauge is located just north of Mill Creek and may not be the best indicator of current levels. Often, a better indicator is the Turner Bend Web site, http://www.turnerbend.com/river_gauge.html. This gauge is updated daily by a sight-reading at Turner Bend.
Minimum: 4.5 *Optimum:* 5.0–6.5 *Dangerous:* >7.0

difficulty	II–III
distance	2.75
time	1
gauge	Turner Bend (USGS)
level	4
scenery	A
water	Excellent
gradient	20
latitude	35 42.0557N
longitude	93 38.4300W

B

OZARK HIGHLANDS TRAIL BRIDGE TO AR 215

DESCRIPTION: Little Whiplash is the most imposing rapid on the creek and solid class III. It is easy to see from the shuttle road, but the land surrounding it is private, so respect the landowner's rights. Large boulders block the creek, but there is a narrow center-left chute. It is a straight run if you are lined up properly. The major hazard here could be pinned boats. The far-left channel can also be run.

The right chute below the first bridge is blocked by a tree and is impassable at higher levels.

Take-out on river right just below the bridge at AR 215.

SHUTTLE: To reach the take-out from the put-in, head south from the bridge over the Little Mulberry for 3.26 miles. Turn right and continue west across the AR 215 bridge over the Little Mulberry.

GAUGE: USGS Mulberry River above Mill Creek and Turner Bend gauge.
Minimum: 4.5 *Optimum:* 5.5–6.5 *Dangerous:* >7.0

MIDDLE FORK OF THE WHITE RIVER

The Middle Fork of the White River begins near the small community of Heath, Arkansas, and flows to the northeast to Lake Sequoia near Fayetteville, Arkansas. Paddlers can expect a small stream that flows through a narrow, remote valley that is untouched by the population sprawl of northwest Arkansas. The upper sections reach class III in difficulty and the lower section is class II+ in difficulty. Most of the river runs through private land, so please respect the landowners' rights. Ask permission if there is any question concerning access.

MAPS: Brentwood, Sulphur City (USGS); Madison, Washington (County)

UPPER PASCAL ROAD LOW-WATER BRIDGE TO ARNETT

difficulty	II–III+
distance	1.8
time	1.5
gauge	Visual
level	See gauge text
scenery	A
water	Good
gradient	25
latitude	35 52.164N
longitude	94 00.661W

DESCRIPTION: Buckle your chinstrap! The run starts off with a good class III rapid at the put-in, with waves in the approach and several ledges that end with a 3-foot ledge and a sticky hole. If you have trouble here, consider running the lower sections.

The remainder of the run is a continuous series of class II drops and waves to play.

The low-water bridge at the take-out is dangerous, approach it with caution. Take-out on river left.

SHUTTLE: From the intersection of US 71 and AR 74, you reach the put-in by going northeast 2.5 miles on AR 74 to Whitehouse Road (note that AR 74 and Whitehouse are the same road). Go 2.4 miles on Whitehouse Road to the intersection with CR 118. From the intersection, go east on CR 118 2.9 miles to Pascal Road and turn north (left). Go 0.7 mile on Pascal Road to the low-water bridge. If the river is runnable, you will not be able to cross the low-water bridge. To reach the take-out, reverse your course to Whitehouse Road and turn north (right) on Whitehouse Road. Go north 1.4 miles to Pascal Road and turn east (right). Go 1.1 miles to the low-water bridge.

GAUGE: USGS White River near Fayetteville, Arkansas. Online at http://waterdata.usgs.gov/nwis/uv/?site_no=07048600. This gauge should be used as a general guide to rainfall in the area only. Local inquiry or visual inspection is the only sure way to determine the proper level for a safe paddle. The low-water bridge at the upper put-in should have at least 12 inches flowing over it.

Minimum: 9.0 *Optimum:* 9.5–12.0 *Dangerous:* >14.0

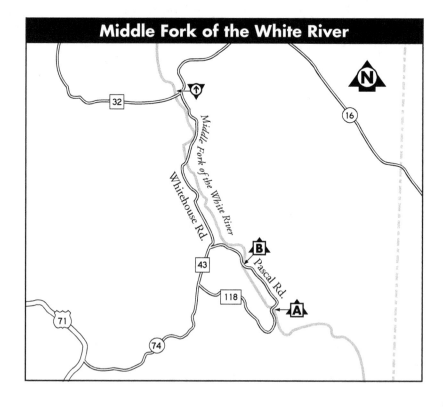

difficulty	II—II+
distance	5.6
time	2.5
gauge	Visual
level	See text
scenery	A—B
water	Good
gradient	24
latitude	35 53.979N
longitude	94 1.5680W

B

ARNETT TO EAST CR 32 (TRACE BRANCH RD)

DESCRIPTION: There are several class II drops in the first part of this section, but the main difficulty is downed trees that have built up during recent floods.

The small bridge for Whitehouse Road is 3.4 miles from the put-in. Be careful and make sure you can paddle safely under the bridge at higher levels.

The frequency of the rapids increases in the next 3 miles. Below the bridge 0.8 mile, the river makes a hard left turn into a rapid with rock ledges on both sides of the river. The waves increase as the river rises. This rapid is visible from the highway.

One mile downstream, paddlers encounter Reese Cemetery Rapid. The river drops over several ledges with holes to avoid, the largest on far river left. Most of the current crashes into a huge boulder on river right. It is easy to avoid with the proper

Middle Fork of the White River

strokes. This spot can easily be reached by parking at the cemetery and taking the trail to the rock overlook. This is a great viewing spot.

Take-out a short distance downstream at the CR 32 bridge on river left, on the downstream side of the bridge. There is a nice parking area with a small trail to the river. The landowner has been nice enough not to post NO TRESPASSING signs, but has placed a sign on the tree asking everyone's help keeping the area clean. Please respect his wishes.

SHUTTLE: From the put-in on Pascal Road, you reach the take-out by going west on Pascal Road for 1.1 miles and turning right on Whitehouse Road. Go 4.8 miles north on Whitehouse Road to CR 32 and turn west (left). Go 0.2 mile and park on the west side of the bridge in a small parking area on the downstream side of the bridge.

GAUGE: White River near Fayetteville, Arkansas. See notes in section A.

Minimum: 9.0 *Optimum:* 9.5–12.0 *Dangerous:* >13.0

MULBERRY RIVER

The Mulberry River rises near the small town of Salus, Arkansas, in the southwest corner of Newton County and flows southwest for 70 miles to its confluence with the Arkansas River at Mulberry, Arkansas.

The Mulberry River flows through many menacing willow jungles and rock gardens, and over moderate drops that create class II and II+ rapids. Willow jungles that act as strainers constitute the greatest challenge for paddlers. The powerful force of water flowing through these willow jungles can pin a boat or a person against the willows with disastrous results.

The Mulberry's water quality is excellent, and the milky green water so distinctive in the Ozarks seems to be more obvious on the river. Oak, pecan, elm, and other hardwood trees cover the riverbanks in the upper sections, and forests alternate with pastureland in the lower sections. Paddlers can expect to find the river flowing swifter, with more rapids, in the upper sections above AR 23, but do not discount the lower sections, which tend to be slower but have some of the biggest drops.

The canoeing put-in is Wolf Pen Recreation Area. One can also put-in at AR 103 and numerous low-water bridges upstream in periods of high water.

MAPS: Ozone, Oark, Yale, Cass, Cravens, Mountainburg SE (USGS); Newton, Johnson, Franklin (County)

difficulty	II—II+
distance	8.4
time	5
gauge	Turner Bend (USGS)
level	2.3
scenery	A
water	Excellent
gradient	20
latitude	35 40.375N
longitude	93 39.9583W

WOLF PEN RECREATION AREA TO BYRD'S CAMPGROUND

DESCRIPTION: Paddlers encounter Toljuso, a sporty class II drop immediately below the pool at the put-in. Good eddies are on both river left and right, with a clear run down the center.

The Little Mulberry enters on river right 2.12 miles below Wolf Pen. This site can be used as an alternate access (GPS: latitude 35 40.372N, longitude 93 39.909). There is a dirt road just west of the bridge over the Little Mulberry. Put-in here and paddle one-third mile to the Mulberry.

Moonshine Ford is just below the confluence with the Little Mulberry. The best run is just left of center, but be aware of rebar in the riverbed at lower levels.

Half a mile downstream, paddlers encounter a fast chute on river left. This is the former site of a rapid called P.H.D., but over the years the river has cut left and most of the current avoids the right channel that formed P.H.D. This spot is still exciting

and can swamp an open boat at higher levels.

One mile downstream is Chainsaw Jungle, a willow jungle that can cause serious problems in high water (3–5 feet). The main channel takes a sharp bend to river left and then a sharp bend to the right approximately 50 yards downstream. The current is swift at all levels, and the sharp turns can cause serious problems for those with little or no boat control. The best advice is to scout the obstacle every time, because the ever-changing river conditions and flooding can wash logs and debris into the channel. If the channel is clear, there are many good eddies to catch, waves to surf, and numerous ferry opportunities.

The Forest Service has provided an excellent access at High Bank on river right a short distance below Chainsaw Jungle. (GPS: latitude 35 40.7267, 93 41.3257 longitude)

Jump Start, a very exciting class II rapid, is just below the High Bank access. The waves build and finish when the river crashes into boulders on river right. Numerous eddies are available for those who wish to practice their skills.

Zeke's Headache is approximately 1.5 miles below Jump Start. This is a fun class II drop that flows from river left to right. At the bottom of the drop are several larger boulders on river right that the current crashes into. Behind the first boulder is the famous eddy, Room of Doom; it is fun but powerful.

At 1.3 miles below Zeke's Headache, paddlers encounter another series of large standing waves. This rapid is known as Whoop and Holler, and at optimum levels can create standing waves 3.5–4 feet high. There are great opportunities for surfing, and large crowds congregate on the rock slab on river right on most weekends.

Bryd's Campground, the take-out, is on river right 1.5 miles below Whoop and Holler. They charge a nominal fee to park, and it is well worth it. They also have a good campground and can shuttle your vehicle.

SHUTTLE: Return to the put-in via AR 215, a paved road that runs beside the river. The distance to the Little Mulberry is almost 5 miles, and the distance to Wolf Pen is 6 miles.

GAUGE: USGS Mulberry River above Mill Creek. Online at http://waterdata.usgs.gov/nwis/uv/?site_no=07252000. Turner Bend has a gauge on its Web site that is updated each morning. This gauge tends to give a more accurate reading of levels upstream of Turner Bend.

Minimum: 2.3 Optimum: 2.5–3.8 Dangerous: >5.

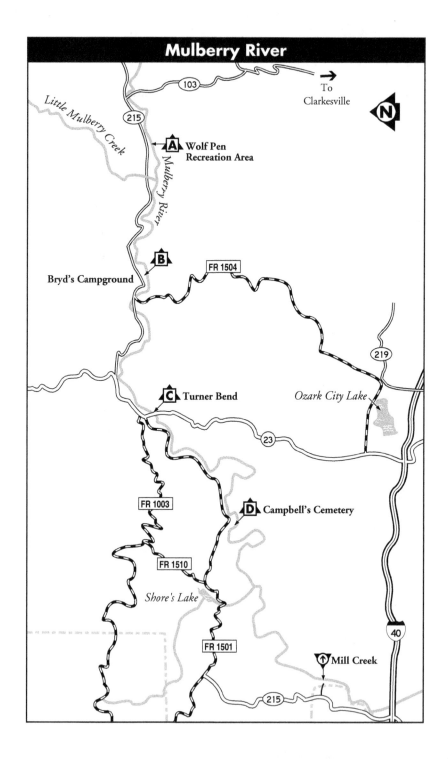

Mulberry River

103

215

To
Clarkesville

N

Little Mulberry Creek

Mulberry River

A Wolf Pen
Recreation Area

B
Bryd's Campground

FR 1504

219

C Turner Bend

Ozark City Lake

23

FR 1003

D Campbell's Cemetery

FR 1510

Shore's Lake

40

FR 1501

↑ Mill Creek

215

BYRD'S CAMPGROUND TO TURNER BEND

difficulty	II
distance	7.25
time	4–5
gauge	Turner Bend (USGS)
level	1.8
scenery	A
water	Excellent
gradient	12.4
latitude	35 40.7209N
longitude	93 44.539W

DESCRIPTION: Troll Shoal is approximately three-quarters of a mile below Byrd's Campground and just above the low-water bridge at FR 1504. Passage under the bridge is possible on river right only. The left side poses extreme danger: A boat could be pinned under this lowest part of the bridge.

Redding Camp and canoe access (GPS: latitude 35 40.1170N, longitude 93 47.1992W) is on river right 3.67 miles below Byrd's Campground. This is a good access for a short trip to Turner Bend. The Forest Service charges $3 per vehicle to park here.

Three-quarters of a mile downstream of Redding Camp, paddlers encounter a narrow chute that ends at a large rock outcropping. The rapid is fast and fun with numerous eddies to test your skills.

Sacroiliac is 1.5 miles below. When you see Fain Creek entering on river right, pull up and scout this drop. The river turns sharply left, then right, with the full force of the current slamming into a house-sized boulder. Good boat control is a must. A sneak route forms at higher levels allowing one to avoid the current directed at the boulder.

Turner Bend is 1.4 miles below Sacroiliac, where AR 23 crosses the Mulberry River. Many people use Turner Bend as a base for canoeing on the Mulberry River. There is a small grocery store that has supplies and beer, canoe rentals, shuttles, gas, and campsites. They will also be glad to give you the latest river conditions if you call (479) 667-3641. The store charges a nominal fee for boat access at its put-in.

SHUTTLE: From the put-in at Byrd's Campground, proceed 6 miles west on AR 215 then turn left on AR 23. Continue 2 miles to the take-out.

GAUGE: USGS Mulberry River above Mill Creek and Turner Bend.
Minimum: 1.8 *Optimum:* 2.2–4.5 *Dangerous:* >5.0

difficulty	I—II
distance	10.5
time	5
gauge	Turner Bend (USGS)
level	1.8
scenery	AA
water	Excellent
gradient	13.9
latitude	35 40.230N
longitude	93 49.676W

TURNER BEND TO CAMPBELL'S CEMETERY

DESCRIPTION: Approximately 1.5 miles below Turner Bend is a willow jungle that can be very difficult. High water makes this spot even more dangerous and it should be scouted for the safest route.

Big Eddy (GPS: latitude 35 39.3753N, longitude 93 51.5402W) is a good access point on FR 1501 2 miles west of AR 23. This is an excellent short run to Campbell's Cemetery, a distance of 8 miles. The access is just west of the Baptist Vista Camp, which is marked by a gravel road.

Three and a half miles below Big Eddy, paddlers encounter Rocking Horse Rapid and then, within sight, Picture Book Rapid. Rocking Horse is fun, with good eddies just below the left turn, but the real fun is at Picture Book. A bluff on river right and boulders on river left constrict the channel, causing the current to pick up speed and the waves to increase. There are several good eddies to catch, especially the one behind the pyramid rock at the top of the drop on river right.

There is a large rock slab just below on river right that is a great lunch stop. Just downstream paddlers find one of the best eddies on the river on river right at Azalea Rapid, named for the wild azaleas that bloom in the spring.

SOB is about a mile below Azalea Rapid. The best route is a narrow chute on river left with a blind curve. Caution is advised due to the possibility of strainers. Several large boulders create a tight course that requires good boat control.

Milton Ford (GPS: 35 37.727N, 93 53.182W) is 1.3 miles below SOB and is a good alternate access point, but if you take-out here, you will miss Hamm's Ford Falls.

Hamm's Ford Falls, a mile below Milton Ford, is one of the best play spots on the Mulberry River. An island splits the river, with the best run on river right. Paddlers enter a narrow chute that ends in a ledge of 2–3 feet with a great surfing hole. Many Arkansas paddlers have honed their surfing skills here.

Just below Hamm's Ford, the river turns left. Then, a long sweeping right turn ends in large waves. This is another great play spot on the Mulberry. This combination of rapids (class II+) makes the short section from Milton Ford to Campbell's Cemetery a classic skills-honing section when time is short.

The Campbell's Cemetery access is a short three-quarter mile below Hamm's Ford.

SHUTTLE: The take-out at Campbell's Cemetery is reached by going approximately a mile north on AR 23 and turning left on AR 215. Go 6.44 miles on AR 215 to the access road at Campbell's Cemetery. Turn left and proceed to the access. The Milton Ford alternate access is 5.33 miles west of AR 23. You will notice several large culverts under AR 215 and a gravel road just to the west that leads south to the river. The Big Eddy alternate access is 2 miles west of AR 23.

GAUGE: USGS Mulberry River above Mill Creek and Turner Bend.
Minimum: 1.8 *Optimum:* 2.4–4.5 *Dangerous:* >5.0

CAMPBELL'S CEMETERY TO MILL CREEK

difficulty	I–II
distance	12.7
time	6-7
gauge	Tuner Bend (USGS)
level	1.6
scenery	AA
water	Good
gradient	9.3
latitude	35 37.4057N
longitude	93 54.6266W

DESCRIPTION: This section of the river tends to be slower, with longer pools, but the pools end in some of the larger drops on the river.

At 2.2 miles below Campbell's Cemetery, paddlers encounter Hell Roaring Falls, a 3-foot drop that can be run almost anywhere with little difficulty. Surfing opportunities are abundant, especially on river left.

Spirits Creek enters on river right, 1.8 miles below Hell Roaring Falls. Spirits Creek (GPS: 35 38.2812N, 93 54.6266W) can be used as an access, but the road is narrow, rough, and muddy. A four-wheel drive vehicle is recommended. Look for the dirt road about 1.2 miles west of Campbell's Cemetery.

V Notch Rapid is 0.4 mile below Spirits Creek.

Hurricane Creek (GPS: 35 36.62N, 93 57.10W) enters on river right, a mile below V Notch Rapid. The adventuresome paddler can float or drag a boat about a mile down Hurricane and use it as an alternate access for a 6.5-mile float to Mill Creek.

Wrecking Rock Rapid is just downstream of Hurricane Creek. This rapid is good even at lower levels. The current pushes your boat towards a large boulder on the left, and you must have just the right stroke to avoid it.

The river enters a beautiful canyon section approximately a mile below Wrecking Rock.

The Shoe is a house-sized boulder in midstream, about 3 miles below Wrecking Rock. Appropriately, it looks like a huge shoe.

Stem Winder, a rapid alongside an island, is a short distance below The Shoe and midway through the canyon section. Over

the years, the current has moved to the left of the island, and in low water it is sometimes difficult to find a good way through the shallow rock garden. Notice the waterfall on river right just below Stem Winder.

Split Willow begins a short distance below Stem Winder. The river turns to the right and drops through an exciting course with plenty of waves and eddies.

Bow Dipper is a mile below Stem Winder. This rock-strewn course is best run on river right.

Mill Creek enters on river right a mile below Bow Dipper.

SHUTTLE: Take-out at Mill Creek. Go 0.6 mile on Plymouth Road from AR 215. The shuttle is 15 miles to Campbell's Cemetery.

GAUGE: USGS Mulberry River above Mill Creek and Turner Bend.
Minimum: 1.6 Optimum: 2.0–4.0 Dangerous: >5.0

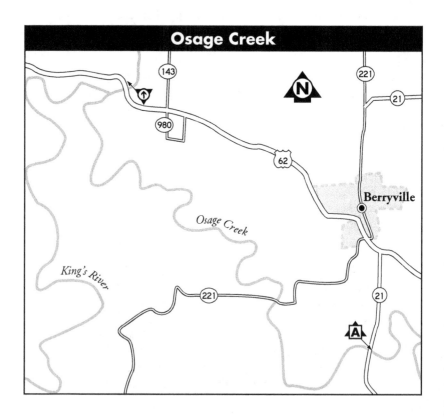

OSAGE CREEK

The headwaters for Osage Creek are north of the Ponca Wilderness near Compton, Arkansas. It flows many miles before the access at AR 21. There are some exciting stretches in the upper section during periods of heavy rain, but the route described here is a class I with great fishing possibilities.

Osage Creek merges into the King's River just upstream of the US 62 Arkansas Game and Fish Commission Access.

Paddlers can expect good scenery and a good current. The only hazards are from trees and willows.

MAPS: Berryville, Rockhouse, Eureka Springs (USGS); Carroll (County)

AR 21 TO US 62

difficulty	I
distance	11.25
time	6
gauge	King's (USGS)
level	3.5
scenery	A
water	Good
gradient	8.4
latitude	36 20.246N
longitude	93 33.852W

DESCRIPTION: The scenery is good, and you will rarely see another boat. This is a great section for testing your fly-fishing skills.

Check with King's River Outfitters for water levels and shuttle information.

SHUTTLE: The put-in is 1.7 miles south of Berryville, Arkansas, on AR 21. To reach the take-out from the put-in, go north 1.7 miles on AR 21. Turn east on US 62. Go east 5.5 miles on US 62 to the bridge over the King's River. Take the first right past the bridge. Follow the Arkansas Game and Fish Commission signs to the access.

GAUGE: USGS King's River near Berryville. Online at http://waterdata.usgs.gov/ar/nwis/uv/?site_no=07050500&PARAmeter_cd=00065,00060. The actual gauge is near Grandview, so local inquiry with King's River Outfitters is your best bet for up-to-date levels. Their number is (479) 253-8954

Minimum: 3.5 Optimum: 4.0–5.5 Dangerous: >6.0

UPPER WHITE RIVER

The White River rises in the Ozark National Forest near Boston, Arkansas, and flows along AR 16 until it is impounded at Lake Sequoyah near Fayetteville. The river's upper stretches flow through small shoals and willow jungles that present little difficulty to experienced paddlers. The speed of the current slows as the stream approaches the lake. The landscape that surrounds the stream is more open due to the proximity of AR 16, and this diminishes the wilderness scenery slightly. Water quality on the Upper White is on par with most Ozark streams.

MAPS: Boston, Pettigrew, St. Paul, Delaney, Durham, Goshen, Elkins (USGS); Madison, Washington (County)

difficulty	I—II
distance	12.8
time	6
gauge	None
level	See gauge text
scenery	A
water	Good
gradient	10
latitude	35 49.106N
longitude	93 38.880W

St. Paul to Crosses

DESCRIPTION: There are several low-water bridges to watch out for in high water, when dangerous backwashes can form on the downstream side. Portaging is necessary in low water.

SHUTTLE: From AR 16, turn on CR 112 and put-in at the river, which is within sight of the turn. To reach the take-out at Crosses, Arkansas, go west on AR 16 for 11.2 miles and turn right onto CR 328. Proceed 0.6 mile to the river.

GAUGE: None. This is a very easy class I float under most conditions, but flooding can cause dangerous situations near low-water bridges and in sharp bends. If the shoals visible from AR 16 have many visible rocks, the river is too low to paddle.

difficulty	I—II
distance	8.71
time	4
gauge	None
level	See gauge text
scenery	A
water	Good
gradient	7.5
latitude	35 52.697N
longitude	93 54.525W

Crosses to Durham

DESCRIPTION: Watch out for downed trees and the ever present willow jungles on this otherwise easy stretch.

SHUTTLE: From Crosses, take CR 328 0.6 mile and go west (right) on AR 16 for 7.1 miles and turn right on Durham Road. Proceed 0.1 mile to the river.

GAUGE: None. See section A above.

DURHAM TO AR 74

difficulty	I–II
distance	7.25
time	3.5
gauge	None
level	See gauge text
scenery	A
water	Good
gradient	10
latitude	35 57.109N
longitude	93 58.756W

DESCRIPTION: This is a straightforward class I float. It is more developed than the preceding sections, but still scenic. Take-out at the AR 74 bridge on river right on the upstream side of the bridge.

SHUTTLE: From Durham, go west on AR 16 for 6.5 miles and turn right on AR 74. Proceed 0.4 mile to the AR 74 bridge. Take-out at the bridge on river right, on the upstream side of the bridge

GAUGE: None. See section A above.

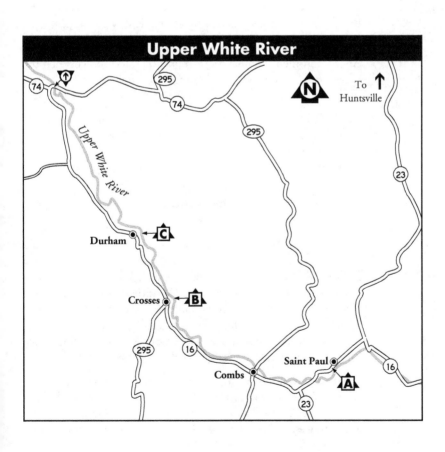

Upper White River

WAR EAGLE CREEK

War Eagle Creek rises just east of Boston, Arkansas, and flows northwest to Beaver Lake. War Eagle Creek is class II, with the exception of the upper reaches in the Ozark National Forest, which can approach class III at high water.

   Hardwood forests line the banks along the creek's upper sections, and the forests alternate with farmland in the lower sections. Water quality is good, and the current moves at a moderate to good pace. Water levels can become problematic in the summer, so be careful.

MAPS: Boston, Witter, Huntsville, Forum, Hindsville, Spring Valley (USGS); Madison, Washington, Benton (County)

difficulty	I—II
distance	10
time	5
gauge	War Eagle (USGS)
level	2
scenery	A
water	Good
gradient	7.2
latitude	36 2.496N
longitude	93 42.310W

AR 23 TO HUNTSVILLE (AR 68)

DESCRIPTION: There are no major difficulties along this stretch, but the scenery is good and the paddling is very pleasant.

SHUTTLE: The put-in is 4 miles south of Huntsville, Arkansas, on AR 23 and then 0.7 mile south (right) on CR 186. To reach the take-out from Huntsville, go northeast 3.8 miles on US 412 and turn north (left) on CR 53. Reach the creek in less than 1,000 feet.

GAUGE: USGS War Eagle Creek, Hindsville. Online at http://waterdata.usgs.gov/ar/nwis/uv/?site_no=07049000&PARAmeter_cd=00065,00060.
   Minimum: 1.8 Optimum: 2.0–3.0 Dangerous: >3.5

difficulty	I—II
distance	6.9
time	8
gauge	War Eagle (USGS)
level	2
scenery	A
water	Good
gradient	2.5
latitude	36 7.293N
longitude	93 41.649W

HUNTSVILLE (AR 68) TO ROCKY FORD

DESCRIPTION: Along this stretch, AR 23 crosses War Eagle Creek 4.5 miles below the put-in at Withrow Springs State Park. The park can be used an access point for a short trip from AR 68. There are excellent camping facilities at the park as well.

   Rocky Ford is located 2.4 miles below Withrow Springs State Park. The creek can be accessed at this point via CR 40.

SHUTTLE: From the put-in, to reach the take-out go southwest on US 412 2.6 miles and turn north (right) on AR 23. Go 4.5 miles northeast to AR 23W and turn northwest (left). Continue 0.8 mile and turn west (left) on CR 40. Go west 1.5 miles to Rocky Ford.

GAUGE: USGS War Eagle Creek, Hindsville.
Minimum: 1.8 *Optimum:* 2.0–3.0 *Dangerous:* >3.5

ROCKY FORD TO AR 45

DESCRIPTION: This is a scenic paddle through alternating pastoral land and scenic bluffs.

SHUTTLE: From the put-in at Rocky Ford, go east 1.5 miles on CR 40 to AR 23W. Follow AR 23W to AR 23 and turn north (left). Go north 11 miles on AR 23 and turn southwest (left) on AR 12. Go 6.3 miles southwest on AR 12 to AR 45 and turn south (left). Continue 3.3 miles on AR 45 to take-out.

difficulty	I
distance	10.2
time	5
gauge	War Eagle (USGS)
level	2
scenery	A
water	Good
gradient	3.2
latitude	36 9.672N
longitude	93 45.648W

GAUGE: USGS War Eagle Creek, Hindsville.
Minimum: 1.8 *Optimum:* 2.0–3.0 *Dangerous:* >3.5

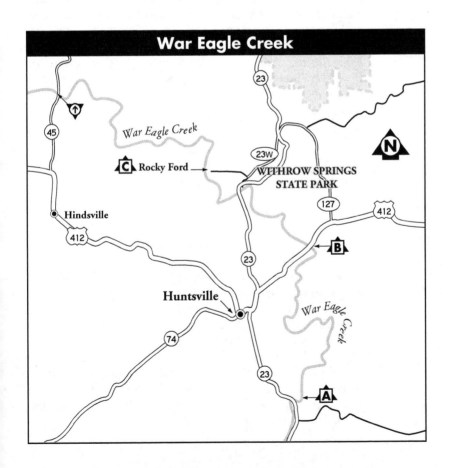

War Eagle Creek

WEST FORK OF THE WHITE RIVER

The West Fork of the White River begins near Winslow, Arkansas, and flows along US 71 to Fayetteville and on to Beaver Lake. A class I–II paddle with a few class III drops in the upper section, the stream flows through willow thickets in the upper stretches and farmland as it nears Fayetteville.

Water quality on the West Fork of the White is good, but the wilderness experience is somewhat limited due to the stream's proximity to US 71 and the constant noise of vehicles on this highway. The completion of I-540, however, diverted most of the heavy traffic and returned some serenity to the valley. Gently sloping banks are tree-lined in the upper stretches but give way to large open fields as the stream approached Fayetteville.

Except in periods of very high water, the normal beginning point for paddling is the Roadside Park just north of Brentwood, Arkansas.

Runs are possible in the 5-mile stretch above the Roadside Park, but this stretch is very sensitive to water levels and the river is a small, narrow creek that drops an average of 36 feet per mile with a difficulty of class II+–III. In fact, a class III drop is visible from put-in just beyond a small private bridge. The other class III rapid is visible from the road just before the junction with AR 74. The put-in for this upper stretch is at Winslow Park, just beyond the Final Gas Station on the east side of the highway. There is plenty of parking available.

MAPS: Winslow, Brentwood, West Fork, Fayetteville, Elkins (USGS); Washington (County)

difficulty	I–II+
distance	7
time	3
gauge	White River (USGS) near Fayetteville
level	5.0
scenery	A–B
water	Good
gradient	19
latitude	35 51.992N
longitude	94 7.067W

ROAD SIDE PARK TO WEST FORK

DESCRIPTION: Watch for willow jungles in the first few miles. There are also several class II shoals to contend with.

Winn Creek enters on river left just upstream of the Woolsey Bridge, adding considerably to the volume of the river.

There is an alternate access at Woolsey, Arkansas, 3.7 miles below Road Side Park (GPS: latitude 35 53.125N, longitude 94 1.177W). A large steel bridge across the river is accessible from US 71. Parking is very limited, however, and it is a good idea to unload you boats on the east side of the bridge and park at the Woolsey Cemetery at the junction of Woolsey Road and US 71. This access is a good choice when the water level is questionable at Road Side Park.

There is a major hazard just upstream of the AR 156 bridge at West Fork. The city of West Fork constructed a low-head dam at Riverside Park. When you see the park on river left, pull out and portage around the dam. Do not attempt to run the low-head dam at West Fork. Take-out well above it. It is a river-wide hydraulic that can kill at any floatable level!

SHUTTLE: Put-in at the rest area on US 71 just north of Brentwood on the west side of the highway. The take-out is in West Fork, 7 miles north on US 71. Turn west (left) at AR 170 and go half a mile to the river. Cross the river and turn left into Riverside Park. There is plenty of parking.

GAUGE: USGS White River near Fayetteville. Online at http://waterdata.usgs.gov/nwis/uv/?site_no=07048550.
Minimum: 5.0 *Optimum:* 5.5–7.0 *Dangerous:* >8.0

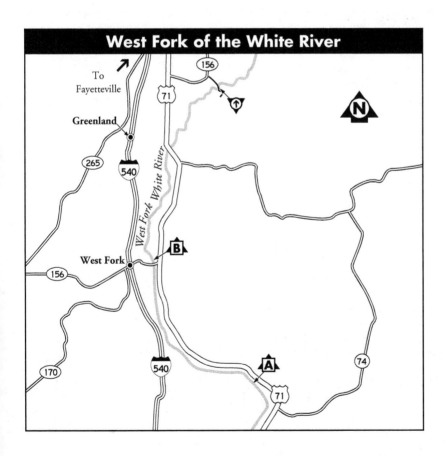

difficulty	I—II
distance	8
time	3.5
gauge	White River (USGS) near Fayetteville
level	5.0
scenery	A—B
water	Good
gradient	13.6
latitude	35 55.689N
longitude	94 11.060W

WEST FORK TO FAYETTEVILLE

DESCRIPTION: This is a good class I–II run, especially if you live in the Fayetteville area and want to paddle close to home.

There is an access just west of US 71 on Jones Road 4.4 miles below the put-in. If you decide to use this access, park at Baptist Ford Church on the south side of the bridge.

Take-out at Wilson Hollow Road just off AR 56 on river left, upstream of the bridge. Vehicles can go over this bridge, but it is narrow and in disrepair. It is best to park on the north side in the parking area.

SHUTTLE: Reach the take-out from West Fork, Arkansas, by going east on AR 170 to US 71 and turning north (left). Go 6.8 miles north on US 71 to AR 156 and turn east (right). Go east 1.5 miles on AR 156 to South Wilson Hollow Road and turn southeast (right). Continue 1.3 miles to the access.

GAUGE: USGS White River near Fayetteville.
Minimum: 5.0 *Optimum:* 5.5–7.0 *Dangerous:* >8.0

ALUM FORK OF THE SALINE RIVER

The Alum Fork rises in the Alum Creek Experimental Forest east of Iron Springs National Forest Campground on AR 7 and flows to the southeast to join the North, South, and Middle Forks of the Saline River near Benton, Arkansas. There are few rapids en route, but numerous willow jungles, downed trees, and deadfalls keep paddlers alert at all times in the nearly constant current.

MAPS: Paron, Lonsdale NE, Haskell, Benton (USGS); Saline (County)

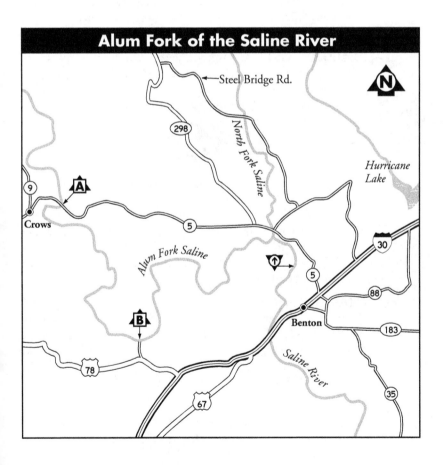

difficulty	I—II
distance	9.5
time	5
gauge	Saline (USGS)
level	5.8
scenery	B
water	Good
gradient	6.8
latitude	34 36.973N
longitude	92 45.040W

CROWS (AR 5) TO SMITH FORD ROAD

DESCRIPTION: There are no major difficulties along this stream section, but paddlers must watch for willow jungles and brush piles that can create dangerous strainers.

The Middle Fork of the Saline enters on river right 3.6 miles below the put-in, and the South Fork of the Saline enters on river right 8 miles below the put-in.

SHUTTLE: From Benton, Arkansas, the put-in is 10.7 miles west on AR 5. To reach the take-out from the put-in on AR 5, go west 1.5 miles on AR 5 and turn south (left) on Narrows Road. Go south 4.9 miles on Narrows Road to Walnut Ridge Road. Go southeast (left) 2.1 miles on Walnut Ridge Road to US 70. Go east (left) 4.7 miles on US 70 and turn north (left) on Smith Ford Road. The take-out is 0.8 mile down Smith Ford Road.

GAUGE: USGS Saline River at Benton. Online at http://water-data.usgs.gov/ar/nwis/uv/?site_no=07363000&PARAmeter_cd=00065,00060.
Minimum: 5.8 *Optimum:* 7.0–12.0 *Dangerous:* >14.0

difficulty	I
distance	11
time	6
gauge	Saline (USGS)
level	7.0
scenery	B
water	Good
gradient	3.7
latitude	34 33.065N
longitude	92 42.066W

SMITH FORD ROAD TO THE BENTON CITY PARK

DESCRIPTION: Watch out for willow jungles and deadfalls along this stretch. The North Fork of the Saline combines with the Alum Fork to create the Saline River 9.6 miles below the put-in

Take-out at Benton City Park, which is reached via Lyledale Road from South AR 5 in Benton.

SHUTTLE: From the put-in on Smith Ford Road, go south 0.4 mile to US 70 and continue east (left) 1.2 miles to Interstate 30 (Exit 111). Go 5.4 miles northeast on I-30 and get off at Exit 117. Turn right on AR 35, then make a quick left on Old Hot Springs Road. Go 1.2 miles on Old Hot Springs Road and turn west (left) on Lyledale Road. Continue 0.9 mile to the river access.

GAUGE: USGS Saline River at Benton.
Minimum: 5.8 *Optimum:* 7.0–12.0 *Dangerous:* >14.0

BAKER CREEK

Baker Creek begins in the Caney Creek Wilderness Area on Porter Mountain at an elevation of 1,600 feet and drops over 400 feet before combining with Harris Creek and emptying into the Cossatot River below AR 278. This is a very tough and technical run that should only be attempted by experienced paddlers who are completely comfortable with the Five Falls area of the Cossatot River. Make sure that you have good maps of the area before trying to take on the myriad roads that Weyerhaeuser is constantly cutting in the area. These roads become very slick in wet weather due to the clay-based soil.

The stream is very narrow, and the water flows very swiftly through a small gorge lined with pines, which creates a feeling of complete isolation. The put-in and take-out are totally uncharacteristic of the run; at each, the stream recalls the typical, small creeks that one often passes on rural roads. Don't be fooled.

MAPS: Baker Springs (USGS); Howard (County)

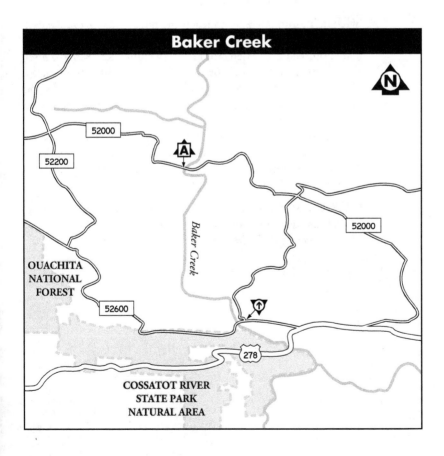

difficulty	III–IV
distance	3.2
time	2
gauge	Cossatot (USGS)
level	5
scenery	A
water	Good
gradient	59.1
latitude	34 19.912N
longitude	94 11.094W

WEYERHAEUSER ROAD 52000 TO WEYERHAEUSER ROAD 52600

DESCRIPTION: The put-in looks very innocent, but this is a challenging run for even skilled paddlers. When the creek turns from east to south, get ready for the meat of the run.

One-quarter mile downstream, the creek drops over an 8-foot waterfall in the middle of a 90° turn. Several decked boaters have experienced piton pins here in low water! This is a solid class IV drop.

Class III rapids follow for a short distance before paddlers encounter another 15-foot waterfall. This can be very fun but caution should be exercised.

The balance of the run is exciting with many class II–III rapids but no major difficulties.

SHUTTLE: From AR 278, to reach the put-in take Weyerhaeuser Road 52600 to the intersection with Weyerhaeuser Road 52200. Then, proceed north (left) to the intersection with Weyerhaeuser Road 52000 and go east on 52000 a short distance to Baker Creek. A small wooden bridge crosses the creek and marks the put-in. Recently, a locked gate has sometimes prevented access, so check with other boaters before attempting this run if possible.

Take-out at the low-water bridge at Weyerhaeuser Road 52600 (GPS: longitude N34 18.171, latitude W94 10.390). This road is impassable due to high water when the Cossatot River is over 5.7 on the Cossatot gauge.

GAUGE: USGS Cossatot near Vandervoort, Arkansas. Online at http://waterdata.usgs.gov/nwis/uv/?site_no=07340300.
Minimum: 5.0 *Optimum:* 5.5–7.5 *Dangerous:* >8.0

BIG CREEK (OKLAHOMA)

Big Creek is located approximately 15 miles south of Heavener, Oklahoma, and 17 miles west of Mena, Arkansas, on US 270/59 in a narrow gorge squeezed by Black Fork Mountain to the north and Rich Mountain on the south. Park at the State Line Bar located at the Arkansas and Oklahoma Line. This is among whitewater paddling's great put-ins, a beer joint on the Arkansas-Oklahoma border! Drag your boat across the road and the railroad tracks to the creek.

Good scenery, especially the maple trees in the fall, and the backdrop of the mountains on both sides of the creek make this a special run.

MAPS: Mountain Fork, Arkansas, Page, Oklahoma (USGS); Le Flore, Oklahoma (County)

US 270 (OKLAHOMA STATE LINE) TO PAGE, OKLAHOMA

difficulty	II–III
distance	6.3
time	3.5
gauge	Black Fork (USGS)
level	8.5
scenery	A
water	Good
gradient	49
latitude	34 42.439N
longitude	94 27.306W

DESCRIPTION: Paddlers encounter a class II+ rapid just below the state-line put-in. The creek drops over several ledges that require good boat control. Strainers and willow jungles with downed trees present a significant hazard. It is best to run this one with someone that has experience on Big Creek.

Class II+ and class III rapids continue almost nonstop for the next 6 miles. It would be easier to count the pools than the rapids.

There are numerous blind turns that require paddlers to be very cautious. One of the most noteworthy of these turns is at Volkswagen Rapid (which gets its name from a large rock that looks like a Volkswagen when viewed from downstream). The creek turns to the right and is constricted by willows on both sides as it turns back to the left. Paddlers need to stay on the inside of the left turn and bear to the left of the midstream boulder. Do not go to the right of the rock because pyramid rocks choking the channel can pin or upset your boat. Eddy behind the first rock and get ready for the Volkswagen Rock, 75 yards downstream. The proper course is to the left of Volkswagen Rock, with a good eddy behind the rock at moderate levels, but be careful at higher levels when a mean hydraulic forms behind the Volkswagen.

Strong eddies and surfing waves are too numerous to count on the creek downstream.

The last bit of excitement is at the take-out. Each paddler has to make Last Chance Eddy or risk being swept downstream over the old bridge abutment.

SHUTTLE: To reach the put-in, cross US 270 at the WELCOME TO OKLAHOMA sign and carry over the Kansas City Southern Railroad tracks to the creek. The take-out is located approximately 7.5 miles west at Page, Oklahoma. Turn north at the sign that points to Big Creek Baptist Church. There is parking on the northwest side of the bridge.

GAUGE: USGS Black Fork below Big Creek near Page, Oklahoma. Online at http://waterdata.usgs.gov/ok/nwis/uv/?site_no=07247250&PARAmeter_cd=00065,00060.
 Minimum: 8.5 *Optimum:* 9.5–11.50 *Dangerous:* 12.0

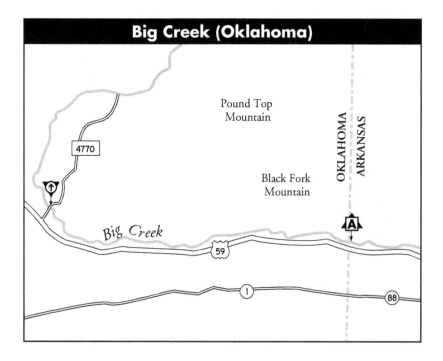

BRUSHY CREEK

Brushy Creek's headwaters are near Smoke Rock Mountain south of AR 375 and just east of the Cossatot River watershed. Brushy Creek is a major tributary of the Cossatot and flows into that river just above the Brushy Creek Access in the Cossatot River State Park Natural Area. In many ways, Brushy is a miniature version of the Cossatot, with the same characteristics but a smaller watershed.

Paddlers will find the creek resembles the upper stretches of the Cossatot, with class II–II+ rapids in a very pristine setting. The Ouachita National Forest protects the entire watershed and there are few signs of civilization. This is a hidden jewel that few have paddled. This is also a great run when the main Cossatot route is too high to paddle.

MAPS: Eagle Mountain (USGS); Polk (County)

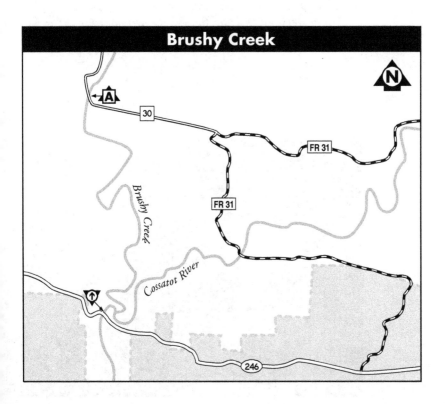

difficulty	II–II+
distance	5.9
time	3
gauge	Cossatot (USGS)
level	6
scenery	A
water	Good
gradient	26.8
latitude	34 25.540N
longitude	94 14.362W

A

CR 30 TO AR 246

DESCRIPTION: Paddlers encounter class II–II+ rapids at medium levels on this run. The difficulty increases at higher levels due to swifter current and the likelihood of downed trees.

The pour-over at the confluence with the Cossatot can approach class III in high water conditions.

SHUTTLE: To reach the put-in from the Brushy Creek Access on AR 246 (the take-out), go east on AR 246 4 miles and turn north (left) on FR 31 (there is a sign for the west trailhead of the Caney Creek Wilderness at this turn). Proceed north on FR 31 6.9 miles to CR 30 and turn east (left). Go 2.2 miles to the low-water bridge at Brushy Creek.

GAUGE: USGS Cossatot River near Vandervoort. Online at http://waterdata.usgs.gov/nwis/uv/?site_no=07340300.
Minimum: 6.0 *Optimum:* 6.5–8.0 *Dangerous:* >9.0

Photo by Mike Stanley

CADDO RIVER

The Caddo River begins south of AR 8 near the Missouri Mountains and flows to the southeast, passing near Norman, Caddo Gap, and Glenwood before entering the backwaters of Degray Reservoir. The reservoir destroyed some of the Caddo's best whitewater, but the remaining river still offers some good class II runs when spring rains are sufficient.

The Caddo River is a small stream in its upper sections that races to the east over moderate drops and through numerous willow thickets, which present an ever-present danger to the unsuspecting paddler. The stream begins to widen and slow as it turns south at Norman. Water quality is excellent in the upper sections and good in the middle and lower sections. Dense forests protect the headwaters and the river flows through many open fields as it nears Degray Reservoir.

MAPS: Athens, Glenwood, Amity, Point Cedar (USGS); Montgomery, Pike, Clark(County)

FR 73 TO NORMAN

difficulty	II (II+)
distance	7.3
time	3
gauge	Caddo (USGS)
level	Local Inquiry
scenery	A
water	Excellent
gradient	19
latitude	34 26.902N
longitude	93 46.944W

DESCRIPTION: Be on the lookout for strainers and wire fences in the upper stretch. There is a low-water bridge 2 miles below put-in. Approach with caution and portage if there is any question about the safety of running it.

There is another low-water bridge 2.8 miles below the first that paddlers should also be cautious of.

Take-out in Norman, Arkansas, alongside AR 8.

SHUTTLE: To reach the put-in from the intersection of AR 27 and AR 8 in Norman, go west 6.4 miles on AR 8 and turn south (left) on FR 73. Go south 0.3 mile to the access.

GAUGE: USGS Caddo River near Caddo Gap, Arkansas. Online at http://waterdata.usgs.gov/ar/nwis/uv/?site_no=07359 610&PARAmeter_cd=00065,00060.

This is a new gauge and there is not yet enough data to determine the minimum, ideal, and dangerous levels. Local inquiry with one of the many area outfitters is still the best way to determine appropriate levels. Check the Arkansas Department of Parks and Tourism Web site for links to outfitters in the area: http://www.arkansas.com/outdoors_sports/float/.

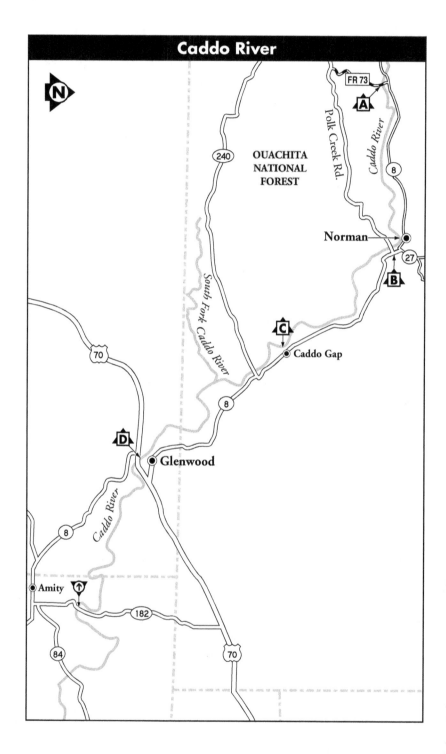

Caddo River

FR 73

A

Polk Creek Rd.

Caddo River

240   OUACHITA
NATIONAL
FOREST

8

Norman

27

B

South Fork Caddo River

70

C

Caddo Gap

8

D

Glenwood

Caddo River

8

Amity

182

84

70

NORMAN TO CADDO GAP

difficulty	I—II
distance	6.63
time	3
gauge	Caddo (USGS)
level	Local Inquiry
scenery	A
water	Good
gradient	12
latitude	34 27.233N
longitude	93 40.955W

DESCRIPTION: The scenery along this stretch is pleasant, and the river moves at a good pace. Class I rapids are scattered along this section. Watch for brush snags and downed trees.

SHUTTLE: From the put-in at Norman, go south on AR 8 6.3 miles to Caddo Gap and turn west (right) on Manfred Road. Go west 0.3 mile to the access.

GAUGE: USGS Caddo River near Caddo Gap. See Section A.

CADDO GAP TO GLENWOOD

difficulty	I (II-)
distance	9
time	4
gauge	Caddo (USGS)
level	Local Inquiry
scenery	A—B
water	Good
gradient	7
latitude	34 23.920N
longitude	93 37.317W

DESCRIPTION: Famous for its natural springs and as the westernmost point of Desoto's travels, Caddo Gap is a town worth exploring before or after your paddling trip.

Half a mile below the Gap, AR 240 crosses the river. This spot can serve as an alternate access.

One and three-quarter miles below AR 240, the South Fork of the Caddo enters and adds to the river's flow.

SHUTTLE: From the put-in at Caddo Gap, go south 7.1 miles on AR 8 to Glenwood, Arkansas. The take-out is located in the town.

GAUGE: USGS Caddo River near Caddo Gap. See Section A.

GLENWOOD TO AMITY

difficulty	I
distance	8.76
time	5
gauge	Caddo (USGS)
level	Local Inquiry
scenery	A
water	Good
gradient	5
latitude	34 19.298N
longitude	93 33.171W

DESCRIPTION: This section moves at a good pace and is floatable more often than the upper sections due to the addition of the South Fork of the Caddo and several creeks.

SHUTTLE: From the Glenwood put-in, go 0.2 mile west on US 70 and turn south (left) on AR 8. Go south 7.4 miles on AR 8 to Amity, Arkansas, and turn east (left) on AR 84. Go 3.3 miles east on AR 84 to the Caddo River access.

GAUGE: USGS Caddo River near Caddo Gap. See Section A.

COSSATOT RIVER

The Cossatot River rises southeast of Mena, Arkansas, and is one of the most difficult whitewater streams in the state. The river originally flowed uninterrupted for 87 miles to its confluence with the Little River, but with the completion of Gillam Dam, it has now been broken into two sections. The upper section offers paddlers 22 miles, from AR 375 to AR 278. The Cossatot River State Park Natural Area now protects the section from AR 246 to AR 278, and this is where the shut-ins are located.

The shut-ins are strictly for experienced whitewater paddlers who are comfortable on class III–IV rapids. Some say this is a river for decked boats only, but canoes filled with adequate flotation and experienced paddlers have successfully negotiated the Cossatot River.

The landscape of the Cossatot departs dramatically from the typical Ozark stream as it cuts through topography that one might expect to find in the Western states. Stark-gray rock outcroppings are covered with pine trees as a result of many years of clear-cutting and replanting. The water quality is good due to protection of the watershed by the Ouachita National Forest and the Cossatot River State Park Natural Area.

MAPS: Eagle Mountain, Nichols Mountain, Baker Springs, Wickes (USGS); Polk, Umpire (County)

difficulty	II–II+
distance	9
time	4.5
gauge	Cossatot (USGS)
level	5
scenery	A
water	Good
gradient	23
latitude	34 25.326N
longitude	94 8.998W

FR 31 to AR 246

DESCRIPTION: Runs on the upper 12.4 miles above the Brushy Creek Access at AR 246 are possible thanks to numerous access points along FR 31, but the second bridge above AR 246, reached via FR 31, is the best access point. Sufficient water levels above the second bridge make access problematic from the south, and the shuttle would be very long.

Paddlers will encounter a very beautiful run with a swift but manageable current and up to class II+ rapids. Winter trips on this section are very special.

The low-water bridge at Gilliam Spring is 5.5 miles below the put-in. Approach with caution and portage on river left or right. This bridge can be used as an access point, and there's a good parking area on the east side of the bridge. The run from here to AR 246 is 3.4 miles. This access can also be used to paddle to the Ed Banks Low-Water Bridge at lower levels, a distance of 6.4 miles.

SHUTTLE: From the Brushy Creek Access at AR 246, go east on AR 246 4 miles and turn north (left) on FR 31 (there is a sign for the west trailhead of the Caney Creek Wilderness at this turn). Proceed north on FR 31 a total of 10.6 miles to reach the uppermost access. You will pass the first bridge 4 miles from AR 246.

GAUGE: USGS Cossatot River near Vandervoort. Online at http://waterdata.usgs.gov/nwis/uv/?site_no=07340300.
   Minimum: 5.0 *Optimum:* 5.5–7.0 *Dangerous:* >7.5

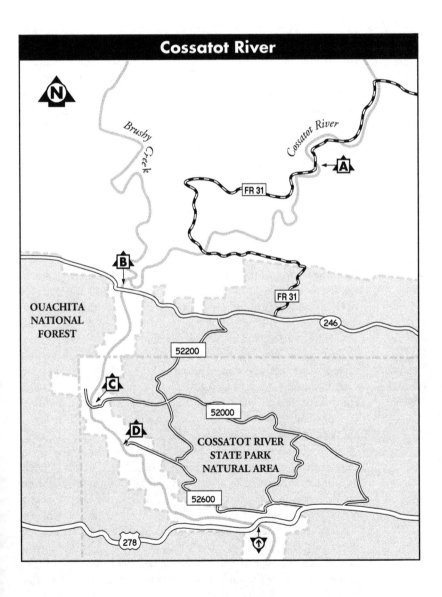

difficulty	II–II+
distance	3
time	1.5
gauge	Cossatot (USGS)
level	3.4
scenery	A
water	Good
gradient	21
latitude	34 22.853N
longitude	94 14.063W

AR 246 TO ED BANKS LOW-WATER BRIDGE (WEYERHAEUSER ROAD 52200)

DESCRIPTION: This section is characterized by many tight turns through rock gardens that create a natural slalom course of class II rapids. This is a good warm-up for the more difficult sections below.

SHUTTLE: The put-in is the parking area on the upstream west side of the Brushy Creek Access at the AR 246 bridge. To reach the take-out, go east from the AR 246 bridge for 1 mile and turn south at the state park sign. Go 4.5 miles, turn right, then proceed 2 miles to the Ed Banks Low-Water Bridge access. The state park has done an excellent job of marking the route, and gates now close many of the Weyerhaeuser roads that were so confusing.

GAUGE: USGS Cossatot River near Vandervoort.
Minimum: 3.4 Optimum: 3.6–5.0 Dangerous: >5.5

difficulty	II–III (IV)
distance	3
time	1.5
gauge	Cossatot (USGS)
level	3
scenery	A
water	Good
gradient	20
latitude	34 20.389N
longitude	94 15.047W

ED BANKS LOW-WATER BRIDGE TO SANDBAR BRIDGE

DESCRIPTION: One-quarter mile below the put-in, paddlers encounter Zig-Zag, a class III rapid. It is run with an approach on river left with an option to eddy out above the drop before making a 90° turn into a 4-foot drop surrounded by boulders. Zig Zag can be surfed, and enders are possible at levels above 4 feet.

Just below Zig-Zag there is a small ledge with a nice surfing wave at levels above 4.2 feet. Beware of the rocks below!

A hundred yards downstream, the river turns to the left and is constricted into a tight channel. For the next 200 yards, paddlers encounter the Esses. The Esses can approach class IV at levels above 5.5 feet, and at lower levels the danger of pinning your boat increases. Enter the Esses to the left of the boulders and work to river right. There are good eddies throughout the run. Watch out for a boulder jumble in mid-river about midway through the rapid. Just below the boulder jumble is a 3.5-foot drop midway through the rapid that should be run on river left at levels below 4.7 feet. The remainder of the run has nice waves and a turn to the right to negotiate. At lower levels, avoid the right side as you near the end of the run—several boats have been pinned on rocks hiding just below the surface, at least one of which required fast

action by several rescuers to avoid serious consequences.

Approximately 100 yards below the Esses, there is a class III rapid with several ledges and boulders strewn in the way. Approach on river right and work left to avoid a large rock. There are also several holes to contend with in the rapid.

A short distance downstream, paddlers encounter a class III double-drop ledge. Approach to the left of center and eddy behind the first ledge. There is a good hole to play before dropping over the second ledge.

Just above the low-water bridge, there is a good class II rapid where the river turns to the left. Paddlers should enter this rapid on river right and work to the left to avoid rocks at the top and bottom. A short distance below, the river splits, with most of the flow going left of a large rock outcropping. At higher levels, a good play spot develops in the smaller right-hand channel.

As you approach the low-water bridge, move to the left and prepare to portage. At minimum flows, some boats can pass safely under the bridge, but this is not a recommended practice. At medium and higher flows, safety dictates staying far to the left and portaging. Seal launches off the downstream side of the bridge are fun and the most common reentry method, but peer over the edge first to be sure you will not land on the broken concrete found in some places.

SHUTTLE: From Ed Banks Low-Water Bridge on Weyerhaeuser 52000, to reach the take-out go east for 2 miles and turn south on Weyerhaeuser Road 52200. Go 1.7 miles and turn west on Weyerhaeuser Road 52600. Continue 1.8 miles to the Sandbar Bridge access. The state park signs are excellent in this section also.

GAUGE: USGS Cossatot River near Vandervoort.
Minimum: 3.0 Optimum: 3.3–5.0 Dangerous: >5.5

SANDBAR BRIDGE TO AR 278

difficulty	III–IV
distance	4.5
time	4
gauge	Cossatot (USGS)
level	3
scenery	AA
water	Good
gradient	26
latitude	34 19.340N
longitude	94 14.127W

DESCRIPTION: This section of the Cossatot is strictly for advanced paddlers who have a sure roll in class IV whitewater or expert open boaters with plenty of flotation. It is comparable in difficulty to the Five Falls area of the Chattooga River in Georgia, but due to a forgiving geology lacks the deadly undercuts and has fewer foot entrapment threats than the famous Five Falls.

One hundred yards below the put-in is a good class II rapid with numerous waves to warm up on before venturing into the Cossatot Falls.

In the next one-third mile, the Cossatot River drops 80 feet over six major falls:

1) **Cossatosser (class III)** is a big drop that bears right with large waves and strong currents. Watch for a pinning boulder on river left at the run out. There is a large eddy where you can collect your thoughts and scout the remaining drops from the left shore.

2) **Eye Opener (class III)** is a 5-foot drop with a large hole at the bottom. This is a good place to do enders, if you dare. If you swim, recover quickly to prevent going over the right side of BMF below. Ferry to the left to approach BMF. At levels above 5 feet, a serious hydraulic forms, and many experienced boaters begin running an alternate route in the far-left channel. Just below Eye Opener, you may want to consider beaching on the left bank and setting up throw ropes below BMF for your group.

3) **BMF (class III)** is a rapid with a diagonal approach and sharp turn to the right at the bottom. It can be run straight at levels over 4.5 feet. Eddy quickly to avoid being swept through the Washing Machine. Ropes set here may prevent a nasty swim of the Washing Machine just below! There is also a good class III route on far river right that averts the danger of being swept over the Machine if you have a mishap. This alternate route is found by working right instead of left just as you leave Eye Opener and should be considered by those who are still testing their wings. Good boat control is essential in the next 30 feet.

4) **Washing Machine (class IV)** is a drop of 7–8 feet with a long diagonal approach from river right to left. The current runs into "Pappy's Rock," a large rock outcropping at the bottom of the slide, and paddlers can successfully negotiate the drop with an effective draw stroke at the precise moment. Cut the corner too soon or with too much draw and you will end up in the Washing Machine Hole—not a good place to swim! Local boaters have explored several alternate routes in addition to the "traditional" run described here. This rapid is more difficult at lower levels, because the "Cannonball" rock is exposed and exit from the Machine becomes more problematic. At levels above 4.5 feet, the Washing Machine can be run over the top, a sudden 8-foot drop. *Note:* Rescue lines should be set before running the Washing Machine. Eddy out behind Pappy's Rock and climb up on the rock to set ropes and watch others make the run.

5) **Whiplash (III–III+)**, a very fast double drop, is immediately below. You may want to catch the small right side eddy just as you enter the rapid, but a barely submerged shelf rock may catch your bow at lower levels. There is a major eddy on river left past the drop and numerous rocks appear at levels below 3.7 feet. Avoid a swim here or it will be a bruiser!

6) **Last One** (**class III**) is a fitting finish to the Five Falls. It has one of the best ender holes around on river right at the bottom of the drop. Optimum levels for enders are 3.3–4.2 feet. A second ender hole forms at levels above 5 feet on river left. Just downstream on river left is a good gravel bar to recover on or stop at for lunch. At levels below 4 feet, local kayakers often opt to carry back upstream from this point and take-out at the Cossatot Falls Campground. Five hundred yards downstream is a very lively class II rapid with numerous standing waves to surf and play.

Approximately a mile downstream, paddlers encounter Deer Camp Rapids (class III), with many rocks to avoid. Pinnings are a danger here, but there are also a number of play spots, including a fun side-surf hole near the bottom on river right.

Devil Hollow Rapid (III–IV) is half a mile downstream where the river picks up speed and turns to the right. There is an eddy on river left where you can stop and scout your course. Run the rapid to river right to avoid the rock garden on river left. The rapid then turns back to the left, with several large waves to surf at the bottom. This rapid merits caution because it is shallow enough to have caused several facial injuries to upside-down boaters.

Just downstream is Devil Hollow Falls, a class IV drop of 6–8 feet that is often run or portaged along the far right channel. The safe routes vary with the water level and cannot be easily described, so scouting or consultation with local boaters is highly recommended. *Caution:* River-left and -center routes that may appear safe can be extremely dangerous due to sharp rocks hidden in the foam pile below the falls. Numerous pinnings and other mishaps have resulted in close calls, cuts, sprains, and even a broken bone or two at several locations in this rapid.

The short paddle to the take-out is a welcome rest from the whitewater paddlers have just navigated.

SHUTTLE: To reach the take-out, follow the state park signs from the put-in to AR 278 (note that all signs refer to AR 278 as AR 4, its former designation) and turn west (right). Go a short distance and park on the west side of the bridge along the road. A small road leads to a primitive parking lot, which may also be open. The climb from the river is steep. You may elect to take-out just downstream of the AR 278 bridge at a low-water bridge. A new Visitor Center and much improved access is being constructed on river right, just south of the river. Once it is opened (which is scheduled for 2004), it is likely that the river-left access will again be closed.

GAUGE: USGS Cossatot River near Vandervoort.
Minimum: 3.0 *Optimum:* 3.3–4.2 *Dangerous:* >5.5

EAGLE FORK CREEK

Eagle Fork Creek, known locally as simply Eagle Fork, begins on the northeast slope of Little River Mountain northwest of Octavia, Oklahoma, and flows to the southeast approximately 20 miles to its confluence with the Mountain Fork River. Eagle Fork's length is short, but it gets help from Cucumber Creek just above the put-in and Little Eagle Creek just below.

Eagle Fork Creek is very remote and scenic along the section from OK 144 to Smithville. Paddlers can expect a class II–II+ stream protected by hardwoods and bluffs in the upper section. Several small waterfalls add to the excitement in this stretch.

MAPS: Ludlow, Octavia, Smithville (USGS); Le Flore, McCurtain (County)

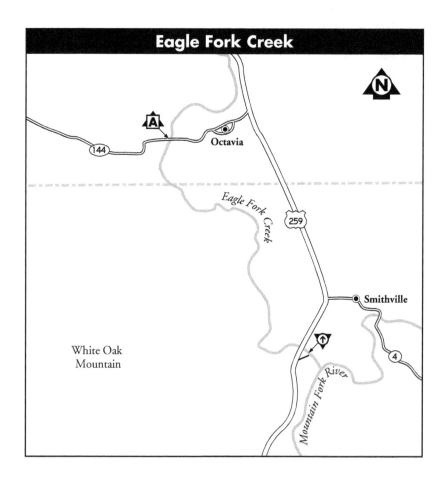

OK 144 TO SMITHVILLE

difficulty	II–II+
distance	8.5
time	4-5
gauge	Visual
level	Local inquiry
scenery	A
water	Good
gradient	18.8
latitude	34 31.305N
longitude	94 43.361W

DESCRIPTION: There is a fun class II rapid just above the Eagle Fork's confluence with Little Eagle Creek, approximately a mile below the put-in

Class II shoals are common, separated by short pools with good current. The scenery in the upper section is beautiful and remote.

Approximately 3.5 miles below the put-in, there is a good class II waterfall that drops into a shallow, fast chute below. If you swim, it can be bouncy. Remember to keep your feet in front of you and slightly out of the water if you are so unlucky as to capsize.

There is a low-water bridge 4.2 miles below the put-in that may need to be portaged depending on the water level.

Take-out at a small bridge just downstream of the US 259 bridge on river right.

SHUTTLE: To reach the put-in from the intersection of US 259 and OK 144, go 3.1 miles on OK 144 to the bridge over Eagle Fork Creek, which is the access point. From the put-in, backtrack 3.1 miles to US 259 and turn south to reach the take-out. Proceed 5.8 miles on US 259, cross Eagle Fork Creek just south of Smithville, and take the first road past the bridge on the left. It goes a short distance to the take-out.

GAUGE: None. Local inquiry is required, and area outfitters may be able to help with river levels. River Edge cottages may be helpful with levels in the area; their Web site is www.riversedge cottages.com.

JACK CREEK

Jack Creek, born on the southwest side of Petit Jean Mountain, flows northeast in a narrow gorge 700 feet deep between Hogan Mountain and North Petit Jean Mountain. Jack Creek breaks out of the gorge just above a small low-water bridge 3 miles east of the Jack Creek Recreation Area on Jack Creek Road. This is the standard put-in for the run.

Paddlers will find a creek that is very scenic and remote with rapids up to class III in difficulty. Jack Creek is normally runnable after heavy rains in the area. Check the Internet rain gauges before you venture to this creek, unless you know someone in the area who can give you a visual reading.

Class III experience is a must before attempting this run. If Sugar Creek is too high, Jack Creek is a good alternative run. In some cases, when you finish the short run on Jack Creek, Sugar Creek will have dropped enough for a safe run.

MAPS: Sugar Grove (USGS); Scott, Logan (County)

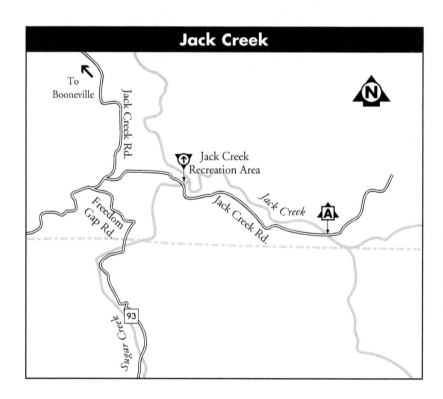

Photo by Mike Coogan

JACK CREEK ROAD LOW-WATER BRIDGE
TO JACK CREEK RECREATION AREA

difficulty	II–III
distance	2.9
time	2
gauge	Sight
level	1.8
scenery	AA
water	Good
gradient	65
latitude	35 1.394N
longitude	93 48.705W

DESCRIPTION: This is a fast run on a narrow and scenic creek. Class II–III rapids abound. Watch out for downed trees.

SHUTTLE: From the intersection of AR 22 and AR 23 in Booneville, Arkansas, head south 1.2 miles on AR 23 to Jack Creek Road and turn southeast (left). Proceed 10.4 miles to the Jack Creek Recreation Area. There is a small parking lot on the east side of the bridge over Sugar Creek, this is the take-out. The put-in is 2.4 east of the Jack Creek Recreation Area on Jack Creek Road.

GAUGE: There is a sight gauge painted on the downstream side of the Jack Creek Road Bridge. Because water levels change quickly on Jack Creek, an on-site inspection is the only reliable means of ascertaining the level.

Minimum: 1.8 *Optimum:* 2.0–2.5 *Dangerous:* >3.0

LITTLE MISSOURI RIVER

The Little Missouri River begins in the Caney Creek Wildlife Management Area and flows southeast to Greeson Lake. The river cuts through the Ouachita Mountains, creating the spectacular Little Missouri Falls near its headwaters and class II, III, and occasionally IV rapids below. Besides the rapids, there's dramatic scenery in store for paddlers due to the remoteness of the river and the geology of the Ouachita Mountains.

The Little Missouri River is for experienced paddlers comfortable in class III whitewater and able to negotiate large standing waves. The river is more technical than most in the state, requiring complex maneuvers in many of the rapids.

The canoe run begins at Albert Pike Campground, except in periods of very high water when paddlers can put-in at numerous spots along FR 73. Be cautious of downed trees and numerous willow jungles if you attempt the upper reaches of the Little Missouri. The area surrounding Albert Pike is lined with vacation homes, mostly on river right, for approximately a mile below the put-in. Below this section the river is very fast and narrow, dropping through several willow-lined chutes with good standing waves. It then widens slightly, and the stark bluffs of the Ouachitas and the pine forests typical of this region greet paddlers. Water quality on the Little Missouri is the best the author has experienced in the Ozark or Ouachita Mountains.

MAPS: Athens (USGS); Montgomery, Pike (County)

ALBERT PIKE CAMPGROUND TO AR 84 BRIDGE

difficulty	II—III- (IV)
distance	8.5
time	4
gauge	Little Missouri (USGS)/AR 84 bridge
level	4.5'/12"
scenery	AA—A
water	Excellent
gradient	24
latitude	34 22.444N
longitude	93 52.642W

DESCRIPTION: The first mile of this run is very exciting, with constant class II rapids, moderate standing waves, and sharp turns. Paddlers can expect to find several rapids with large boulders in the river that require the ability to use eddies for scouting purposes.

One and a half miles below the put-in, the river makes a left turn and then a quick right. Paddlers will notice a boulder garden just downstream with an eddy on river left just above Eye of the Needle (class III), also known as Pinball. The best run is the slot on river left. A straight run is possible on the left at levels above 6 feet. Lower levels require maneuvering. This rapid is more difficult in lower water, and pinnings your boat is a real concern.

One and a half miles downstream, paddlers encounter a long class II rapid. At the bottom of this rapid, Blaylock Creek enters on river right, adding considerably to the volume of the river.

Half a mile below Blaylock Creek, the river turns right. Approach from the left and run The Slalom Course (class III) on left-center. There are numerous places to make eddy turns. Be aware of the holes on river right and -center in high water.

Three-quarters of a mile below The Slalom Course, the river divides around an island that marks the approach to Winding Stair Rapid. This series of four drops is class II–III and possibly class IV at higher levels. Take the left chute around the island for the best run through Winding Stair Rapid. There is an opportunity to scout by stopping on river left just above the first drop. The first drop is a 2-foot ledge that should be run on river left near the willows. Avoid river right, as there is a possible hydraulic along the ledge. You are then in position to ferry into the best chute of the second drop. This is a 2-foot ledge that can be run almost any-where in high water and on river left in low water. Large standing waves form below, with good eddies on both sides for playing the river or recovering swamped canoes. Twenty-five yards below the second drop is a twisting drop that can be run on river right or left in high water but only on river right in low water. Several boulders are in position to catch swamped canoes. The final drop is dotted with several boulders in midstream that should be avoided. This drop is done easily at high levels by staying to river right. The drop is a more difficult at low levels, and an S-turn is required. If time

permits, stop and have lunch at Winding Stair Creek on river left. The short climb up the boulders is well worth the effort. The creek flows over solid bedrock here, creating a special place.

Approximately one-quarter mile below the Winding Stair, paddlers encounter a series of class II waves ending in a very interesting rapid known as Edgar's Surprise (class III+). A large ledge in midstream creates a hidden diagonal bar obscured by standing waves. Do not be fooled, use the series of eddies on river right and avoid the hidden diagonal hole on river left at the end of the wave train. The hole is nasty and a keeper at all levels. It gets worse and more difficult to avoid at high levels.

Vines Branch Creek enters on river right half a mile below. This is another good spot to have lunch or gather your equipment.

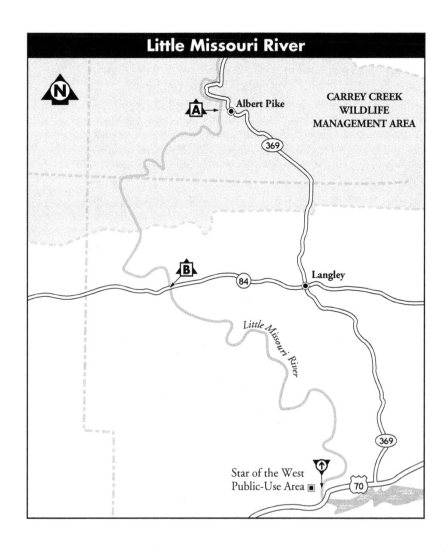

A short distance below Vines Branch Creek, the waves increase and can fill an open boat before the real fun begins at Boulder Garden (class III). Run this rapid on river right to avoid the holes that form on river left at levels above 6 feet.

Two and a quarter miles downstream, the river turns to the left and then back right. The waves increase in intensity for the next half mile at Acceleration Rapid (class III). There are plenty of eddies at levels below 6 feet, but above 6 feet eddies become scarce. This stretch is one of the most fun on the river!

There are several class II rapids in the final 1.5 miles. Just above the take-out is a nice ledge with several play spots.

SHUTTLE: Albert Pike Campground is 5.5 miles north of Langley, Arkansas, on AR 369. The take-out is on river left just below the AR 84 bridge, 3.4 miles west of Langley.

GAUGE: USGS Little Missouri near Langley, Arkansas. Online at http://waterdata.usgs.gov/nwis/uv/?site_no=07360200. The USGS gauge is located at the AR 84 bridge. There is also a homemade gauge painted on an abutment of the AR 84 bridge on the east side of the river. A simple conversion system between each gauge is to subtract 42" from the USGS gauge reading to correlate the visual reading at the AR 84 bridge.
Minimum: 4.5' USGS / 12" visual gauge *Optimum:* 5.0–6.0' / 18–24" *Dangerous:* 6.5+'/36"

AR 84 Bridge to US 70 Bridge

DESCRIPTION: There are no major difficulties in this section, but there are many class II rapids in the first 3 miles.

Some of the largest standing waves are encountered in the last 5 miles. They can easily swamp an open boat, especially if it is tandem, so exercise caution when the river is at higher levels.

SHUTTLE: From the put-in at AR 84, to reach the take-out go east 3.5 miles to AR 369 and turn south (right). Go south 6 miles to US 70 and turn west (right). Continue approximately 1.4 miles to the Star of the West Public-Use Area. Proceed to the access on the Little Missouri.

GAUGE: USGS Little Missouri near Langley and visual gauge on the AR 84 bridge.
Minimum: 4.5' USGS / 12" visual gauge *Optimum:* 5.0–6.0'/ 18–24" *Dangerous:* 6.5+'/36"

difficulty	II (II+)
distance	11.5
time	6.5
gauge	Little Missouri (USGS)/AR 84 bridge
level	4.0'/6"
scenery	A–B
water	Good
gradient	16.5
latitude	34 18.695
longitude	93 53.980

LOWER OUACHITA RIVER

Locally, the section from Remmel Dam to Rockport is simply known as the Rockport Run. The actual run is rarely done, as there is but one class II drop and that is at the takeout at Rockport. The Rockport Ledge, just upstream of the I-30 bridge, has become a favorite for paddlers in the Little Rock area, however. Most paddlers simply put-in at the Rockport Ledge. There is a very small ledge downstream, just past the bridge, and another class II drop at the old Tanner Street Bridge. It is common to see a multitude of brightly colored kayaks playing in the upper ledge on most weekdays and every weekend throughout the summer. They are attracted by the holes and waves that form at the class II ledge thanks to a dependable flow from Remmel Dam. You can find boaters who spend all day honing their river skills at the Rockport Ledge.

A study by the Arkansas Canoe Club determined that it is very feasible to enhance the riverbed to provide multiple world-class play spots at full flow and at least one at the minimum flow near the old Tanner Bridge site. Efforts towards that end are underway, but their implementation is not yet certain. Entergy, which controls the dam, has also played a very positive role by working closely with the Arkansas Canoe Club to further the recreational aspects of this section of the river. The dam is now obliged to provide full recreational release flows for three hours between noon and 5 p.m. from Memorial Day to Labor Day. Typically, they start at noon and in wet years often run much longer than the three-hour minimum. In addition, the dam provides up to four special releases of six hours each any time of year. The dam is also required to release a small continuous flow at all times. This flow is low, but floatable. Finally, Entergy publishes its flow release plan weekly. This information can be obtained via e-mail subscription; from a recorded phone message at (501) 620-5760; or on the Web site www.entergy.com/Corp/utilitypower/data.asp.

The river run from Remmel Dam to the Rockport Ledge is a scenic class I float. At higher levels, you need to be aware of swift current that can wash you into trees. At the normal full-generation/recreational-release flow, the river is reasonably swift in the first couple of miles and then slows down for the last few miles. There are only a couple of riffles and one side channel at the top. At the lower, continuous-flow levels, paddlers must pick the correct course through several small rock gardens, and at the very lowest flow you might have to get out and drag over a very short shoal if you don't pick a good line.

MAPS: Lake Catherine, Malvern North (USGS); Hot Spring (County)

difficulty	I (II)
distance	5.95
time	2–3
gauge	Ouachita (USGS) Remmel Dam
level	4.0
scenery	A–B
water	Good
gradient	3.4
latitude	34 25.631N
longitude	92 53.560W

DESCRIPTION: The actual run is easy class I water with a good current and plenty of great scenery. There are some signs of civilization as the river approaches an area a few miles downstream of the put-in with several very nice houses on river left. There are a few nice bluffs, and you cannot hear the sound of the highway until you get within a mile of the takeout.

The Upper Rockport Ledge, above the I-30 bridge, is a great place to learn ferries and eddies and to get that first combat roll in easy moving water. The area is often used by swift-water rescue training classes and by decked boaters who want to learn and practice rodeo skills. It is not uncommon to see open boats surfing the ledge among the multitude of kayakers. This is the sight of the annual Arkansas Canoe Club Rendezvous Rodeo in mid-September.

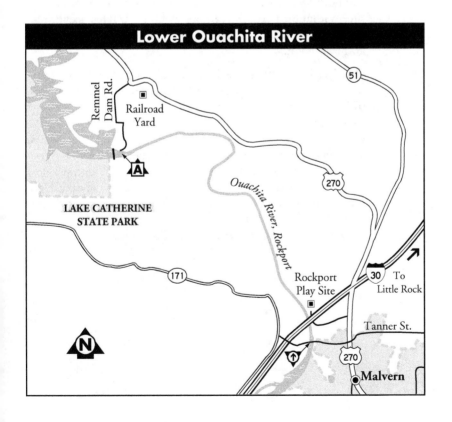

There is a take-out at the concrete boat ramp on the left in the new Millennium Park, or you can proceed downstream and take-out just below the I-30 bridge at the old Tanner Bridge site on river right. The Arkansas Highway and Transportation Department will be replacing this bridge in 2004 through 2005.

SHUTTLE: Reach the put-in by taking Exit 98B on I-30 and heading west 5.7 miles on US 270 to Jones Mill. Turn south (left) on Remmel Dam Road. Go 1.3 miles to the access area below Remmel Dam. There are multiple river-access points and a concrete boat ramp if you need it. From the put-in, to reach the Upper Rockport Ledge take-out, head 1.3 miles north on Remmel Dam Road and turn right on US 270. Go south 5.7 miles on US 270, continue over the interstate, and take the first right into the new Malvern Industrial Park. Follow the road south and west until you pass under the I-30 bridge and continue to the parking area for the play ledge. The Malvern Water Works will soon build a new water treatment plant here. You can also take-out at the old Tanner Bridge site by going south one exit on I-30 (Exit 97). Go a short distance to AR 171 and turn south (left), cross over I-30 and head back toward the river a short distance to the old bridge site. Within the next few years, a new bridge will replace the old, and hopefully the City of Malvern will provide better river access at this location.

GAUGE: USGS Ouachita River at Remmel Dam below Jones Mill. Online at http://waterdata.usgs.gov/nwis/uv/?site_no= 07359002. From www.entergy.com/hydro click on "Entergy Real Time Lake Level Data" to reach the Entergy Web page showing the flow at Remmel Dam in 15-minute increments. You can hear this data on a recorded message at (501) 620-5760, option 3. Approximately 6 feet (3600 CFS) is the optimal flow for playing at the ledge. Entergy rarely releases flows between the minimum continuous and the optimum flow for playing. So it is typically either up or down.

Minimum: 3.0 Optimum: 5.5–6.5 Dangerous: >7.0

NORTH FORK OF THE SALINE RIVER

The North Fork of the Saline River begins near Crystal Mountain in the Ouachita National Forest and flows to the south to join the Alum Fork of the Saline just below AR 5 near Benton, Arkansas. The upper sections above CR S are full of deadfalls that require paddlers to carry over many of these spots.

Paddlers can expect a river that flows through hardwood forests, creating a sanctuary for wildlife. The pools move at a good pace at normal flows, and the river's proximity to Little Rock makes it a favorite for a Sunday afternoon paddle to stretch the muscles. Water quality is relatively good.

MAPS: Paron SW, Paron, Fourche SW, Lake Norrell, Congo, Benton (USGS); Saline (County)

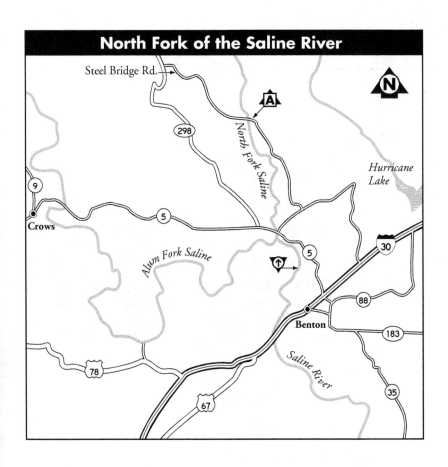

difficulty	I—II
distance	6.5
time	3
gauge	Saline (USGS)
level	5.8
scenery	B
water	Good
gradient	9.7
latitude	34 39.642N
longitude	92 38.116W

STEEL BRIDGE ROAD TO BENTON

DESCRIPTION: Expect a continuous flow except in short pools separated by willow jungles and brush piles.

Take out at Benton City Park.

SHUTTLE: To reach the put-in go northwest 2.1 miles on AR 5 and turn northeast (right) on Mulberry Salem Road. Go 1.2 miles on Mulberry Salem Road to Brazil Road and turn north (left). Go 3.5 north on Brazil Road and turn west on Steel Bridge Road. Proceed 1 mile to the river.

GAUGE: USGS Saline River at Benton, Arkansas. Online at http://waterdata.usgs.gov/ar/nwis/uv/?site_no=07363000& PARAmeter_cd=00065,00060.

Minimum: 5.8 *Optimum:* 7.0–12.0 *Dangerous:* >14.0

OUACHITA RIVER

The Ouachita River begins west of Mena, Arkansas, near Rich Mountain and flows to the east before it is impounded to form Lake Ouachita. The river itself is not too difficult but offers paddlers a chance to experience the remoteness of the area in the upper stretches and a chance to fish in the sections closer to the lake.

The Ouachita appears rather lazy as it flows under the bridge at AR 71. This site is indicative of the overall characteristics paddlers will find on the river. The Ouachita National Forest protects its watershed, and there are virtually no large communities along the Ouachita's entire length. Consequently, paddlers and anglers are treated to a quiet, peaceful stream away from the frantic city.

MAPS: Rich Mountain, Alcorn, Mena, Board Camp, Pine Ridge, Oden, Mt. Ida, Sims, Story (USGS); Polk, Montgomery (County)

MCGUIRE ACCESS TO CHERRY HILL

difficulty	I
distance	6.7
time	3
gauge	Ouachita (USGS)
level	3
scenery	A
water	Good
gradient	3.6
latitude	34 33.818N
longitude	94 3.894W

DESCRIPTION: The river is small and narrow along this section. Paddlers should be on the watch for downed trees and logjams.

SHUTTLE: From the intersection of AR 88 and US 59 in Mena, Arkansas, reach the put-in by going 8.6 miles east on AR 88 and turning south (right) on CR 63. Go 1.3 miles to CR 68. Go 0.6 mile southwest (right) on CR 68 to the McGuire Access. Reach the take-out by backtracking to AR 88 and turning east. Go 4.2 miles east on AR 88 and turn south (right) on CR 67. Go 0.8 mile to the Cherry Hill Access.

GAUGE: USGS Ouachita River near Mt. Ida, Arkansas. Online at http://waterdata.usgs.gov/ar/nwis/uv/?site_no=07356000&PARameter_cd=00065,00060.
Minimum: 3.0 Optimum: 3.5-5.0 Dangerous: >7.0

difficulty	I-II
distance	19.5
time	7
gauge	Ouachita (USGS)
level	3
scenery	A
water	Good
gradient	5.5
latitude	34 34.531N
longitude	93 59.908W

CHERRY HILL TO SHIRLEY CREEK ACCESS

DESCRIPTION: This is a long float, but the current moves pretty well. Paddlers will seldom have to contend with crowds in this section. The Forest Service float camp is an excellent base camp. There are campsites with picnic tables and rest rooms.

SHUTTLE: To reach the take-out from the put-in at Cherry Hill, go 0.8 mile north on CR 67 to AR 88 and turn east (right). Go 10.5 to the Shirley Creek Access sign and turn south (right) and proceed 1.2 miles to the Shirley Creek Access.

GAUGE: USGS Ouachita River near Mt. Ida.
Minimum: 3.0 *Optimum:* 3.5–5.0 *Dangerous:* >7.0

difficulty	I—II
distance	3.5
time	5.5
gauge	Ouachita (USGS)
level	3
scenery	A
water	Good
gradient	4.6
latitude	34 34.897N
longitude	93 53.026W

SHIRLEY CREEK ACCESS TO ODEN

DESCRIPTION: There are several class II rapids to keep paddlers' attention in this section, not to mention beautiful scenery.

SHUTTLE: From the put-in at Shirley Creek, reach the take-out by going 1.2 miles north to AR 88 and turning east (right). Go 4.2 miles to Oden and turn south (right) on AR 379. Go south 0.6 mile on AR 379 to the Oden Access.

GAUGE: USGS Ouachita River near Mt. Ida.
Minimum: 3.0 *Optimum:* 3.5–5.0 *Dangerous:* >6.0

difficulty	I—II
distance	9.5
time	5
gauge	Ouachita (USGS)
level	2.5
scenery	A+
water	Good
gradient	4.7
latitude	34 36.670N
longitude	93 46.664W

ODEN TO ROCKY SHOALS

DESCRIPTION: Brushy Creek enters on river left just downstream of the put-in. This is one of the more popular sections of the river. Paddlers can expect many good rapids and several very scenic bluffs, which add to the wilderness experience.

SHUTTLE: To reach the take-out from the put-in at Oden, go north 0.6 mile on AR 379 and turning east on AR 88. Go east 2.8 miles to Pencil Bluff, Arkansas, and turn southeast (right) on

Ouachita River

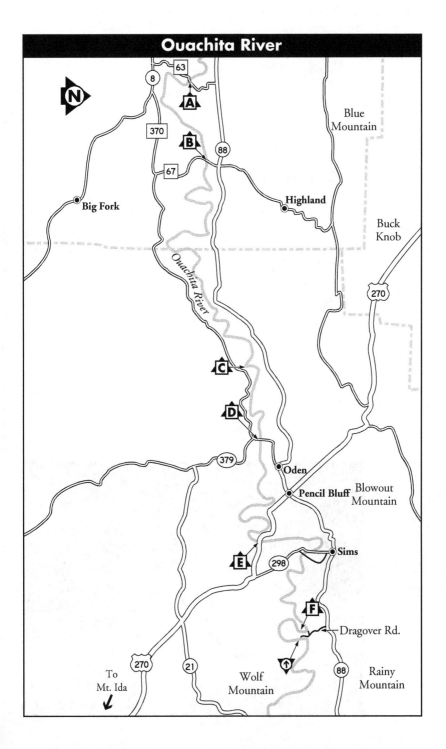

US 270. Go 3.1 miles on US 270 and cross the Ouachita River to access the Rocky Shoals Access off US 270 to the left.

GAUGE: USGS Ouachita River near Mt. Ida.
Minimum: 2.5 Optimum: 3.0–5.0 Dangerous: >6.0

difficulty	I-II
distance	9.3
time	5
gauge	Ouachita (USGS)
level	2.5
scenery	A+
water	Good
gradient	4.6
latitude	34 36.674N
longitude	93 41.866W

ROCKY SHOALS TO DRAGOVER FLOAT CAMP

DESCRIPTION: Sims Float Camp is 4 miles below the put-in. Fulton Branch Float Camp is 3 miles below Sims, and Dragover Float Camp is 2.3 miles below Fulton Branch.

SHUTTLE: From the put-in at Rocky Shoals, reach the take-out by going 3.8 miles northwest on US 270 and turning east (right) on AR 88. Go east 7.3 miles on AR 88 and turn south at the Dragover access road. Go 1.5 miles to the campground.

GAUGE: USGS Ouachita River near Mt. Ida.
Minimum: 2.5 Optimum: 3.0–5.0 Dangerous: >6.0

DRAGOVER LOOP

difficulty	I—II (II+)
distance	3.25
time	2
gauge	Ouachita (USGS)
level	2
scenery	AA
water	Good
gradient	7.7
latitude	34 38.512N
longitude	93 38.059W

DESCRIPTION: This is one of the most unique river trips to be found. You can put in at Dragover Campground and paddle just over 3 miles to the take-out and walk approximately 0.25 mile back to the put-in. This is the easiest shuttle anywhere in this area!

This section is a fun class I–II run with a good current. There is a good class II rapid with a drop and a nice hole not far from the put-in and one class II+ rapid about 2.4 miles from the put-in. Large boulders block the channel and the paddler is required to maneuver through the boulders for a safe passage.

There are several more class II rapids before the take-out. This run can be paddled several times in a day.

Take-out on river left where a small dirt road leads to the river. If you've never paddled this section, it is a good idea to go to the take-out before the run and leave a marker (GPS: 34 38.275N, 93 37.599W). You can take-out just downstream at River Bluff Campground, but why bother? That involves a real shuttle.

SHUTTLE: Hike a quarter mile back up the trail to the put-in.

GAUGE: USGS Ouachita River near Mt. Ida.
Minimum: 2.0 *Optimum:* 3.0–5.0 *Dangerous:* >6.0

SALINE RIVER

The Saline River originates near the Caney Creek Wilderness Area in the Ouachita Mountains and flows a short distance to Shady Lake. Do not confuse this stream with the Saline River in Saline County. When rains cause sufficient water to spill over the overflow dam at Shady Lake Reservoir, paddlers are treated to a very narrow and fast class III run below the lake. The stream is constricted by limbs and bushes that often cause obstructions, so be careful when attempting this run. The run is for experienced paddlers who are comfortable with eddy turns and have good boat control.

Paddlers can expect hardwood forests lining the banks, which totally restrict the views of the surrounding land. Abundant plant and animal life are also part of the landscape.

MAPS: Udall (USGS); Howard (County)

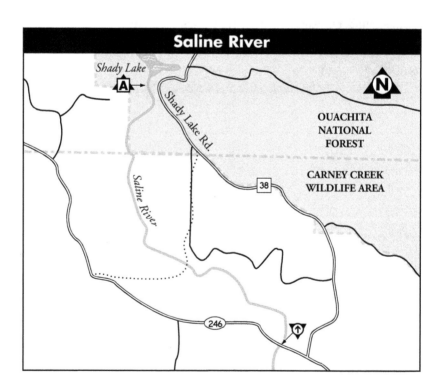

SHADY LAKE TO AR 246

difficulty	II–III
distance	2.9
time	1
gauge	None
level	See description
scenery	A
water	Good
gradient	61
latitude	34 21.508N
longitude	94 01.654W

DESCRIPTION: If there is plenty of water to run the first shoals below the dam, there should be sufficient water for the run.

The river drops over 180 feet in less than 3 miles with no major waterfalls, creating a very fast current similar to the Nantahala River in North Carolina. The Saline is narrower and has about 50 percent more drop, so paddlers should be comfortable with catching small eddies and have a bomb-proof roll. Advanced skills are a must for this run.

Be very careful on this swift, narrow course, as there are few eddies, and downed trees can be a significant hazard.

There is a challenging ledge-boulder field located just above the take-out, which is at the AR 246 bridge.

SHUTTLE: Put-in below the spillway at Shady Lake. To reach the take-out, go south 2.3 miles on Shady Lake Road to AR 246 and turn west (right). Go 0.6 mile to the AR 246 bridge. There is a small parking area on the northeast side of the bridge. No trespassing signs are abundant in other locations surrounding the bridge, so respect the landowners' rights.

GAUGE: There is no real gauge. Water flowing over the spillway at Shady Lake usually means there is enough water to paddle this section. A rough indicator of enough water is a level over 6 feet on the Little Missouri. This stretch is often runnable when the Cossatot is too high.

SOUTH FOURCHE LAFAVE RIVER

The headwaters of the South Fourche Lafave River are near Bear Head Mountain just west of Onyx, Arkansas. The South Fourche Lafave River flows generally east to its confluence with the Fourche Lafave River near Aplin, Arkansas, a distance of approximately 40 miles. The river flows along the base of the mountains rather than cutting abruptly through the mountains. The drop is less dramatic than you find on some of the other Ouachita streams in the area.

The section to paddle is from Hollis to the community of Deberrie near Aplin. This section can be divided into three parts. The first is a fun class I–II stream with good current separated by a few pools. The middle stretch is a small gorge area with several class II+ rapids, and in the final section the pace slows through several long pools separated by class I and II drops.

MAPS: Onyx, Steve, Nimrod SW, Nimrod Dam, Nimrod SE, Nimrod, Aplin (USGS); Yell, Perry (County)

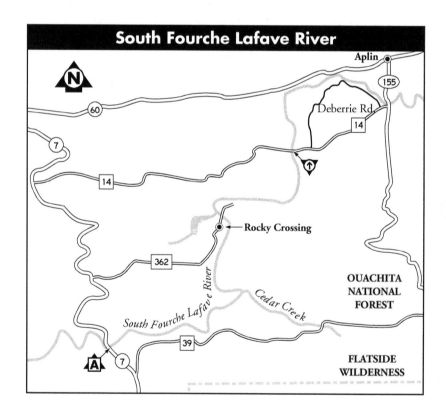

difficulty	I–II (II+)
distance	11.2
time	6
gauge	S. Fourche (USGS)
level	3.5
scenery	A
water	Good
gradient	13.5
latitude	34 52.263N
longitude	93 6.621W

DESCRIPTION: The first 3 miles offer fun class I–II rapids separated by short pools.

Just below a cabin on river left, the river makes a sharp bend to the left and enters the Willow Jungle. The current braids through trees and brush. Be careful and scout if you cannot see an open course.

The river enters a canyon 5 miles below the put-in. Cedar Creek enters on river right at the base of a 300-foot bluff. This is a very scenic spot and a good place to stop and enjoy the scenery.

Blockhead Rapid is just downstream of Cedar Creek. Blockhead is a class II+ rapid with a rock in the middle of the drop and a large boulder on river right. The best course is the wave train on river left. This rapid is similar to the Cascades on Big Piney but with the features reversed.

The action continues for the next mile through several fun rapids with standing waves and rocks to avoid.

The river gauge is approximately 2 miles below Blockhead Rapid. There is a Forest Service road that leads to the gauge and can be used for access. You could put-in here for a 4.5–mile paddle to the low-water bridge at Deberrie, but you would miss the best part of the river!

Just over half a mile downstream, you will come to an island. Take the right chute and enjoy Bounce, a class II+ rapid. The creek is constricted and drops about 8 feet over 50 yards.

Half a mile below Bounce, the river turns sharply to the right and slows. There are several nice class II drops in the final 4.5 miles, but the pools are longer in this section.

There is a good surfing ledge just above the take-out.

SHUTTLE: The put-in is at the Forest Service campground just south of the bridge on AR 7 near Hollis, Arkansas. To reach the take-out, go north on AR 7 for 11.6 miles to AR 60 and turn east (right). Continue 10.6 miles to AR 155 and turn south (right). Go 1.2 miles on AR 155 and turn right on the first road south of the Fourche River. Proceed 2.3 miles to the low-water bridge at Deberrie.

GAUGE: USGS South Fourche Lafave River near Hollis, Arkansas. Online at http://waterdata.usgs.gov/nwis/uv/?site_no= 07263000.

Minimum: 3.5 *Optimum:* 4.0-5.5 *Dangerous:* >6.0

SUGAR CREEK

The headwaters of Sugar Creek are east of US 71 and north of AR 248 near White Oak Mountain in the Ouachita National Forest. Sugar Creek flows east, then turns abruptly north near Bee Mountain. The gradient of the creek increases to almost 50 feet per mile, and a class III whitewater stream is born.

Paddlers can expect a very slender creek that weaves through a narrow gorge. Downed trees are a problem due to ice storms in recent years.

Sugar Creek has some significant hazards, including one of the most dangerous low-water bridges in the area. Paddling with someone who knows the run and can identify the hazards will add a significant margin of safety.

MAPS: Bee Mountain, Sugar Mountain, Sugar Grove (USGS); Scott, Logan (County)

difficulty	III—III+
distance	6.1
time	3
gauge	Sight
level	1
scenery	A
water	Good
gradient	48
latitude	34 59.899N
longitude	93 51.427W

SECOND LOW-WATER BRIDGE ABOVE KNOPPER'S FORD TO JACK CREEK RECREATION AREA

DESCRIPTION: The Ouachita National Forest mostly surrounds this stream, but parcels of private land with livestock and fences also abut the water. Much of the upper run is in a pristine setting reminiscent of some wilderness runs in the Ozark Mountains.

When you put-in, use the small eddy on river left just below the low-water bridge to get set. Just a few yards downstream you will encounter the first major rapid of Sugar Creek. The Creek takes a sharp left turn over several boulders, and then most of the water tries to push paddlers into a rock wall on river right. This first rapid is a great introduction to a superb creek run.

Paddlers must watch out for downed trees, narrow willow-choked passages, blind turns, and cables that remain in the riverbed from the ice storm of December 2000. But the most dangerous hazard on the creek is the first low-water bridge 2.45 miles below the put-in. The bridge is difficult to identify from upstream, and paddlers must be on the alert to pull off the creek on river left or right well upstream of the bridge. Look for surveyor's tape tied to willows on river left as a signal to get into an eddy. The easier boat carry down to the bridge is on river left. If you miss the opportunity to take-out well above the bridge, the continuous whitewater for 100 yards or so above the bridge presents little opportunity to get off the creek. A small eddy at

the bridge on river left presents a desperate last chance before the water carries your boat into the low-water bridge.

Also be on the lookout for Knopper's Ford Low-Water Bridge, 4.5 miles below the put-in, and Jack's Creek Bridge, 6.1 miles below the put-in.

Several ledges create great play spots along the run. The most significant drop is a creek-wide ledge with drop of 4 feet or so about half a mile above the take-out. Get out and scout if you cannot see the line, which is left of center. If the water is low enough, you can paddle under the third low-water bridge just above Jack

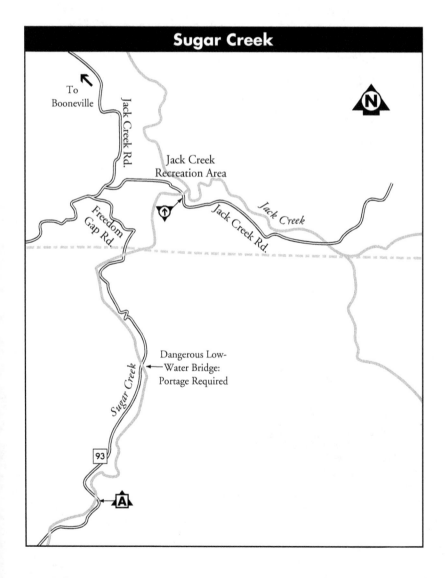

Sugar Creek

To Booneville

Jack Creek Rd.

Jack Creek Recreation Area

Freedom Gap Rd.

Jack Creek Rd.

Jack Creek

Dangerous Low-Water Bridge: Portage Required

Sugar Creek

93

N

Creek Recreation Area. Jack Creek will enter on your right. Just below this confluence is a large pool that offers an easier take-out alternative to the rougher terrain at the low-water bridge.

SHUTTLE: From the intersection of AR 22 and AR 23 in Booneville, Arkansas, go south 1.2 miles on AR 23 to Jack Creek Road and turn southeast (left). Proceed 10.4 miles, following the signs to the Jack Creek Recreation area. There is a small parking lot on the east side of the bridge over Sugar Creek. This is the take-out. To reach the put-in from the take-out bridge at Jack Creek Recreation Area, go west 1.3 miles and turn south (left) on Freedom Gap Road. Continue 4.4 miles, passing the low-water bridge at Knopper's Ford Recreation Area and one more low-water bridge. The put-in is at the second low-water bridge south of Knopper's Ford.

GAUGE: There is a sight gauge on the downstream side of Jack Creek Bridge at the take-out.
   Minimum: 1.0 *Optimum:* 1.25–1.75 *Dangerous:* >2.0

part**Five**

BRYANT'S CREEK

Bryant's Creek is a relatively untamed stream that begins north of MO 76 in Douglas County and flows approximately 40 miles to Norfork Lake. It is spring-fed but lacks the volume found on many other Missouri streams. Your chances of spying wildlife are excellent, and you can be assured of beautiful scenery.

Expect a wilderness experience on this stream flowing through the Ozark foothills, passing bluffs in one bend and farmland in the next as the watercourse swings away from the hills. The velocity of the current is relatively mild, leaving time to enjoy the many species of wildflowers and wildlife along the gently sloping riverbanks. Trappist Abbey is not on the river, but if you are in the area, it's worth a visit to try the renowned bread baked by resident monks.

MAPS: Sweden, Brushy Knob, Rockbridge, Gentryville, Sycamore, Udall (USGS); Douglas, Ozark (County)

BELL SCHOOL LOW-WATER BRIDGE (MO 95) TO AID-HODGSON MILL (MO 181)

difficulty	I (II)
distance	10.6
time	5
gauge	None
level	NA
scenery	AA
water	Good
gradient	4.34
latitude	36 46.98N
longitude	92 22.00W

DESCRIPTION: There are no major difficulties awaiting on this stretch, but direct caution to the many rocky shoals and willow thickets. Be aware of high water, because even relatively easy streams can become extremely dangerous at high levels.

Take-out at MO 181 at Aid-Hodgson Mill. The mill is perched against a rocky cliff with a beautiful green pool in front of it. Several years ago Euell Gibbons did a Grape Nuts commercial from the mill, which is powered by the fifteenth largest spring in the state of Missouri.

SHUTTLE: From Tecumseh, Missouri, go west 9.7 miles on US 160, then turn northwest (right) on MO 5 and go 13.5 miles to MO 95. Go east 11.7 miles to the access at Bryant's Creek. From Tecumseh, go west on US 160 8.3 miles and turning northeast (right) on MO 181 to reach the take-out. Continue 14.5 miles on MO 181 to the bridge over Bryant's Creek.

GAUGE: None. However, the spring-fed stream is floatable except during extreme dry spells. Be sure to make a local inquiry if you plan to float the upper sections of the stream.

difficulty	I
distance	7.4
time	3
gauge	None
level	NA
scenery	A
water	Good
gradient	4.6
latitude	36 42.81N
longitude	92 16.01W

AID-HODGSON MILL (MO 181) TO WARREN LOW-WATER BRIDGE

DESCRIPTION: The Narrows is 3.5 miles from the put-in. A narrow island less than one-quarter mile wide separates the creek. Take-out at the Warren Low-Water Bridge 3.9 miles downstream.

SHUTTLE: From the put-in, go north and east on MO 181 4 miles and turn south (right) on SR H. Go south 5.4 miles on SR H and turn west (left) on CR 328. Go west 2.5 miles to Warren Low-Water Bridge.

GAUGE: None.

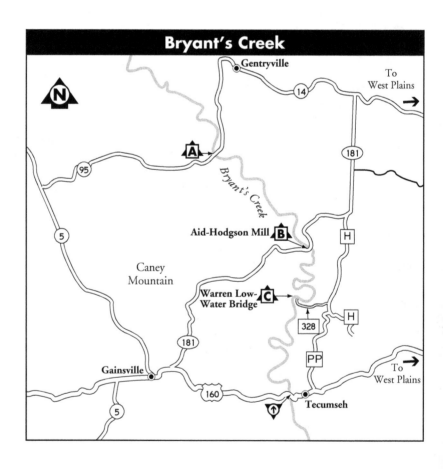

WARREN LOW-WATER BRIDGE TO NORFORK LAKE

DESCRIPTION: Bryant Creek merges with the North Fork of the White approximately half a mile above Norfork Lake. This final stretch is an easy class I float.

Take-out at the U.S. Army Corps of Engineers access in Tecumseh, Missouri.

SHUTTLE: From the put-in at Warren Low-Water Bridge, go east on CR 328 2.5 miles and turn south (right) on SR H. Go south 0.5 mile to SR PP and bear right. Go south for 5.3 miles and turn west on US 160. Go west 1.76 miles on to the access at Norfork Lake.

GAUGE: None.

difficulty	I
distance	9.7
time	5
gauge	None
level	NA
scenery	A
water	Good
gradient	3.71
latitude	36 40.09N
longitude	92 16.89W

CURRENT RIVER

The Current River begins near Licking, Missouri, and flows southeast for 133 miles to its confluence with the Black River in Arkansas. The Current River is blessed with more springs than any other in the Ozarks, as well as excellent water quality. The Current, along with its tributary, the Jack's Fork River, was protected by the Ozark National Scenic Riverways Act on August 27, 1964. Passage of the Riverways Act empowered the U.S. Department of the Interior to preserve many unique plants, animals, and geological formations. Today, the river is managed by the National Park Service for everyone's enjoyment. For paddlers, that means camping opportunities and ample facilities at most access points.

The Current River flows through the heart of the Ozarks. Paddlers can expect a relatively easy stream. There are some challenges in the Current's uppermost sections, but for the most part it should be considered a float stream that meanders between hills and farmland. Healthy hardwood forests along its entire length protect the Current River. The stream begins to widen and deepen considerably below the junction with the Jack's Fork River, and motor-powered boats become common. Locals have been known to water ski on the lower sections of the Current.

MAPS: Montauk, Cedargrove, Lewis Hollow, Round Spring, The Sinks, Eminence, Powdermill Ferry, Stegal Mountain, Van Buren North, Van Buren South, Big Spring, Grandin S.W., Donniphan (USGS); Dent, Shannon, Carter, Ripley (County)

CEDARGROVE TO AKERS FERRY

difficulty	I
distance	7.7
time	3
gauge	Current River (USGS) Akers Ferry
level	2.0
scenery	A
water	Excellent
gradient	8
latitude	37 25.329N
longitude	91 36.507W

DESCRIPTION: Cedargrove, the site of an old gristmill and community, is now primarily an access point for the Current River.

Approximately 4.7 miles downstream of Cedargrove, Welch Spring enters on river left. The spring is named for Thomas Welch, the first man to settle in the area.

Akers Ferry is 3 miles from Welch Spring. This is also very popular access for canoeists.

SHUTTLE: To reach the put-in at Cedargrove from Eminence, Missouri, go north on MO 19 24 miles and to SR KK. Turn west (left) on SR KK and go southwest for 6 miles to SR K. Turn north (right) on SR K and go 6.67 miles to CR 650 (White Oak Hollow Road). Turn Southwest on CR 650 and proceed 3.5 miles to the access at Cedargrove.

From the put-in at Cedargrove, to reach the take-out at Akers Ferry go 3.5 miles northeast on CR 650 to SR K. Go south (right) 6.67 miles on SR K to the Akers Ferry access.

GAUGE: USGS Current River above Akers Ferry. Online at http://waterdata.usgs.gov/mo/nwis/uv/?site_no=07064533&PARAmeter_cd=00065,00060. The minimum water level for running the Current River is 2 feet on its upper stretch and 1.5 feet downstream. The stream-fed Current rarely dips below minimum water level and the relatively easy route is dangerous only in times of torrential flooding.

AKERS FERRY TO PULLTITE SPRING

difficulty	I
distance	9.5
time	5
gauge	Current River (USGS) Akers Ferry
level	1.5
scenery	AA
water	Excellent
gradient	6.8
latitude	37 22.494N
longitude	91 33.224W

DESCRIPTION: Akers Ferry, easily reached via SR KK from MO 19, has extensive facilities, including campsites, picnic tables, drinking water, rest rooms, a ranger station, and a store.

Cave Spring is located approximately 5 miles from Akers Ferry. Beautiful blue-green water flows from the cave, into which several canoes can paddle. The daily flow from the spring is 32 million gallons. Have your camera ready to take pictures.

SHUTTLE: To reach the take-out from the put-in at Akers Ferry, go east 6 miles on SR KK and turn south (right) on MO 19. Head south 7 miles on MO 19 and turn west (right) on SR EE. Continue 4 miles to the Pulltite Spring access.

GAUGE: USGS Current River above Akers Ferry. See Section A.

PULLTITE SPRING TO ROUND SPRING

difficulty	I
distance	9
time	4
gauge	Current River (USGS) Akers Ferry
level	1.5
scenery	AA
water	Excellent
gradient	4.77
latitude	37 20.478N
longitude	91 28.909W

DESCRIPTION: Facilities at Pulltite include campsites, picnic tables, drinking water, rest rooms, a ranger station, and a store.

Pulltite Spring, with a daily flow of 38 million gallons, is located a short distance downstream from the access on river right.

Fire Hydrant Spring is just downstream. Just like a fire hydrant, it flows into the river from a rock wall.

The Alton Club is located on river left 4 miles from the Pulltite access. This is a private club, so respect the owners' rights.

Merritt Rock Cave is a short distance downstream on river right. There is a nice rapid in front of the cave.

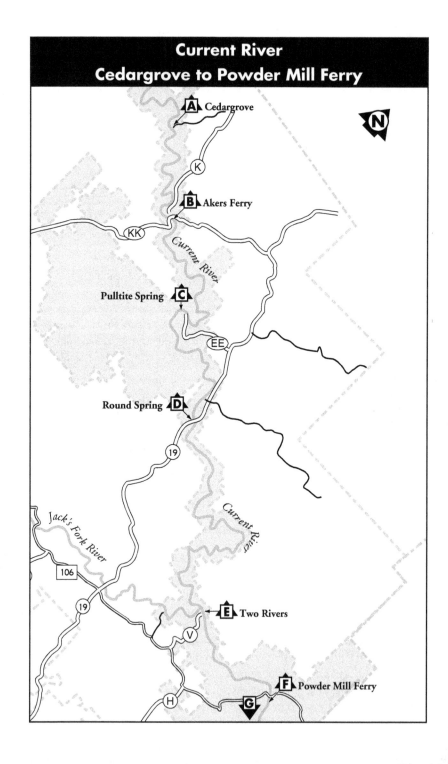

Current River
Cedargrove to Powder Mill Ferry

A Cedargrove

N

K

B Akers Ferry

KK

Current River

Pulltite Spring **C**

EE

Round Spring **D**

19

Jack's Fork River

106

19

Current River

E Two Rivers

V

F Powder Mill Ferry

H   **G**

Round Spring is located on river right. Deep blue water flows from a pool at a rate of 26 million gallons per day. The Park Service conducts tours daily of the cave located near the spring.

SHUTTLE: To reach the take-out at Round Spring from the put-in at Pulltite Spring, go northeast 4 miles on SR EE to MO 19 and turn south (right). Proceed south 6 miles to the access at Round Spring.

GAUGE: USGS Current River above Akers Ferry. See Section A.

ROUND SPRING TO TWO RIVERS

difficulty	I
distance	17.3
time	7–8
gauge	Current River (USGS) Akers Ferry
level	1.5
scenery	A
water	Excellent
gradient	5.1
latitude	37 17.010N
longitude	91 24.328W

DESCRIPTION: Big Creek enters on river left 8 miles downstream. Jerktail Landing is located on river right approximately a mile below Big Creek. This spot can serve as an intermediate take-out, and is accessible via MO 19 north of Eminence, Missouri.

Two Rivers, the take-out, is at the junction of the Jack's Fork and Current Rivers. Facilities there include campsites, picnic tables, drinking water, rest rooms, and a store.

SHUTTLE: To reach Two Rivers from the put-in at Round Spring, go south 16 miles on MO 19 to Eminence and turn east (left) on MO 106. Go east 5.4 miles on MO 106 and turn north (left) on SR V. Continue 3.1 miles to the access at Two Rivers.

GAUGE: USGS Current River above Akers Ferry. See Section A.

TWO RIVERS TO POWDER MILL

difficulty	I
distance	7.3
time	2.5
gauge	Current River (USGS) Van Buren
level	1.5
scenery	A
water	Excellent
gradient	3.9
latitude	37 11.401N
longitude	91 16.627W

DESCRIPTION: Coot Chute is not far downstream from the put-in. This is a narrow, fast chute at the foot of Coot Mountain. Blair Creek enters on river right 4.7 miles from the put-in.

Owl's Bend, named for the area's barred and screech owls, is located 2.5 miles below Blair Creek.

The take-out access is just downstream of the MO 106 bridge at Powder Mill Landing. Facilities there include campsites, picnic tables, drinking water, rest rooms, and a ranger station.

SHUTTLE: From the put-in at Two Rivers, the take-out at Powder Mill is south 3.1 miles on SR V and east (left) on MO 106. Go 11.5 miles east on MO 106 to Powder Mill.

GAUGE: USGS Current River above Akers Ferry. See Section A.

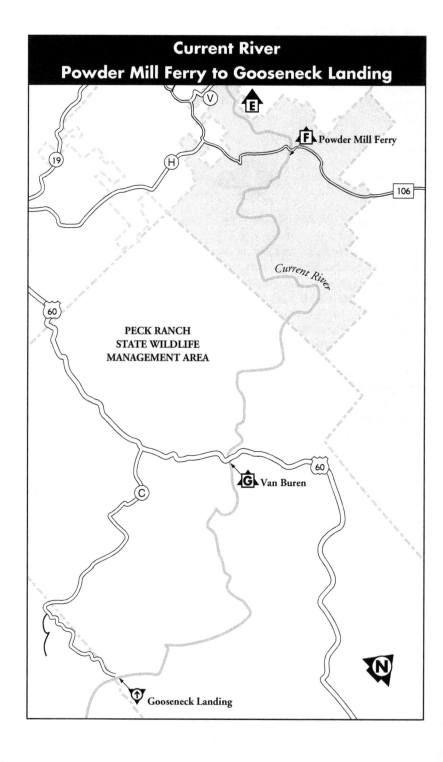

Current River
Powder Mill Ferry to Gooseneck Landing

Powder Mill Ferry

Current River

PECK RANCH
STATE WILDLIFE
MANAGEMENT AREA

Van Buren

Gooseneck Landing

POWDER MILL TO VAN BUREN

difficulty	I
distance	26.1
time	12
gauge	Current River (USGS) Van Buren
level	1.5
scenery	A
water	Good
gradient	3.5
latitude	37 10.887N
longitude	91 10.538W

DESCRIPTION: Blue Spring is 1.3 miles below Powder Mill Ferry on river left. The spring has an average daily flow of 72 million gallons and is known for its beautiful blue water.

The Log Yard, 9 miles from Owl's Bend, and Beal Landing, 11 miles, can be used as alternate access points. Both are reached via SR HH and MO 106 east of Owl's Bend.

Paint Rock Bluff is 1.7 miles below Beal Landing. A small gravel spring is at the end of the bluff.

Chilton Creek is 5.2 miles downstream on river right. Camping and picnicking are permitted there. Camping is also allowed at Mill Creek, a short distance downstream on river right.

Watercress Park is 6.6 miles below Chilton Creek. Facilities include campsites, picnic tables, drinking water, and rest rooms.

The take-out is at Van Buren at the US 60 bridge.

SHUTTLE: From the put-in at Powder Mill, reach the take-out at Van Buren by going southwest 8 miles on MO 106 to SR H and turn left. Go southwest 13 miles to Winona, Missouri, and turn east (left) on US 60. Head east 20 miles to the access at Van Buren.

GAUGE: USGS Current River above Akers Ferry. See Section A.

VAN BUREN TO GOOSENECK LANDING

difficulty	I
distance	19.3
time	8
gauge	Current River (USGS) Van Buren
level	1.5
scenery	A
water	Good
gradient	3.5
latitude	36 59.475N
longitude	91 0.841W

DESCRIPTION: Big Spring, the world's largest single spring, is located 4.3 miles below Van Buren. The daily flow is 277 million gallons. Facilities there include campsites and lodging, food service, picnic tables, drinking water, rest rooms, and a ranger station.

Hickory Landing and Cataract Landing are both 8.6 miles below Big Spring. Hickory Landing is accessible via SR E and US 60, and Cataract Landing is reached via SR Z, MO 103, and US 60 south of Van Buren.

Gooseneck Landing, the take-out, is 8.4 further downstream.

SHUTTLE: To reach Gooseneck Landing from the put-in at Van Buren, go southwest 5 miles on US 60 to SR C and turn south (left). Continue 9 miles on SR C and turn east (left). Follow the signs 7 miles east to Gooseneck Landing.

GAUGE: USGS Current River above Akers Ferry. See Section A.

ELEVEN POINT RIVER

The Eleven Point begins as a series of small creeks that unite just to the west of Thomasville, Missouri. One of the many theories about how the Eleven Point was named holds that 11 small creeks form its headwaters. Another theory states that someone shot an eleven-point deer on the river and the name was derived from that great event. Many more theories circulate in this area, but no two people can agree on which is correct.

The Eleven Point River was listed in the National Wild and Scenic Rivers Act upon its initial passage by Congress in 1968, and it is thereby protected from Thomasville to MO 142, a distance of 45 miles. The Forest Service is in charge of managing the river and maintaining access points, float camps, campgrounds, and visitor centers.

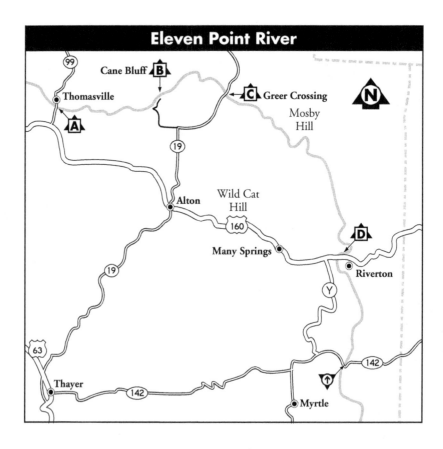

Paddlers on the Eleven Point are blessed with some of the best scenery and wildlife in Missouri. This run is a personal favorite for the author, especially in the fall and winter months when there are few other people on the river. Sightings of wild turkey, deer, and beaver are common, and on a recent trip a group of paddlers reported sighting a bald eagle. Trout also abound from Greer Crossing to Riverton, so make sure you have a fishing license and trout stamp. The cold, deep green water that emanates from Greer Spring gives the river most of its volume as well as the famous fog that hangs above the river until mid-morning on hot summer days. Densely forested banks that slope gently away from the river are mixed with steep rocky bluffs, usually on the opposite side of the river. The river speed is a pleasant 4 miles per hour, just enough for an occasional rapid and to keep one from paddling too much.

The warm summer months bring out many paddlers, tubers, and swimmers, drawn by the icy cold water from Greer Spring. Canoe camping is also a favorite option on the Eleven Point River.

MAPS: Birchtree, Wilderness, Riverton, Billmore (USGS); Oregon (County)

THOMASVILLE TO CANE BLUFF

difficulty	I
distance	9.3
time	3
gauge	None
level	NA
scenery	AA
water	Good
gradient	6.34
latitude	36 47.09N
longitude	91 31.65W

DESCRIPTION: There are no major difficulties on this section, but narrow chutes can always catch branches that clog the channel. There is little chance of seeing other paddlers in this section.

Denny Hollow Float Camp is located 7 miles from the put-in and 2.3 miles from the take-out.

SHUTTLE: From Alton, Missouri, to reach the put-in go 11.1 miles northwest on US 160 and turn north (right) on MO 99. Go 1.5 miles north on MO 99 to the river access. To reach the take-out at Cane Bluff from Alton, go 5.1 miles north on MO 19. Turn west (left) on CR 410 and go 1.2 miles to CR 405. Go north (right) CR 405 for 2.1 miles to FR 3189. Proceed 0.6 mile to the Cane Bluff Access.

GAUGE: There is a visual gauge at the Greer Crossing access. It is on the retaining wall and indicates levels from 1.5 feet to 5 feet. The Forest Service warns that levels above 4 feet are too dangerous to put-in. The author has never seen the level too low to float, even in the driest years. The sections above Greer Crossing are more water-sensitive, so check with the Forest Service or area

outfitters before attempting to float these sections. The Army Corps of Engineers' Bardley gauge tracks water-levels on the Eleven Point. It is online at http://www.swl-wc.usace.army.mil/WCDS/plots/Web/Bardley.htm.

Minimum: 1.5 *Optimum:* 2.0–3.5 *Dangerous:* >4.0

difficulty	I
distance	7.3
time	3.5
gauge	None
level	NA
scenery	AA
water	Good
gradient	5.9
latitude	36 47.78N
longitude	91 24.33W

CANE BLUFF TO GREER CROSSING

DESCRIPTION: Cane Bluff is a 250-foot dolomite cliff that gets its name from the cane that grows in the area. Camping with picnic tables and sanitary facilities is available at Cane Bluff.

Three miles from the put-in, Spring Creek enters the Eleven Point on river left.

Greer Spring, with a daily flow of 220 million gallons, enters on river right 4.3 miles from Spring Creek. The addition of the spring doubles the flow of the river and ensures water in even the driest years.

There is a fun riffle just above the MO 19 bridge with eddies to play in.

SHUTTLE: From Alton, Missouri, to reach the access at Greer Crossing drive north on MO 19 for 9.5 miles. Turn right at access just past bridge over the Eleven Point River.

GAUGE: The Army Corps of Engineers' Eleven Point gauge at Bardley. See Section A above.

difficulty	I (II)
distance	19
time	9
gauge	None
level	NA
scenery	AA
water	Good
gradient	5.6
latitude	36 47.58N
longitude	91 19.89W

GREER CROSSING TO RIVERTON

DESCRIPTION: Approximately a mile from the put-in, the river divides around an island. Take the left channel: It is much easier and less prone to snags.

The river current moves at approximately 4 miles per hour en route to Bliss Spring. This creates many class I–II rapids that make the trip fun but not difficult.

Mary Decker Shoal is 3.3 miles from the put-in. Large boulders scattered across the river constrict the water's flow. There are routes on river right and left. The route on river right is safer.

Turner's Mill is a mile below Mary Decker Shoal. This is the site of an old mill and Surprise Schoolhouse. All that remains are

a giant steel wheel and a crumbling rock flume. Both, however, are worth seeing, and the hike to the cave from which Spring Creek emanates is a must. The cave is blocked, but the surrounding area is beautifully cloaked in wildflowers and watercress. Turner's Mill is also an optional access point, reached via FR 3190 on the north side of the river and FR 3153 on the south side of the river.

Stinking Pond Camp is 0.8 mile downstream from Turner's Mill.

There is an interesting cave visible from the river approximately 2 miles from Stinking Pond Camp. At one time, there was a house in front of the cave that utilized the cool cave air for natural air conditioning.

Horseshoe Bend Camp is one mile from the cave, and Barn Hollow Camp is 0.9 mile below Horseshoe Bend. Both sites are excellent for overnight camping if you put-in at Greer Crossing.

Just downstream from Barn Hollow, Bliss Spring enters on river left. The Forest Service has reclaimed this former camping area for revegetation after heavy use in this stretch.

White's Creek Camp is located 1.4 miles from Bliss Spring. Whether you camp or not, you should see White's Creek Cave. Take the trail that leads to the outhouse and continue until it forks. Take the left fork and continue for 150 yards to a trail that leads up the hill to White's Creek Cave. This is one of the largest caves in the vicinity, and in the very back you will find stalactites and stalagmites.

Back on the water, Greenbriar Float Camp is 2.4 miles below White's Creek. Boze Mill Camp is 2.4 miles from Greenbriar Float Camp. Here you will find a very interesting millpond, campsites, sanitary facilities, and picnic tables.

The river divides around an island 1.3 miles from Boze Mill. Over the years, the channel has meandered from the right chute to the left chute. This rapid can reach class II at times.

The take-out is a mile downstream at Riverton.

SHUTTLE: The put-in is on river left just above the US 160 bridge. From Alton, the take-out is 12.9 miles east on US 160 at the Riverton access.

GAUGE: The Army Corps of Engineers' Eleven Point gauge at Bardley. See Section A above.

RIVERTON TO MO 142

difficulty	I
distance	8.6
time	3
gauge	None
level	NA
scenery	A
water	Good
gradient	4.9
latitude	36 38.93N
longitude	91 12.05W

DESCRIPTION: Piney Creek enters on river left 1.7 miles from the put-in.

Morgan Spring Float Camp is 4.7 miles below and is the only Forest Service campground on this stretch of the river.

Blue Spring contributes 91 million gallons daily a mile below Morgan Spring Float Camp. This area is known as the Narrows because of the narrow strip of land that separates Frederick Creek and the Eleven Point River.

SHUTTLE: To reach the take-out at the MO 142 bridge from Riverton, go west on US 160 for 0.9 mile and turn south (left) on Missouri Y. Go south on Missouri Y 8.3 miles and turn southeast (left) on MO 142. Go 3.2 miles to the MO 142 bridge (GPS: 36 33.02N, 91 11.58W).

GAUGE: The Army Corps of Engineers' Eleven Point gauge at Bardley. See Section A above.

JACK'S FORK RIVER

The Jack's Fork Rive, the major tributary of the Current River, offers approximately 46 miles of canoeable water. The two rivers make up the Ozark National Scenic Riverways, administered by the National Park Service. Expect a remote wilderness experience on the Jack's Fork in the fall, winter, and early spring, but armies of paddlers invade the river during the warm summer months, aided by a multitude of canoe-rental concessionaires and campgrounds. Everyone comes to enjoy the crystal-clear water that emanates from an abundance of springs along the route.

Put-in at The Prongs, where two small tributaries combine to form the Jack's Fork River. Access the river where SR Y crosses it. This section is normally canoeable only after good rains or a wet spring. The stretch from The Prongs to Alley Spring includes some of the wildest riparian scenery in the region. There are few signs of civilization in the upper sections, where crystal-clear water courses between the famous Ozark hardwood forests and stark bluffs formed by the never-ending erosion of the streambed. Paddlers feel as though they are navigating through a gorge, thanks to dense forest that blocks any view of pastoral land nearby. The only signs of civilization are the remnants of early settler homesteads and several bridges that cross the river at Alley Spring and Eminence. Below Eminence the river passes several campgrounds, which detract slightly from the wilderness experience.

MAPS: Pine Crest, Jam-up Cave, Bartlett, Alley Spring, Eminence, Powder Mill Ferry (USGS); Texas, Shannon (County)

THE PRONGS TO BUCK HOLLOW (MO 17)

difficulty	I–II
distance	11.6
time	5.5
gauge	Jack's Fork (USGS) near Mt. View
level	1.5
scenery	AA
water	Excellent
gradient	7.5
latitude	37 4.610N
longitude	91 43.946W

DESCRIPTION: One mile downstream of the put-in, you will see Chimney Rock Cave on river right. Just below this point, the waterway enters the protected land of the Ozark National Scenic Riverways.

SHUTTLE: From Mountain View, Missouri, reach the put-in by going north 5.8 miles on SR Y. From Mountain View, the take-out is a mile east on US 60 and then 4 miles north (right) on MO 17 at Buck Hollow.

GAUGE: USGS Jack's Fork near Mountain View. Online at http://waterdata.usgs.gov/mo/nwis/uv?dd_cd=01&format=gif&period=7&site_no=07065200. This gauge, located at the MO 17 bridge, is a good indicator of levels on the river's upper sections. *Minimum: 1.5 Optimum: 2.0–4.0 Dangerous: >5.0*

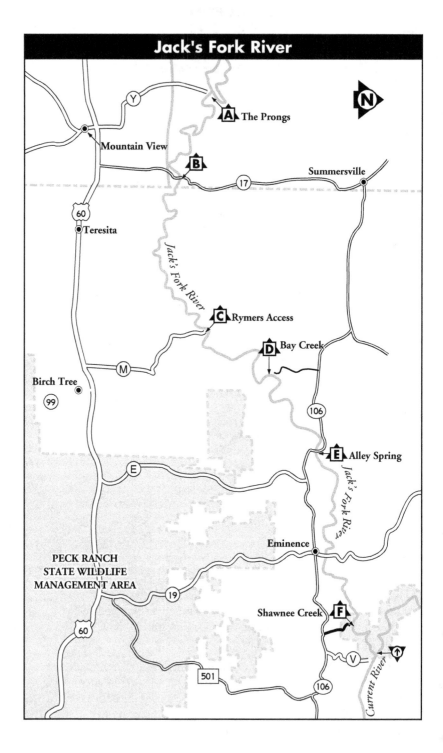

Jack's Fork River

BUCK HOLLOW (MO 17) TO RYMERS ACCESS

difficulty	I–II
distance	11.6
time	5.5
gauge	Jack's Fork (USGS) near Mt. View
level	1.5
scenery	AA
water	Excellent
gradient	9.6
latitude	37 4.551N
longitude	91 40.050W

DESCRIPTION: Blue Spring, 2.8 miles below the put-in, offers camping, picnicking, and rest rooms. It is accessible via SR OO after a left turn from US 60.

Jam-Up Cave is located on river right 3.1 miles below Blue Spring. This is one of the most spectacular caves in the region. A very large opening is visible from the river; it leads into a cave that slopes downward to a waterfall cascading from a sinkhole. The waterfall is visible without the aid of flashlights due to the size of the cave opening. There is a gravel bar across the river that is an excellent spot for lunch or camping. Lucky paddlers may find wild melons growing nearby in the autumn months.

Ebb and Flow Spring is located on river left 2.7 miles below Jam-up Cave. There are many theories on what causes the volume of water issuing from this spring to fluctuate, but the only reasonable answer is that the spring is very sensitive to changes in the water table.

SHUTTLE: To reach the take-out from the put-in at Buck Hollow, go south 4 miles on MO 17 and turn east (left) on US 60. Continue 5 miles to SR M and turn north (left). Go 6 miles to Rymers Access.

GAUGE: USGS Jack's Fork near Mountain View.
Minimum: 1.5 *Optimum:* 2.0–4.0 *Dangerous:* >5.0

RYMERS ACCESS TO BAY CREEK

difficulty	I
distance	9.4
time	5
gauge	Jack's Fork (USGS) near Alley Spring
level	1.5
scenery	AA
water	Excellent
gradient	5.1
latitude	37 4.551N
longitude	91 32.522W

DESCRIPTION: Bunker Hill Resort (privately owned by the Missouri Teachers' Association) is located 1.3 miles below the put-in on river left.

Chalk Bluff is 4.4 miles downstream of Bunker Hill. This 200-foot bluff is an awesome sight.

SHUTTLE: From the put-in at Rymers Access, reach the take-out by going south 6 miles on SR M and turning east (left) on US 60. Continue east 9 miles to SR E and turn north (left). Proceed 10 miles to MO 106 and turn east (right). Go 7 miles and turn south (right). Go 1.8 miles to the Bay Creek access.

GAUGE: USGS Jack's Fork near Alley Spring. Online at http://waterdata.usgs.gov/mo/nwis/uv?dd_cd=03&format=gif& period=7&site_no=07065495. The gauge is located at Alley Spring and is a good indicator of levels near the mid-river sections.

Minimum: 1.5 Optimum: 2.0–3.0 Dangerous: >4.5

difficulty	I
distance	5.7
time	2.5
gauge	Jack's Fork (USGS) near Alley Spring
level	1.5
scenery	AA
water	Excellent
gradient	7.1
latitude	37 6.940N
longitude	91 30.320W

BAY CREEK TO ALLEY SPRING

DESCRIPTION: The Grandma Rocks, located approximately 1.5 miles below the put-in, are the most notable geological feature on this stream section.

SHUTTLE: To reach the take-out from the put-in at Bay Creek, backtrack north 1.8 miles and turn east (right) on MO 106. Go east 5.2 miles on MO 106 to the Alley Spring Access.

GAUGE: USGS Jack's Fork near Alley Spring.

Minimum: 1.5 Optimum: 2.0–3.0 Dangerous: >4.5

E

difficulty	I
distance	11.9
time	6
gauge	Jack's Fork (USGS) near Alley Spring
level	1.5
scenery	A
water	Good
gradient	6.3
latitude	37 8.902N
longitude	91 26.694W

ALLEY SPRING TO SHAWNEE CREEK

DESCRIPTION: A short distance from the put-in, Alley Spring Branch enters on river left. Alley Spring, located a short distance up the branch, is one of the largest in the state, with a daily flow of 81 million gallons.

Next you'll see Red Mill, which is still operating just as it was before the turn of the century and is open to visitors. Check with the Park Service for operating hours at the mill.

The river leaves the park boundary just above Eminence, so remember to respect the rights of landowners.

The town of Eminence is located 6.5 miles below the put-in, and it can serve as an intermediate take-out. On river left, just downstream of the MO 19 bridge, is a large gravel bar that is used as a parking area and access. It can be reached from the north side of the MO 19 bridge via a county road that parallels the river.

For paddlers who stay on the river, Hole in the Wall Bluff is located on river right 2.6 miles below Eminence.

SHUTTLE: To reach the take-out from the put-in at Alley Spring, go east 8.4 miles on MO 106 and turning north (left) at the Shawnee Creek access. Proceed 2.2 miles to the access.

GAUGE: USGS Jack's Fork near Alley Spring.
Minimum: 1.5 *Optimum:* 2.0–3.0 *Dangerous:* >4.5

SHAWNEE CREEK TO THE CURRENT RIVER

difficulty	I
distance	3.4
time	2
gauge	Jack's Fork (USGS) near Alley Spring
level	1.5
scenery	AA
water	Good
gradient	5
latitude	37 10.351N
longitude	91 17.844W

DESCRIPTION: Little Shawnee Creek enters on river right approximately half a mile from the put-in.

The Jack's Fork joins the Current River 2.7 miles from the put-in. There is a gravel bar located at the junction that's a good spot to rest or have lunch.

SHUTTLE: To reach the take-out from the put-in at Shawnee Creek go south 2.2 miles to MO 106. Go east a short distance to SR V and north to the access at Two Rivers.

GAUGE: USGS Jack's Fork River near Eminence, Missouri. Online at http://waterdata.usgs.gov/mo/nwis/uv?dd_cd=04&format=gif&period=7&site_no=07066000. The gauge is located at the MO 19 bridge and is a good indicator of levels on the lower Jack's Fork.
Minimum: 1.5 *Optimum:* 2.0–3.5 *Dangerous:* >4.5

NORTH FORK OF THE WHITE RIVER

The North Fork of the White River begins in the Mark Twain National Forest and flows to the south for approximately 78 miles before it empties into Norfork Lake. It is similar to the Eleven Point, Jack's Fork, and Current Rivers but contains more exciting class II rapids than the others. An abundance of springs keeps the water level almost constant year-round and the water quality excellent.

Canoe outfitters and swimmers are numerous during the spring and summer months. At times, you can see as many people floating in the crystal-clear water as paddling in boats. Paddlers can expect a

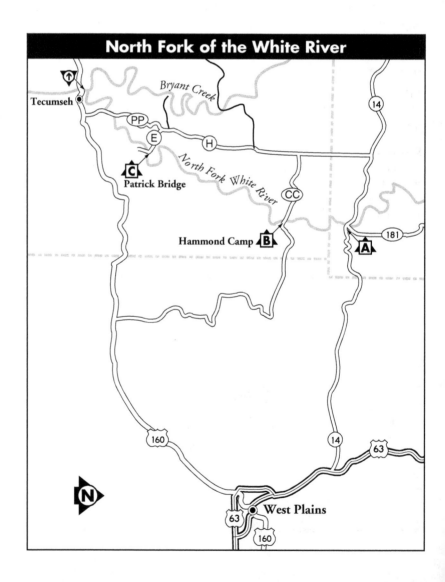

relatively swift current that moves at approximately 4 miles per hour over moderate drops to form small standing waves and rapids. The banks are lined with hardwood trees, and there are few manmade structures visible from the river. Its national forest surroundings add to the feeling of a wilderness float.

MAPS: Nichols Knob, Dora, Bakersfield, Udall (USGS); Douglas, Ozark (County)

MO 14 (TWIN BRIDGES) TO HAMMOND CAMP

difficulty	I (II-)
distance	5.1
time	2
gauge	None
level	NA
scenery	A
water	Excellent
gradient	7.8
latitude	36 48.66N
longitude	92 08.95W

DESCRIPTION: Spring Creek enters on river left 1.8 miles from the put-in and Hicks Spring is just downstream on river right.

SHUTTLE: To reach the put-in from West Plains, Missouri, head north on US 63 4.2 miles and turn west (left) on MO 14. Go 15.7 miles to access the river at the MO 14 bridge. To reach the take-out from the put-in, go 4.9 miles west on MO 14, which runs concurrent with MO 181, and turn south (left) on MO 181. Go 3.8 miles on MO 181 and turn east on SR CC. Go 4.9 miles to the Hammond Camp access.

GAUGE: None. However, natural springs along the route ensure a reliable flow.

HAMMOND CAMP TO PATRICK BRIDGE

difficulty	I–II
distance	12.9
time	5
gauge	None
level	NA
scenery	A
water	Excellent
gradient	6.2
latitude	36 38.58N
longitude	92 13.50W

DESCRIPTION: Blue Spring, less than a mile from the put-in on river left, is named for the deep-blue tint of the water it emits. North Fork Spring is 3.4 miles downstream on river left.

In the next few miles are several nice class I rapids that prepare you for the Falls.

The Falls is a 3-foot ledge that extends across the river. At this spot, the author took one of the sport's most memorable pictures of a canoe mishap, dubbed the "gunnel push-up" by members of the Bluff City Canoe Club. John Johnson and his son Scott Johnson were pinned on a rock in the Falls, so John stepped out to free the boat. Loosed, their craft headed downstream without Mr. Johnson, who panicked and tried to jump back into the canoe. The result was priceless.

Below the Falls 3.2 miles is Blair Bridge, a wooden low-water

bridge that must be portaged. Avoid getting too close to the bridge, as the current could pin your boat sideways.

SHUTTLE: To reach the take-out from the put-in, go west on SR CC 4.2 miles and turn south (left) on MO 181. Go south on MO 181 2.8 miles and veer south on SR H and proceed 7.7 miles to the Patrick Bridge access

GAUGE: None.

difficulty	I–II
distance	7.4
time	3
gauge	None
level	NA
scenery	A
water	Excellent
gradient	3.91
latitude	36 40.09N
longitude	92 16.89W

PATRICK BRIDGE TO NORFORK LAKE

DESCRIPTION: Althea Spring is just downstream from the put-in on river left. It is located on private property, and the owner has dammed the spring and built a small hydroelectric plant to provide power for his farm. Excess power generated from such private plants can be sold to the state.

SR PP crosses the river 2 miles from the put-in and can be used as an access.

Dawt Mill is approximately 1.5 miles below SR PP. Approach the dam with caution and portage on river left or right well above the dam. In very high water, daring canoeists have run the break near the middle of the dam. A more common choice is to stop and visit and photograph the still-operating Dawt Mill.

Dawt Mill Bridge is just downstream of the mill, and caution is advised when approaching it in high water.

Repeating Riffle is 2 miles from Dawt Mill. This is a fun place to play the waves and then paddle back up the eddy and do it again.

Just above the take-out at the Corps of Engineers campground is a good drop, provided the lake is low.

SHUTTLE: From the put-in, to reach the take-out go northwest on SR H 1.7 miles and turn south (left) on SR PP. Go south on SR PP 5.5 miles to US 160. Turn west (right) and continue 1.9 miles to the access at Tecumseh, Missouri.

GAUGE: None.

part**Six**

THE ST. FRANCOIS MOUNTAINS

BIG CREEK

This quiet little tributary of the St. Francis is not a whitewater run; however, this creek has many things going for it. Located near the southern end of the St. Francois Mountains, it flows through two small shut-ins. The stream's pristine lower half flows through Sam A. Baker State Park. Granite bluffs, deep pools, crystal-clear water, steep hills with glades above, and the scenic shut-ins make up for the lack of large rapids. There are only a few outfitters renting canoes on the creek, so this float trip can be quiet compared with more popular Ozark streams.

MAPS: Des Arc, Brunot (USGS); Iron, Wayne (County)

DES ARC TO THE FORD AT SAM A. BAKER STATE PARK

difficulty	I–II
distance	9.3
time	6
gauge	Visual
level	Local inquiry
scenery	AA
water	Excellent
gradient	12.7
latitude	37 17.556N
longitude	90 37.729W

DESCRIPTION: From the put-in below the MO 143 bridge at Des Arc, the creek's gravel bottom and constant current recall many Ozark streams. The first few small drops over granite shoals should offer no problems. A concrete low-water bridge, at mile 2.4, should be portaged. This is the alternate put-in (see directions below).

Below the concrete bridge is a real eyesore on an otherwise picturesque float. Old, junked cars have been used to stabilize the riverbanks for the next quarter-mile.

One mile below the bridge, hills compress the creek to form the first shut-in. In low water, the shut-in appears to be a mine-field of rocks. One way to test your paddling skills is to try maneuvering through without hitting any of the rocks. The creek opens up after the shut-in. After 4.5 miles, the creek swings around a bend to the right, past a spring and cottages linked by a hanging bridge.

You reach the second shut-in at mile 5.4. This one requires less maneuvering than the first. Small drops continue for the next half-mile. The creek slows down again above Crane Pond Creek, but the scenery only gets better. Hills soar 400 feet above the water, and gravel bars tempt paddlers to set up camp. The MO 143 bridge is at mile 9, and the take-out is a short distance beyond on the right.

SHUTTLE: To reach the put-in from Sam A. Baker State Park, go north on MO 143 and cross Big Creek. MO 143 bears west. The gravel road to the alternate put-in is the third left after crossing Crane Pond Creek. The gravel road continues straight as MO 143 makes a sharp right turn. Go 0.5 mile on the gravel road to the concrete low-water bridge. Unload vehicles on the river-right

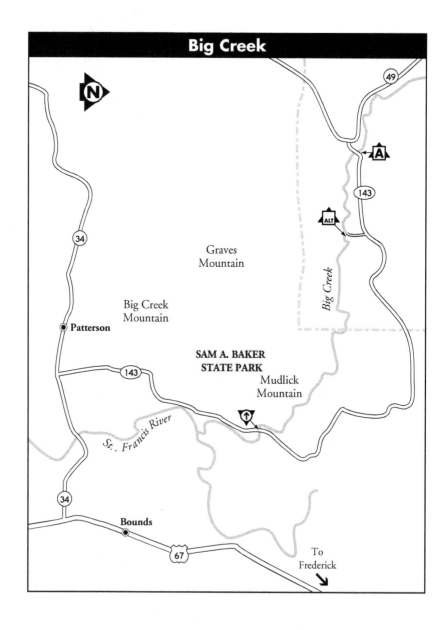

side of the bridge and shuttle all vehicles downstream to avoid conflicts with the local landowner. The access farther upstream is another 2 miles on MO 143, below the bridge on river left.

The take-out is located at Sam A. Baker State Park. From the intersection of US 67 and MO 34, go west 3.9 miles on MO 34 and turn north (right) on MO 143. Go north 3.7 miles on MO 143 to reach the entrance of Sam A. Baker State Park.

GAUGE: None. However, the upper watershed is just southwest of the St. Francis River (also profiled in this section) and Stouts Creek. Big Creek is generally floatable up to one week after the SR D bridge gauge on the St. Francis goes below 0 inches. Personal inspection of the take-out at the old concrete ford should confirm whether or not there is sufficient flow to make the run. You should be able to paddle over the ford without hitting the concrete below. The superintendent's office at Sam A. Baker State Park is also able to tell you if the creek is floatable (call (573) 856-4223). The usual paddling season is from mid-October through May. The park also has cabins for rent. Visit the park website for details: http://www.samabaker.com/index.html.

CASTOR RIVER

The Castor River is on the eastern edge of the St. Francois Mountains. Its upper willow-choked channel offers no clue as to its dramatic change downstream. Hahn's Mill Shut-In is a beautiful miniature gorge, with salmon-colored granite surrounded by shortleaf pine trees. Unfortunately, the shut-in is only a quarter mile long. The Castor is a good chaser after paddling other nearby runs

MAPS: Higdon (USGS); Madison (County)

HAHN'S MILL SHUT-IN SECTION

difficulty	III–IV
distance	1.5
time	1
gauge	None
level	Local inquiry
scenery	AA
water	Excellent
gradient	75
latitude	37 34.223N
longitude	90 .09.427W

DESCRIPTION: Above the shut-in, the river is braided into several willow-infested channels. The river-right channel at the put-in allows the best approach. Follow the channel as it turns left. The large rock on the right signals the top of the first drop.

The first drop is obviously the most difficult—or the best, depending on your sense of adventure. Willows grow within a boat-length from the top of the 4-foot ledge. The key is to get to the center slot and aim left. Be aware that this ledge is prone to vertical pins. Higher water produces a mean, river-wide hydraulic.

Weave your way around the rocks and waves as the river turns to the right.

The last drop in the shut-in is a center-left chute that plows into the bottom hydraulic. The pool below signals the end of the shut-in. You can elect to carry back half a mile to the put-in or run the mile to the take-out.

Downstream, the pool goes left and leads to several chutes and rocky shoals that are no more than class II rapids. Look for a road on the right, which is the take-out.

SHUTTLE: To find the take-out, follow MO 72 east from Fredericktown. Go left (east) on SR J and right (south) on SR W. This road ends in a gravel crossroad. Go left on CR 208 about a mile. The Castor River will be on your right. To get to the put-in, continue upriver from the take-out. Within 200 feet, the road forks. Take the left fork, CR 253. Go 0.75 mile to a left turn with a pull-off on the right. The river-right channel is directly in front of you. Follow the trail 0.25 mile downstream on the right bank to scout the shut-in.

GAUGE: None. In order to run the Castor, streams in the area should be in flood or close to it. Although the watershed is east of the St. Francis, the SR D gauge on that river should be at least 2.5 feet over the bridge. Note that the river has a natural aqua color; a lack of muddy water does not always mean there's not enough water. Inspecting the first drop in Hahn's Mill Shut-In will resolve any doubts about the water level. Scout the entire shut-in from the put-in preceding any run.

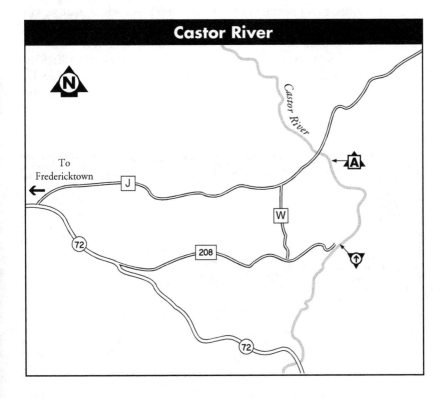

MARBLE CREEK

Marble Creek is the alternate whitewater run for the intermediate paddler when the St. Francis is nearing flood stage or higher. This medium-sized creek alternates between fast-moving pools, tight willow-lined chutes, and small drops and ledges.

Almost the entire creek is protected by the Mark Twain National Forest, enhancing the water quality and scenery tremendously. Paddlers can expect a relatively remote run on this short but exciting creek.

MAPS: Des Arc, Rockpile Mountain (USGS); Madison (County)

difficulty	II–III
distance	3.75
time	2.5
gauge	None
level	Local inquiry
scenery	A
water	Good
gradient	33
latitude	37 26.987N
longitude	90 32.538W

MARBLE CREEK CAMPGROUND TO MADISON COUNTY HIGHWAY 427

DESCRIPTION: Immediately below the put-in is a 5-foot dam. Scout first and run it center or far left. The rapid below the dam leads to a pool that circles around Marble Creek Campground. After going nearly full circle, the river turns left. A roar signals Bridge Rapid. Go right of a diagonal ledge that nearly spans the river. Work left as you paddle under the SR E bridge.

A long series of pools and chutes continues for 1.5 miles. Two rapids appear as hills compress the creek. Both are low class III rapids. Granite glades are visible on the hillsides above. As the hills recede, the creek makes a right turn and pillows up on a

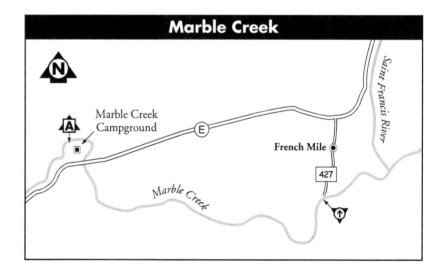

large rock on the left bank. Steer wide of the rock, as a hole develops next to the rock. Watch for some old barbed wire at the bottom in the willows on the right.

Begin looking for the road on the left bank. The river splits around a small island as the road appears. Take the left channel. Watch for the remains of a cattle fence in the creek and carry your gear up the bank to your vehicle.

SHUTTLE: Put-in at the U.S. Forest Service's Marble Creek Campground, 16.4 miles west of US 67 on SR E. Enter the campground, take the far left road, and unload at the parking area just upstream of the dam. To get to the take-out, go east 3 miles on SR E to CR 427. Go south on CR 427, cross Little Rock Creek, and drive slowly and carefully past the houses, on the lookout for children. Stay right as you near the creek and leave as few vehicles as possible. The road ruts out easily.

GAUGE: None. The St. Francis should be at least 6 inches over the SR D bridge before attempting Marble Creek. The ledge just upstream of the SR E bridge (visible from the bridge) should have adequate water, and you should be able to run the dam below the put-in without scraping.

ST. FRANCIS RIVER

The St. Francis River rises from the foothills north of Elephant Rocks State Park and flows northeast before turning south outside of Farmington. It offers paddlers some of the most challenging whitewater in the state of Missouri, with rapids up to class IV in difficulty. Paddlers can expect a river that is unlike most streams in the Missouri Ozarks because it flows through the St. Francois Mountains, some of the oldest and most stubborn igneous bedrock in the area. By the time the river encounters igneous rock outcroppings, it has a sizable watershed.

The western character of the St. Francis River is very apparent when you put-in on the river. In the first section, the current moves swiftly over rocky shoals and drops that fine tune your paddling skills for the more difficult shut-in section, where class III–IV rapids and spectacular scenery await. The final section of the river is more of a float stream with good scenery, especially in the small shut-in section below SR E. Good water quality and stark rock formations make the St. Francis a near-perfect river.

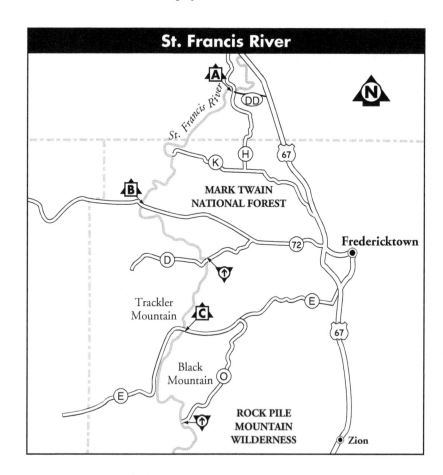

MAPS: Wachita Mountain, Rhodes Mountain, Rockpile Mountain (USGS); St. Francois, Madison (County)

SR H BRIDGE TO MO 72 BRIDGE

DESCRIPTION: Before paddling this section, you should be armed with the skills for intricate weaving among willows and ledges yet have the patience for the seemingly infinite flatwater. Paddlers generally choose to do Section B as well when this upper section is runnable.

SHUTTLE: Put-in at the SR H bridge, which is 3.8 miles south of US 67 in St. Francois County. To reach the take-out, head south on SR H a short distance and turn east (left) on SR DD to go 2 miles to US 67. Turn south (right) on US 67 and continue 8.3 miles to SR 72. Turn west (right) on SR 72 and go 10.2 miles to the access. An optional 6-mile float, which avoids lots of the flatwater in this stretch, may be possible by taking out on private land to reach CR 512. This road continues west after SR K turns south. Inquire with landowners first.

GAUGE: USGS St. Francis River near Roselle, Missouri. Online at http://waterdata.usgs.gov/nwis/uv/?site_no=07034000.
  Minimum: 3.0 *Optimum:* 4.0–5.0 *Dangerous:* >5.5
  See also Section B. The minimum is 1 foot on the SR D bridge gauge (at the section B take-out). Medium to high water is better, although higher levels will increase the risk to inattentive boaters of getting pinned in the willows.

difficulty	I–II
distance	10.75
time	6
gauge	St. Francis (USGS)
level	3
scenery	A-B
water	Good
gradient	8.6
latitude	37 40.878N
longitude	90 24.566W

MO 72 BRIDGE TO SR D LOW-WATER BRIDGE

DESCRIPTION: This section can be divided into two parts, above and below the Millstream Gardens State Forest access at mile 3. From the MO 72 access on river right below the bridge, paddle 0.75 mile to Entrance Rapid. This rapid is a series of ledges. In low water, start in the center, work right, and make a sharp left turn behind some willows to finish off left of center. High water and flood-stage levels produce great surfing waves and two large play holes near the right bank halfway down.
  The next rapid is Kitten's Crossing, a simple chute over a ledge. High water produces a play hole at the very bottom of the rapid.

difficulty	II–III (IV)
distance	5.6
time	3
gauge	St. Francis (USGS)
level	3
scenery	AA
water	Good
gradient	20
latitude	37 35.761N
longitude	90 29.905W

After another pool, the third rapid, Land of Oz (named after Oz Hawksley, noted Ozark river author and conservationist), is recognizable by a boulder on the left that splits the current.

Long pools separated by riffles stretch for the next mile. Mill-stream Gardens' access is on river left below the second island. Anyone experiencing difficulties should consider taking out here. It only gets harder downstream.

Below the access is a long pool that ends with a left turn and increasing gradient. The river then turns right at a ranch-style house on the left bank. Paddlers then enter Tiemann Shut-in, a three-quarter-mile section of almost continuous class III rapids in medium to high water. Start and stay right over the ledges, at normal levels, to reach a small pool. To approach Big Drop Rapid, start left, ferry right, and run the drop about 5 feet out from the large boulder on the right bank. At high water or flood, a left-center run is best. Rescue any errant boats or paddlers quickly, as rapids continue below.

Cat's Paw, 100 yards downstream, is the hardest rapid at most levels, with a high probability of pinning a wayward boat. It is recognizable by the large, shark-fin rock on river left, easily the largest boulder on the river. Scout on the right side. In low to medium water, paddle into "the Paw," and eddy right, across from the shark-fin rock. There are three possible exits. From the right eddy, one can ferry to river-left behind the boulder and run the remainder of the rapid along the left side. If the level is above 1 foot, peel out from the eddy, run just to the right of a small pyramid-shaped rock, and bounce left off the drop below. Brace and maneuver accordingly below. In low water, a Z-shaped route starts diagonally behind the large, flat rock across from the eddy. It really requires just one move, but mess up your left draw and you're pinned. Novices can carry a short distance to the left of the shark-fin rock and safely run the left side of the ferry route. The right eddy almost disappears in high water, with a sizable hole below Cat's Paw.

Double Drop, 200 yards downstream, is just that. Run left at low water, center when it's higher. This rapid is noted for its super ender spot when the river is between 15 and 36 inches. Paddle up the river-left eddy line and kick your bow slightly right as you hit the wall of water. This is a popular lunch spot, where you can watch paddlers' performances from atop the boulders.

A short slow section leads to Rickety-Rack, and you'll have a rickety ride if you don't move fast enough to the right at the bottom ledge.

Paddlers now leave Tiemann Shut-in and proceed through alternate pools and riffles. The one-eighth-mile side hike up Mud

Creek, just below a 40-foot granite bluff on the right, is very rewarding. Mud Creek slides down a beautiful, moss-covered lava dike. Below the Turkey Creek picnic area on the left is Willow Jungle Rapid. Take the right fork in low or medium water and the left fork in higher water.

Another pool brings you to the Silver Mines Dam, built in the late nineteenth century to supply power for the silver mining in the area. Every year the dam deteriorates some more. The breach on the left side is safe to run in low and medium levels. A large hydraulic forms at high water, Once water is flowing over the SR D bridge it is a keeper, class VI. At levels 1.5–3 feet over the SR D bridge, there are low spots on the right side of the dam that water flows through. With careful scouting and alignment, the run is a simple 10-foot waterfall. Stay clear of the huge hydraulic by the dam breach. At levels over 3 feet, carry on the right shore.

Below the dam is the Silver Mines Shut-In. The half mile from the dam to the SR D bridge is a natural slalom course, class II–III. Take-out just above the low-water bridge on river left.

SHUTTLE: Put-in at MO 72 downstream of the bridge on river right. Millstream Gardens State Forest alternate access is off MO 72, 3.75 miles west of SR D. Proceed south on the gravel entrance road. Go left at the first fork, right at the next two forks. Unload and park in the upper lot. Take-out at the SR B low-water bridge, upstream of the bridge on river left. The bridge is 3 miles south of the intersection of MO 72 and SR D, west of Fredericktown.

GAUGE: All the water levels cited above refer to a hand-painted gauge on the SR D low-water bridge. The gauge, in inches, is on a downstream abutment on the north end. The minimum level for a solo run is 0 inches. Medium water starts at 12 inches, high water around 27 (at this point, water is hitting bridge). Flood conditions (class IV) start at 2.5 feet over the top of the bridge. This is the limit for open boats, which will need to skirt all kinds of waves and holes. The usual boating season for this section is from late November to early May. Heavy summer thunderstorms may bring the river up for only a day or two.

Water levels can often be obtained on weekdays from the U.S. Forest Service Fredericktown office at (314) 783-7225 or the St. Louis National Weather Service recordings of daily river stages at (314) 928-1194. Listen for Roselle on the St. Francis, which will be a two-digit number with a decimal. To correlate the Roselle gauge with the SR D gauge, subtract three from the Roselle figure and multiply the result by 15. This really works. A negative number means it's below 0 inches, anything over 40 means the

water is over the top of the SR D bridge. The recording usually reflects a 2 a.m. reading. The levels cited below apply to the Roselle gauge.

Minimum: 2.9 Optimum: 3.8–4.3 Dangerous: >5.5

difficulty	I–II
distance	7.25
time	3.5
gauge	St. Francis (USGS)
level	2.7
scenery	A–B
water	Good
gradient	6
latitude	37 30.142N
longitude	90 27.474W

SR E Bridge to Captain Creek Junction

DESCRIPTION: This section should be considered a float trip. Its short rocky sections are separated by slow pools. The longest pool is encountered where Black and Marlow Mountains flank the river.

About a mile below the Marble Creek junction, the St. Francis enters a spectacular shut-in, The Fish Trap. This three-quarter-mile class II shut-in ends below Lee Bluff, a 380-foot granite bluff on the left. A climb up the hill rewards you with a view of distant forested hills and the canyon below.

The suggested take-out is at Captain Creek. To find the creek, the Rockpile Mountain topo map is helpful. One mile below Lee Bluff, look for two houses about 40 feet up a hill on the right. The creek is just below the houses on the left. Downstream are additional small drops and scenery, but the shuttle becomes very long. There is no public access until Jewett, 8 miles downstream.

SHUTTLE: Put-in at the SR E bridge, 9.5 miles west of its intersection with US 67 just south of Fredericktown. To reach the take-out, go south on SR O from its intersection with SR E 6.25 miles west of US 67. Follow SR O to its end and continue on the gravel-road extension, which is CR 425. Cross the low-water bridge over Captain Creek. Go left, following CR 425 downstream. The road recrosses the creek and ends at a farmer's gate. Ask permission before parking along the side of the road, and do not block the road or any gates. Boats must to be carried and paddled one-eighth mile up the creek when returning to your vehicle.

GAUGE: See section B. The minimum for this section is 4 inches on the SR D bridge gauge or 2.7 feet on the Roselle gauge.

Minimum: 2.7 Optimum: 3.0–4.0 Dangerous: >5.0

TURKEY CREEK

Turkey Creek descends from MO 72 to its junction with the St. Francis River upstream of the Silver Mine Dam. Only 2.5 miles long, the river is flat for the first 1.25 miles and the last 0.6 mile. In between, this little ripsnorter is anything but. It drops 100 feet in 0.75 mile. It is the steepest known creek run in Missouri. When water levels are right (a local flash-flood watch is a clue), it offers five to six class III–IV rapids.

MAPS: Rhodes Mountain (USGS); Madison (County)

MO 72 BRIDGE TO THE ST. FRANCIS RIVER

difficulty	III–IV
distance	2.6
time	1.5
gauge	Visual
level	Flood
scenery	A–B
water	Fair
gradient	46 (100+)
latitude	37 35.156N
longitude	90 26.281W

DESCRIPTION: Below the last livestock fence, there is one-eighth mile of fast water and class II drops.

As the creek swings to the left, you'll notice flat ledges along the shore. Boulder Dance Rapid has no defined route, but staying to the center works best. An eddy separates Boulder Dance from Janney's Jam. Start right-center, work left-center, and be prepared to blast hydraulics in high water. Catching eddies in both rapids requires scrambling at any water level. The drops merge into one rapid in high water.

A pool and a turn to the right signal the approach of Turtle Slide. This starts as a confusion of rocks ending in a chute that tends to scrape paddlers along a large rock on the left. The largest pool yet encountered separates Turtle Slide from Stickey Wicket, where a 12-foot boulder splits the river as it screams around a left turn. Scouting Stickey Wicket on the left is a good idea because of the willows and downed trees that collect here. The safest route is to go right of the boulder and eddy out along the right shore. Look over your right shoulder, find a pair of willows you can blast through, and fire away. The remainder is a fast, rocky chute.

Another pool brings you to a horizon line. At Look Right rapid, prepare to start left, aim right, and bounce off the pillow on the left. Starting right invites a vertical pin. The three ledges immediately below offer few problems. Just beyond is Stoy's Joy. This 8-foot slide is a narrow slot between rock walls only 5 feet apart. Low water means bumping down, carefully staying aligned. High water dictates skirting the top hole to the right, then paddling the drop and the soupy hydraulic on the bottom.

A few more class II drops and the real stuff is over. Watch for a willow thicket, where taking the far-left channel offers the

fewest problems. Paddle over the ford at Turkey Creek Picnic Area, under the bridge for the hiking trail, and onto a swollen St. Francis River just above Willow Jungle Rapid (the St. Francis is always swollen when there's enough water to run Turkey Creek).

SHUTTLE: Although the put-in at MO 72 is easy, at present it's not recommended. Two farmers own property along the creek for the first mile and a half. Boating this stretch means getting their permission (hit or miss), plus navigating around the pigs, cattle, and four livestock fences that span the stream. A safer and more invigorating method is to boat the St. Francis and carry overland about half a mile. Paddle the St. Francis below Rickety-Rack, stopping at a pool with a 40-foot granite bluff on the river-right side. Take-out on the left across from the bluff on a small, sandy beach. Carry upstream on the trail that parallels the river. Look for a brush pile hiding an intersecting old logging road on the right. Carry up the old logging road, now going north. The trail will make a left; follow it to the top of a low, flat rise. When the logging road begins to go downhill very slightly, turn right (east) and start walking approximately one-quarter mile through the woods. Veer to the left (northeast), and ideally you'll intersect Turkey Creek just below the last fence.

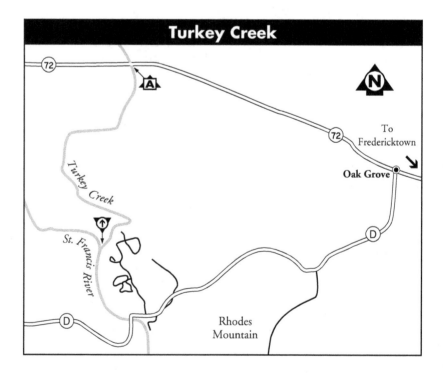

The take-out for this run is the same as that for the middle section on the St. Francis River. Take-out on the upstream, river-left side of the SR B low-water bridge. The bridge is 3 miles south of the intersection of MO 72 and SR D, west of Fredericktown.

GAUGE: None. In low water, the river is passable when all the rocks and gravel bars are covered at the MO 72 bridge. At this stage, the rapids are tight, technical drops that require threading around numerous pin possibilities. Flood conditions mean 1–2 feet of muddy water swirling under the MO 72 bridge. Pinning is still a possibility, especially on the ever-present willows. In addition, there is the added excitement of small stopper hydraulics in some powerful rapids. At any water level, Turkey Creek is unpleasant for inverted boaters, who are likely to lose some skin.

appendices

Appendix A:
Clubs and Organizations

Paddling exploded in the early 1970s, coinciding with the movie *Deliverance,* and grew steadily until the early nineties, when a second growth spurt occurred due to advancements in materials and boat design. Paddling and conservation clubs formed as a result of the early popularity, first as a vehicle to bring people with common interests together and more recently to promote safety, education, and conservation. The Ozark area is fortunate to have many excellent organizations that help accomplish these goals and provide the general public with vital information concerning rivers and the outdoors.

PADDLING CLUBS

Arkansas Canoe Club
P.O. Box 1843
Little Rock, AR 72203
www.arkansascanoeclub.com

The Arkansas Canoe Club is a statewide organization with over 450 members and five chapters throughout the area. The ACC is dedicated to participating in and promoting the sport of paddling by holding paddling schools and clinics, whitewater rescue courses, river cleanups, and by taking an active stand on conservation and river-access issues.

Bluff City Canoe Club
P.O. Box 4523
Memphis, TN 38014
www.bluffcitycanoeclub.org

The Bluff City Canoe Club is located in Memphis, Tennessee, and has a membership of 225 families. Their primary objective is the preservation and enjoyment of area rivers, and their slogan is "Refresh the Spirit with Nature's Bounty." The club schedules canoe and camping trips throughout the year.

Dallas Down River Club
P.O. Box 820246
Dallas, TX 75382-0246
www.down-river.com

This Texas club sponsors regular paddling outings and publishes a monthly newsletter. The group also hosts the annual Trinity Challenge race in Carrollton, Texas.

Kansas Canoe Association

P.O. Box 44-2490
Lawrence, KS 66044
www.tfsksu.net/~tjhittle

This conservation-oriented club, formed in 1975, offers courses and trips for Kansas paddlers, as well as member discounts at some outfitters.

Kansas City Whitewater Club

1009 Brookside Drive
Raymore, MO 64083
www.kcwc.org

This club offers canoeing safety and technique classes. They also organize trips for, and rent equipment to, members.

Memphis Whitewater

www.memphiswhitewater.com

This club promotes camaraderie among Memphis-area paddlers with regular games of boatball, which it describes as "a rather anarchic variation on water polo called boatball."

Missouri Whitewater Association

427 Water Street
St. Charles, MO 63301
www.missouriwhitewater.org

Formerly known as the Arnold Whitewater Society, this club promotes a range of activities, including canoeing, camping, and cross-country skiing. They organize and sponsor the Missouri Whitewater Championships each spring on the St. Francis River, usually held in late March. They have also published an excellent map of the St. Francis River that is a must for area paddlers; the map can be obtained at a reasonable price from local whitewater shops or the association.

Ozark Wilderness Waterways

P.O. Box 16032
Kansas City, MO
http://hometown.aol.com/owwccanoeclub

This is one of the original canoe and conservation groups in the area. Activities include canoeing, camping, and hiking.

Ozark Mountain Paddlers

P.O. Box 1794
Springfield, MO 65805
www.ozarkmtnpaddlers.org

Founded in 1983, this club offers whitewater-skills clinics and monthly overnight paddling excursions. The group promotes volunteerism with an emphasis on education and recreation.

NATIONAL ORGANIZATIONS

American Canoe Association
7432 Alban Station Boulevard, Suite B-226
Springfield, VA 22150
(703) 451-0141
www.aca-paddler.org
    The American Canoe Association is dedicated to safety and education in the sport of canoeing and is the governing body for whitewater and flatwater races in the United States.

American Whitewater Affiliation
P.O. Box 85
Phoenicia, NY 12464
www.awa.org
    The American Whitewater Affiliation is made up of canoe clubs nationwide that promote competition and conservation. Yearly dues include a subscription to *American Whitewater*, the bimonthly journal of the American Whitewater Affiliation.

CONSERVATION GROUPS

The Ozark Society
Membership Chairman
P.O. Box 2914
Little Rock, AR 72203
www.ozarksociety.net
    Dr. Neil Compton founded the Ozark Society in 1962 to preserve the natural resources of the Ozark Mountain region. The group was instrumental in the fight to save the Buffalo River in the early 1970s and still makes its voice heard on all matters of environmental importance in the area. The Ozark Society also actively promotes canoeing and publishes books on area rivers. Several excellent publications are available through Ozark Society Books; see Appendix B.

The Sierra Club
730 Polk Street Street
San Francisco, CA 94109
www.sierraclub.org
Arkansas Chapter: www.arkansas.sierraclub.org/
    The Sierra Club was created in 1892 to protect scenic areas of the United States. The group played a major part in the creation of many of our great national parks, among them Yosemite, Grand Canyon, Rocky Mountain, and Glacier National Parks. The Sierra Club was also the driving force in the creation of the Wild and Scenic Rivers System.

Membership benefits include the group's bimonthly magazine *Sierra,* chapter newsletters, discounts on books and calendars published by the club, and outing programs.

GOVERNMENT COMMISSIONS

The Arkansas Game and Fish Commission
Arkansas Game and Fish Commission
2 Natural Resources Drive
Little Rock, AR 72205
www.agfc.state.ar.us
The Arkansas Game and Fish Commission is charged with managing the state's wildlife resources. They are instrumental in establishing public access points on many streams in the state.

Arkansas Natural and Scenic Rivers Commission
Director, Arkansas Natural and Scenic Rivers Commission
c/o Department of Arkansas Heritage
1500 Tower Building
323 Center Street
Little Rock, AR 72201
The Arkansas Natural and Scenic Rivers Commission was formed by the state legislature. Their duty is to protect the "natural beauty along certain rivers of the state."

The Missouri Department of Conservation
www.conservation.state.mo.us
The Missouri Department of Conservation is charged with preserving the state's natural resources and making them available to citizens for recreational use.

Oklahoma Department of Wildlife Conservation
1801 North Lincoln
Oklahoma City, OK 73105
(405) 521-3851
As the state regulatory agency for hunting and fishing, the Department of Wildlife Conservation is committed to protecting the habitat of wild game.

Appendix B:
Additional Books and Videos

BOOKS OF LOCAL INTEREST

The following titles are available from Ozark Society Books, P.O. Box 3503, Little, Rock, AR 72203:

The Battle for the Buffalo by Dr. Neil Compton.

Buffalo National River Canoeing Guide by Margaret and Harold Hedges.

Buffalo River Country by Ken Smith.

Cadron Creek, a Photographic Narrative and Floating Guide by Lil Janus.

The Mighty Mulberry by Margaret and Harold Hedges.

INSTRUCTIONAL BOOKS

The following titles are available from the American Canoe Association, which offers online ordering via www.acanet.org:

The ACA's Kayak and Canoe Games by Laurie Gullion.

The ACA's River Safety Anthology by Charlie Walbridge.

Canoeing and Kayaking Instruction Manual by Laurie Gullion.

Catch Every Wave . . . Surf Every Eddy by Tom Foster and Kel Kelly.

Introduction to Paddling: Canoeing Basics for Lakes and Rivers by the American Canoe Association.

The Kayaker's Playbook by Kent Ford with Phil Deriemer and Mary Deriemer.

Kayaking by Kent Ford.

Solo Playboating by Kent Ford.

Whitewater Rescue Manual by Charlie Walbridge and Wayne A. Sundmacher Sr.

INSTRUCTIONAL VIDEOS

The following videos are also available from the American Canoe Association:

Cold, Wet and Alive. An internationally acclaimed collaboration between the ACA and filmmaker Russ Nichols, this video follows a group of early-season paddlers down a cold-water stream and documents their encounter with the silent killer hypothermia. Recommended for all paddlers, especially those who push the limits of the paddling season.

Drill Time: Solo Playboating II. This instructional video teaches playboating techniques.

Heads Up! River Rescue for River Runners. An ACA/Nichols award winner, *Heads Up!* emphasizes the need for both self- and group-rescue skills among whitewater paddlers. It features extensive footage of actual entrapments and subsequent rescues.

Retendo! This film teaches precision rodeo skills for whitewater kayaks.

Take the Wild Ride. An informative video introduction to whitewater rodeo.

Whitewater Self-defense. This Performance Video film teaches fundamental safety skills for kayakers.

Appendix C:
Maps

Maps are an important source of information on both rivers and roads leading to the rivers. Listed below are some of the better maps and informational booklets available for the Ozarks area.

TOPOGRAPHIC MAPS

Topographic maps are detailed descriptions covering 7.5 minutes of latitude and 15 minutes of longitude. Each quadrangle is designated by the name of the city, town, or prominent feature on the map. You can obtain ordering information online or request free map indexes by phone or mail:

USGS Information Services
Box 25286
Denver, CO 80225
(888) ASK-USGS
http://ask.usgs.gov/maps.html

Maps can be ordered from:

U.S. Geological Survey
P.O. Box 25286 Federal Center
Denver, CO 80225
http://mcmcweb.er.usgs.gov/topomaps/ordering_maps.html

STATE AND COUNTY MAPS

State road maps for Arkansas and Missouri are free; county maps in Arkansas are about $3.60 each and county maps in Missouri are less. Digitally scanned Oklahoma county maps are free online. Maps are available from the following government departments:

Map Sales, Room 205
Arkansas State Highway & Transportation Department
P.O. Box 2261
Little Rock, Arkansas 72203
(501) 569-2444

Missouri Highway Transportation Department
Division of Surveys and Plans
P.O. Box 270
Jefferson City, MO 65102
(888) 275-6636
http://www.modot.state.mo.us/index.htm

Oklahoma Department of Transportation
Attn. Printing Services
200 Northeast 21st Street
Oklahoma City, OK. 73105
(405) 521-2586

NATIONAL FOREST MAPS

Ozark National Forest The Ozark map shows the entire area managed by the Forest Service as well as adjacent land not owned by the Forest Service. This is especially useful for planning access to a particular area.

A listing of campgrounds and recreation areas is available free from the Forest Service. It gives information about each area and a small map showing its location within the forest.

Supervisor's Office
Forest Supervisor
Ozark-St. Francis National Forest
605 West Main Street
Russellville, AR 72801
www.fs.fed.us/oonf/ozark/

Ouachita National Forest The Ouachita map, as well as maps for special areas including Caney Creek Wilderness, Ouachita River, and Charlton, can be ordered from:

Forest Supervisor
Ouachita National Forest
P.O. Box 1270
Hot Springs, AR 71902
www.fs.fed.us/oonf/ouachita.htm

Mark Twain National Forest Maps of each of the forest's ranger districts are available from:

Forest Supervisor
Mark Twain National Forest
401 Fairgrounds Road
Rolla, MO 64501
(573) 364-4621
www.fs.fed.us/r9/marktwain/so-maps.htm

Appendix D: Recommended Web Sites

Arkansas Canoe Club
www.arkansascanoeclub.com
The club's official site is full of useful information about the
group and its many activities. There are also links to the more
popular river gauges, commercial links, weather information,
and a great message board.

Arkansas Department of Parks and Tourism
www.arkansas.com/outdoors_sports/float/
This is the Parks and Tourism Departments float trip and canoeing page. Here you will find information on some of the rivers
and streams listed in this book, but more importantly if you are
seeking an outfitter for a particular river, there is a comprehensive list of all outfitters and the services they provide. Click the
site map and you can find other valuable recreation information
for Arkansas.

Bluff City Canoe Club
www.bluffcitycanoeclub.org
This is the official site of Memphis's Bluff City Canoe Club,
founded in 1967. Check out their activities schedule, which
includes paddling, hiking, and adventure trips

Buffalo National Hydraulic Data System
www.buffaloriverandrain.com
This site was developed by the National Park Service with the
help of the Arkansas Canoe Club and the Arkansas Game and
Fish Commission. Detailed rainfall reports, watershed maps,
river level plots, and recommended floating levels are all here.
The easy-to-read Current Watershed Map is an interactive map
showing all the river and rainfall gauges.

Dallas Down-River Club
www.down-river.com/index.html#misc
This may be the largest list of cool paddling links online. Check
this out when you have time to surf!

Fort Smith Intellicast Radar
www.intellicast.com/Local/USLocalWide.asp?loc=kfsm&seg=
LocalWeather&prodgrp=RadarImagery&product=Radar&
prodnav=none
This is one of the best sites for real-time radar data for Western
Arkansas.

Kansas City Whitewater Club
www.kcwc.org
At the official site of the Kansas City Whitewater Club, you can find out all you need to know about canoeing in the Kansas City area.

Missouri Canoe Rentals
www.conservation.state.mo.us/cgibin/mdcdevpub/apps/canoes/main.cgi
This site allows you to locate canoe rentals by selecting the river you are interested in paddling.

Missouri Whitewater Association
http://www.missouriwhitewater.org/competition.html
This is a great place to keep up on the annual Missouri Whitewater Championships. There is also plenty of information on area rivers.

Ozark Creek Information Summary
www.ozarkpages.com/cgi-bin/stages.pl
Bill "Fish" Herring compiled a table of all the popular rivers and creeks with a real-time, color-coded water-level system. There is also information about each stream, including links to the real-time gauge and photos. This is cutting edge stuff!

The Ozark Whitewater Page
www.ozarkpages.com/whitewater
If you could only link to one page about paddling in Arkansas, this would be it. Bill "Fish" Herring has compiled a comprehensive Web page with links to all the important places you need for paddling information in Arkansas. My personal favorite is the section titled "Information for Planning your Ozark Paddling Trip." Take some time and explore the links to river gauges, rainfall gauges, photos of your favorite stream, and cool paddling stuff for sale.

Water Resources of Arkansas
http://arkweb.er.usgs.gov
This is the USGS link to a very in-depth look at all aspects of hydrology in Arkansas. Real-time stream data is accessible from the site.

Appendix E: USGS Waterline

The USGS Waterline is a service provided by the United State Geological Survey that allows 24-hour access to the gauges listed below. A gauge level is obtained by calling (800) 452-1737. You will reach an automated system, and by entering the code for the river, will get a current reading. Levels are updated every four hours, and selected past readings for the gauge are also available. This is a nationwide system, and you can get site codes for gauges nationwide online at: www.h2oline.com.

CODE	SITE NAME
051329	Big Piney Creek at AR 164
051242	Buffalo River near St Joe
051249	Cadron Creek near Guy
051253	Cossatot River near Vandervoort
051255	Crooked Creek at Yellville
055114	DeQueen Dam Tailwater
055115	DeQueen Lake Pool
055113	Dierks Dam Tailwater
051259	Dutch Creek at Waltreak
051177	Fourche La Fave S Fork near Hollis
051268	Frog Bayou at Rudy
055111	Gillham Dam Tailwater
051271	Gillham Lake Pool
051139	I llinois Bayou near Scottsville
051281	King's River near Berryville
051142	Lake Greeson at the Narrows
055118	Little Missouri River near Langley
051291	Little Piney Creek near Lamar
051153	Little Red, Middle Fork at Shirley

CODE   **SITE NAME** *(continued)*

051176   Little Red, South Fork at Clinton

051159   Mulberry River near Mulberry

055116   Ouachita below Remmel Dam Jones

051325   Petit Jean River near Booneville

051171   Piney Fork of the Strawberry at Evening Shade

055117   Richland Creek near Witts Spring

051333   Rolling Fork near DeQueen

051182   Strawberry River near Poughkeepsie

051365   War Eagle Creek near Hindsville

051386   White River near Fayetteville

index

Creek and River Difficulty Ratings for each specific segment are indexed under Class (e.g. Class II-III). All river segments and county or state government entities are for Arkansas unless identified as Missouri (MO) or Oklahoma (OK).

A

Access, river. *see also* Fees and donations; Landowners; Outfitters
Alcohol and drugs, 12
Alum Creek Experimental Forest, 137
American Canoe Association, 17, 218
American Whitewater, 10, 218
Archey Creek
  Castleberry Creek to US 65 Bridge, 15–16
  Hartsugg Creek to US 65 Bridge, 15–16
Arkansas Canoe Club, 112–113, 162–164, 216
Arkansas Game and Fish Commission, 219
  Cadron Creek access at Pinnacle Springs, 19
  Cove Creek access at AR 285, 22
  King's River access at Trigger Gap, 110
  King's River access at US 62, 129
Athens Piedmont Plateau, 1

B

Baker Creek
  Weyerhauser Road 52000 to 52600, 139–140
Barkshed Recreation Area, 27
Bear Head Mountain, 174
Bee Mountain, 176
Benton County
  Illinois River, 104–105
Big Creek (AR)
  Low-Water Bridge 3 to Old Iron Bridge, 17–18
Big Creek (MO), 17
  Des Arc to Sam A. Baker State Park, 201–203

Big Creek (OK)
  US 270 to Page, OK, 141–142
Big Piney Creek, 44–49
  Fort Douglas to Helton's Farm, 46–47
  Helton's Farm to Longpool Campground, 47–48
  Limestone to Fort Douglas, 46
  Longpool Campground to Twin Bridges, 49
  Walnut Creek to Limestone, 44–46
Black Fork Mountain, 141
Black River, 33, 36, 182
Blackburn Creek, 112
Blair Creek (MO), 185
Blaylock Creek, 159
Boston Mountains
  Big Piney Creek, 44
  Buffalo National River and, 50
  Clear Creek and, 94
  King's River, 106
  The Ozarks and, 1
  river hydrology and, 7
Brushy Creek, 168
  CR 30 to AR 246, 143–144
Bryant's Creek (MO)
  Aid-Hodgson Mill to Warren Bridge, 180–181
  Bell School Bridge to Aid-Hodgson Mill, 179
  Warren Bridge to Norfolk Lake, 181
Buffalo National River, 50–59
  Big Piney Creek and, 44
  Boxley to Ponca, 52
  Buffalo Point to Rush Landing, 59
  Carver to Mt. Hersey, 55–56
  Gilbert to Buffalo Point, 57–58
  Kyle's Landing to Pruitt, 53–55

Mt. Hersey to Woolum, 56
Ponca to Kyle's Lnading, 52–53
Pruitt to Carver, 55
Rush Landing to Buffalo City, 59
White River and the, 40–42
Woolum to Gilbert, 56–57
see also Hailstone River
Buffalo River. *see* Buffalo National
River
Bull Shoals Recreation Area, 39
Bull Shoals State Park, 39–40

C
Caddo River
Caddo Gap to Glenwood, 147
FR 73 to Norman, 145–146
Glenwood to Amity, 147
Norman to Caddo Gap, 147
Cadron Creek
Pinnacle Springs to US 65
Bridge, 19–20
US 65 Bridge to AR 285, 20–21
Camping, Arkansas
Big Piney Creek, Longpool
Campground, 44, 48–49
Buffalo National River, 52–53,
56–57
Buffalo National River, National
Park Service, 50
Falling Water Creek, Richland
Campground, 65–66
Illinois Bayou, Bayou Bluff
Campground, 74
Illinois Bayou, East Fork, 64
Iron Springs National Forest
Campground, 137
King's River, Trigger Gap, 110
Little Missouri River, Albert Pike
Campground, 158, 161
Mulberry River, Byrd's
Campground, 123
Ouachita River, Dragover
Campground, 170–171
Ouachita River Forest Service
camp, 168
Ouachita River, River Bluff
Campground, 171
Richland Creek, Richland
Campground, 85–86
South Fourche Lavave River, 175
White River, Buffalo City, 42

Camping, Missouri
Big Creek (MO) rental cabins,
203
Current River (MO), 183–187
Eleven Point River (MO),
189–192
Jack's Fork River (MO), 193–195
Marble Creek (MO), 206–207
White River, North Fork (MO),
200
Caney Creek Wilderness Area, 139,
144, 149, 158, 172
Captain Creek (MO), 212
Carroll County
Osage Creek, 128–129
Cassatot River, 148–153
AR 246 to Ed Banks Bridge, 150
Baker Creek and the, 139
Brushy Creek and the, 143
Ed Banks Bridge to Sandbar
Bridge, 150–151
FR 31 to AR 246, 148–149
Sandbar Bridge to AR 278,
151–153
Cassatot River State Park, 139,
143, 148
Castor River (MO)
Hahn's Mill Shut-In Section,
204–205
Cautions
Baker Creek piton pins, 140
Big Creek (AR) guage, 18
Cedar Creek parking, 93
Clear Creek, 94, 96
Cove Creek electric fence, 97
Crooked Creek flash floods, 62
Hailstone River rapids, 67–69
Hurricane Creek rapids, 70–72
Little Mulberry Creek
landowners, 116–118
Little Piney Creek landowners,
76
Mulberry River low bridge, 125
"No Trespassing" signs near Elba,
24
Richland Creek rapids, 82–85
Salado Creek guage, 30
Shoal Creek downed trees and
steep walls, 87–88
South Fork of the Spring River
low water bridges, 32

C *(continued)*
Cautions *(continued)*
  Spring River, Humphries Ford,
    35
  Strawberry River low-water
    bridge, 36–37
  White River, Middle Fork,
    landowners, 119–121
  see also Hazards and safety;
    Portages
Caves
  Buffalo National River, John
    Eddings Cave, 55
  Buffalo National River, Skull
    Bluff, 56
  Current River (MO), Cave
    Spring, 183
  Current River (MO), Merritt
    Rock Cave, 183
  Eleven Point River (MO),
    White's Creek Cave, 191
  Jack's Fork River (MO),
    Chimney Rock Cave, 193
  Jack's Fork River (MO), Jam-Up
    Cave, 195
Cedar Creek, 175
  AR 162 to Rudy, 91–93
Cherokee Wildlife Management
    Area
  Archey Creek and, 15
  Big Creek and, 18
  Salado Creek, 29
Class, river-run, defined, 3–4
Class I
  Bryant's Creek (MO), 180–181
  Buffalo National River, 55–59
  Caddo River, Glenwood to
    Amity, 147
  Crooked Creek, 62
  Current River (MO), 182–187
  Eleven Point River (MO),
    188–193
  Illinois River, 105
  Jack's Fork River (MO), 195–197
  King's River, 108–111
  Osage Creek, 128–129
  Ouachita River, 167
  Saline River, Alum Fork, 138
  Spring River, South Fork, 32

  War Eagle Creek, 133
  White River, 38–43
Class I-II
  Big Creek (AR), 17–18
  Big Creek (MO), 201–203
  Bryant's Creek (MO), 179–180
  Buffalo National River, 50–55
  Caddo River, 146–147
  Cadron Creek, 20–21
  Crooked Creek, 60–61
  Frog Bayou, 99–103
  Illinois River, 104
  Jack's Fork River (MO), 193–195
  King's River, 106–108
  Lee Creek, 114–115
  Middle Fork of the Little Red
    River, 25–26
  Mulberry River, 126–128
  North Sylamore Creek, 28
  Ouachita River, 168–170
  Ouachita River, Lower, 162–164
  Saline River, Alum Fork, 138
  Saline River, North Fork,
    165–166
  Spring River, Dam 3 to Hardy,
    33–35
  Spring River, South Fork, 32
  St. Francis River (MO), SR E
    Bridge to Captain Creek, 212
  St. Francis River (MO), SR H
    Bridge to MO 72, 209
  Strawberry River, 36–37
  War Eagle Creek, 132–133
  White River, North Fork (MO),
    198–200
  White River, Upper, 130–131
  White River, West Fork, 136
Class II
  Big Piney Creek, Ft. Douglas to
    Helton's Farm, 46–47
  Big Piney Creek, Longpool to
    Twin Bridges, 49
  Illinois Bayou, 74
  Mulberry River, 125
Class I-III
  Cadron Creek, 19–20
  North Sylamore Creek, 28
  Ouachita River, Dragover Loop,
    171

South Fourche Lavave River,
174–175
White River, West Fork, 134–135
Class III
Shoal Creek, 87–88
Class II-III
Archey Creek, 16
Big Creek (OK), 141–142
Big Piney Creek, Helton's Farm
to Longpool, 47–48
Big Piney Creek, Walnut Creek
to Ft. Douglas, 44–46
Brushy Creek, 143–144
Caddo River, 145–146
Cassatot River, 148–150
Cedar Creek, 91–93
Clear Creek, 94–96
Cove Creek Barker Gap to Creek
Ford, 97–98
Cove Creek, Martinville to
Mallet Town, 22–23
Eagle Fork Creek, 154–155
Illinois Bayou, 73–74
Illinois Bayou, East Fork, 63–64
Illinois Bayou, Middle Fork,
77–79
Illinois Bayou, North Fork,
80–81
Jack Creek, 156–157
Lee Creek, 112–113
Little Missouri River, 161
Little Mulberry Creek, 116–118
Little Piney Creek, 75–76
Marble Creek (MO), 206–207
Middle Fork of the Little Red
River, 24–25
Mulberry River, 122–123
Salado Creek, 29–30
Saline River, 172–173
Sprada Creek, 89–90
White River, Middle Fork,
120–121
Class II-IV
Cassatot River, 150–151
Falling Water Creek, 65–66
Hurricane Creek, 70–72
Little Missouri River, 158–161
Richland Creek, 86
St. Francis River (MO), 209–212

White River, Middle Fork, 119
Class III-IV
Baker Creek, 139–140
Cassatot River, 151–153
Castor River (MO), 204–205
Hailstone River, 67–69
Richland Creek, 82–85
Sugar Creek, 176–178
Turkey Creek (MO), 213–215
Clear Creek
Chester to Mountainburg, 96
Schaberg to Chester, 94–95
Cleburne County
Big Creek, 17–18
Middle Fork of the Little Red
River, 24–26
Climate, Ozarks, 2
Conway County
Cove Creek, 22
Coot Mountain, 185
Cove Creek, 112
Barker Gap Road to Creek Ford
Road, 97–98
Martinville to Mallet Town,
22–23
Crawford County
Cedar Creek, 91–93
Clear Creek, 94–96
Cove Creek, 97–98
Frog Bayou, 99–103
Lee Creek, 112–115
Crooked Creek
Harman to Pyatt, 60–61
Pyatt to Yellville, 61
Yellville to AR 101, 61
Crystal Mountain, 165
Cucumber Creek, 154
Current River (MO), 182–187
Akers Ferry to Pulltite Spring,
183
Cedargrove to Akers Ferry,
182–183
Jack's Fork River (MO) and the,
193, 197
Powder Mill to Van Buren, 187
Pulltite Spring to Round Spring,
183–185
Round Spring to Two Rivers, 185
Two Rivers to Powder Mill, 185

C *(continued)*
Current River (MO) *(continued)*
Van Buren to Gooseneck
Landing, 187

D
Dams
Big Creek (AR) Pangburn Dam,
17
Cossatot River, Gilliam Dam,,
148
Frog Bayou and Lake Fort Smith,
96, 99
Illinois Bayou, North Fork
proposed, 80
Lee Creek, Pine Mountain Dam,
114
Lower Ouachita River, Remmel
Dam, 162–164
Marble Creek (MO)
campground, 207
Saline River, Shady Lake
Reservoir, 172–173
Spadra Creek, Clarksville Water
Plant, 90
Spring River, Dam 3, 33
St. Francis River (MO) Silver
Mines dam, 211, 213
Strawberry River, Bell Foley Dam
Project, 36
White River, 38
White River, Buffalo City, 42
White River, North Fork (MO),
Dawt Mill dam, 200
White River, West Fork,
Riverside Park, 135
Dent County (MO)
Current River (MO), 182–187
Devil's Den State Park, 112
Difficulty, river, defined
see also specific river segments by
Class
Difficulty scale, river, defined, 3–4
Divide Mountains, 73
Douglas County (MO)
Bryant's Creek, 179–181
White River (MO), North Fork,
198–200
Drugs and alcohol, 12

E
Eagle Fork Creek
OK 144 to Smithville, 154–155
East Cedar Creek. *see* Cedar Creek
East Fork Wilderness Area, 63
Education and safety, 10–12,
220–221
Eleven Point River (MO), 188–193
Cane Bluff to Greer Crossing,
190
Greer Crossing to Riverton,
190–192
Riverton to MO 142, 192
Thomasville to Cane Bluff,
189–190
Environment, protecting the pad-
dling, 13–14, 220–221
Equipment preparedness and safety,
10–12
Etiquette, river, 13–14, 63, 93
Events
Arkansas Canoe Club Rendezous,
163

F
Fall Creek, 112
Falling Water Creek
FR 1205 to Richland
Campground, 65–66
Faulkner County
Cadron Creek, 19
Fees and donations
Cadron Creek, 19
fishing license, 40
King's River, 110
Mulberry River, 123, 125
Salado Creek, 29
see also Access, river; Landowners;
Outfitters
First aid. *see* Safety and hazards
Fishing
Crooked Creek, 60–62
Eleven Point River (MO), 189
King's River, 108–111
Osage Creek, 128–129
Ouachita River, 167
Spring River, 33
White River, 38–43
Flat water. *see* Lakes

Food and supplies
  Buffalo National River, Baker
    General Store, 57
  Current River (MO), 183–187
  Mulberry River, Turner Bend,
    125
  State Line Bar near Big Creek,
    141
Forest Service. *see* U. S. Forest
  Service
Fourche Mountains, 1
Frog Bayou, 99–103
  AR 282 to Grotto, 100–101
  Grotto to Lancaster, 101
  Lancaster to Rudy, 101–103
  Mountainburg to AR 282, 99
  Rudy to US 64, 103
Fulton County
  South Fork of the Spring River,
    31–32
  Spring River, 33–35
  Strawberry River, 36–37

G
Geology, Ozarks Interior
  Highlands, 1
Global Positioning Satellite (GPS),
  5
Gradient, river, 1, 5
Greer's Ferry Lake, 24
Guage, river, 5–9, 226–227

H
Hailstone River
  FR 1463 to Boxley, 67–69
Harris Creek, 139
Hazards and safety
  advice and education, 10–12,
    220–221
  Buffalo City dam and flash
    flooding, 42
  Cedar Creek downed trees, 91
  Clarksville Water Plant dam, 90
  Cove Creek downed trees, 97
  Frog Bayou downed trees, 103
  Illinois Bayou downed trees, 74
  Illinois Bayou, East Fork trees
    and overhangs, 63–64
  Lee Creek barbed wire fence, 114

Lee Creek downed trees and
    overhangs, 112
  Little Mulberry Creek Willow
    Jungle, 116
  Marble Creek (MO), 206–207
  Salado Creek willow overhangs,
    30
  Strawberry River downed trees
    and snags, 36–37
  Sugar Creek, 176–177
  White River, West Fork dam,
    135
  see also Cautions; Portages
Historic sites
  Red Mill, Jack's Fork river (MO),
    196
  White River (AR) moonshine
    operations, 40
  see also Sites of interest
Hogan Mountain, 156
Hot Spring County
  Ouachita River, Lower, 162–164
How to use the Guide, 3–6
Howard County
  Baker Creek, 139–140
  Saline River, 172–173
Hurricane Creek
  Chancel to Fort Douglas, 70–72
  Mulberry River and, 127
Hydrology, river, 7

I
Illinois Bayou
  AR 27 to Hector Bridge, 73–74
  Hector Bridge to Scottsville, 74
Illinois Bayou, East Fork
  FR 1301 to Lindsey Mt. Way
    Road, 63–64
Illinois Bayou, Middle Fork
  Nogo to Snow Creek, 77–78
  Snow Creek to AR 27 Bridge, 79
Illinois Bayou, North Fork
  FR 1310A to FR 1818, 80–81
  Victor to FR 1310A, 80–81
Illinois River
  Chambers Spring Road to AR
    59, 105
  Lake Weddington to Chambers
    Spring Road, 104

I *(continued)*
Independence County
  Salado Creek, 29–30
Information, paddling, 216–219
Information sidebar, defined, 3–6
International Scale of River
  Difficulty, 3
Internet rescources, paddling, 7–9,
  224–225
Iron Springs National Forest, 137

J
Jack Creek, 177–178
  Jack Creek Bridge to Jack Creek
    Rec. Area, 156–157
Jack's Fork River (MO), 182
  Alley Spring to Shawnee Creek,
    196–197
  Bay Creek to Alley Spring, 196
  Buck Hollow to Rymers Access,
    194–195
  The Prongs to Buck Hollow,
    193–194
  Rymers Access to Bay Creek,
    195–196
  Shawnee Creek to Current Tiver,
    197
Johnson County
  Little Mulberry Creek, 116–118
  Little Piney Creek, 75–76
  Mulberry River, 122–128
  Sprada Creek, 89–90

K
Kimes Mountain, 91
King's River, 106–111
  AR 74 to Marble, 107
  Marble to Marshall Ford, 108
  Marshall Ford to Rockhouse, 108
  Rockhouse to Trigger Gap, 110
  Trigger Gap to US 62, 110–111
  US 62 to MO 86, 111

L
Lakes, Arkansas
  Beaver Lake, 132, 134
  Bull Shoals Lake, 38
  Degray Reservoir, 145
  Greer's Ferry Lake, 24
  Greeson Lake, 158

Lake Dardanelle, 44, 73, 75, 87,
  89
Lake Fort Smith, 95, 99
Lake Ludwig, 90
Lake Ouachita, 167
Lake Sequoia, 119, 130
  Shady Lake Reservoir, 172–173
Lakes, Missouri
  Norfork Lake, 179, 198
  Table Rock Lake, 106
Landowners, dealing with
  Big Creek (MO), 203
  Current River (MO), 183
  etiquette and paddler's rights,
    13–14
  Jack's Fork River (MO), 195
  Little Mulberry Creek, 116–118
  Little Piney Creek, 76
  Saline River, 173
  Turkey Creek (MO), 214
  White River, Middle Fork,
    119–121
Le Flore County (OK)
  Big Creek, 141–142
  Eagle Fork Creek, 154–155
Lee Creek
  AR 220 to Lee Creek
    Community, 113
  Devil's Den State Park to AR
    220, 112–113
  Lee Creek Community to AR 59,
    114–115
Legal issues, paddlers and, 13–14,
  77
Littering and trash handling,
  13–14
Little Missouri River
  Albert Pike Campground to AR
    84 Bridge, 158–161
  AR 84 Bridge to US 70 Bridge,
    161
Little Mulberry Creek
  Highlands Trail Bridge to AR
    215, 118
  Mulberry River and, 122
  Spoke Plant to Highland Trail
    Bridge, 116–117
Little Piney Creek
  AR 123 Bridge to Hagarville,
    75–76

Mt. Levi to AR 123 Bridge, 75–76
Little Red River, Middle Fork, 24–26
Little River, 148
Little River Mountain, 154
Logan County
Jack Creek, 156–157
Shoal Creek, 87–88
Sugar Creek, 176–178
Lower Ouachita River. *see* Ouachita River, Lower

M

Madison County (AR)
King's River, 106–111
War Eagle Creek, 132–133
White River, Upper, 130–131
Madison County (MO)
Castor River (MO), 204–205
Marble Creek (MO), 206–207
St. Francis River (MO), 208–212
Turkey Creek (MO), 213–215
Mammoth Springs, 33
Maps
GPS and, 5
legend and list of, viii–ix
sources for, 3, 222–223
Marble Creek (MO)
Marble Creek Campground to Hwy 427, 206–207
Marion County
Crooked Creek, 60–62
White River, 38–43
Mark Twain National Forest (MO), 198, 206
Middle Fork of the Little Red River
Alberg to Shirley, 25–26
Elba to Alberg, 24–25
Missouri Mountains, 145
Missouri Ozarks, 179–200
Montgomery County
Caddo River, 145–147
Mount Magazine, 87
Mountain Fork Creek, 112
Mountain Fork River, 154
Mulberry River, 122–128
Big Piney Creek and, 44
Bryd's Campground to Turner Bend, 125

Campbell's Cemetery to Mill Creek, 127–128
King's River and, 106
Little Mulberry Creek and, 116
Turner Bend to Campbell's Cemetery, 126–127
Wolf Pen Rec. Area to Byrd's Campground, 122–123

N

National Forests
Iron Springs National Forest, 137
Mark Twain National Forest (MO), 198
Ouachita National Forest, 143, 148, 165, 167, 176
Ozark National Forest, 27, 65
see also Ozark National Forest; State Parks; Wilderness Areas
National Oceanic and Atmospheric Administration (NOAA), 7–8
National Park Service, 50, 182, 193
National Weather Service, 7–8
Newton County
Buffalo National River, 50–55
Hailstone River, 67–69
Hurricane Creek, 70–72
Richland Creek, 82–86
North Sylamore Creek
Barkshed to Blanchard Springs, 27–28
Blanchard Springs to Allison, 28

O

Oklahoma
Big Creek, 141–142
Oregon County (MO)
Eleven Point River (MO), 188–193
Osage Creek
AR 21 to US 62, 128–129
Ouachita Mountains, 1, 7, 158, 172
Ouachita National Forest
Brushy Creek and, 143
Cossatot River and, 148
Ouachita River and, 167
Saline River, North Fork, and, 165
Sugar Creek and, 176

O *(continued)*
Ouachita River, 167–171
  Cherry Hill to Shirley Creek
    Access, 168
  Dragover Loop, 171
  McGuire Access to Cherry Hill,
    167
  Oden to Rocky Shoals, 168–170
  Rocky Shoals to Dragover Float
    Camp, 170
  Shirley Creek to Oden, 168
Ouachita River, Lower Remmel
  Dam to Rockport, 162–164
Outfitters
  Cadron Creek Outfitters, 19
  Eagle Fork Creek, 155
  Illinois River, 104
  King's River Outfitters, 108–110,
    129
  Ouachita River, 170
  White River (AR) fishing guides,
    38–39
  White River, North Fork (MO),
    198
Ozark Mountain, 1
Ozark National Forest
  Cove Creek, 97
  Falling Water Creek, 65
  Illinois Bayou, North Fork, 80
  Illinois River, 104
  Lee Creek, 112
  Little Piney Creek, 75
  North Sylamore Creek, 27
  War Eagle Creek, 132–133
  White River, Upper, 130
  see also National Forests
Ozark National Scenic Riverways,
  182, 193
Ozark Society, 36, 218
Ozarks Interior Highlands, 1

P
Paddling Clubs and information,
  216–219
Permits. *see* Access, river; Fees and
  donations; Landowners
Perry County
  South Fourche Lavave River,
    174–175
Petit Jean Mountain, 156

Pike County
  Little Missouri River, 158–161
Polk County
  Brushy Creek, 143–144
  Cassatot River, 148–153
  Ouachita River, 167–171
  Ponca Wilderness Area, 129
Pope County
  Archey Creek, 15–16
  Big Piney Creek, 44–49
  Illinois Bayou, 73–74
  Illinois Bayou, East Fork, 63–64
  Illinois Bayou, Middle Fork,
    77–79
  Illinois Bayou, North Fork,
    80–81
Portages
  Cassatot River, 148
  Cedar Creek, 92
  Clear Creek, 94
  Lee Creek, 114
  South Fork of the Spring River,
    32
  Sprada Creek, 90
  Spring River, Humphries Ford,
    35
  Strawberry River low-water
    bridge, 37
  Sugar Creek, 176
  White River, North Fork (MO)
    Blair Bridge, 200
  White River, North Fork (MO)
    Dawt Mill dam, 200
  White River, Upper, 130
  White River, West Fork, 135
  see also Cautions; Hazards and
    safety
Porter Mountain, 139
Precipitation. *see* Rainfall, Ozarks
Profiles, river-run, 3–6

R
Rainfall, Ozarks, 2, 8–9
Raspberry Mountain, 65
Raymond, Jim, ii, x, 56
Rescue and safety, river, 10–12
Rich Mountain, 141, 167
Richland Creek
  Ben Hur to Richland
    Campground, 82–85

Richland Campground to Stack Rock, 86

Richland Creek Wilderness Area, 65

River etiquette, 13–14, 63, 93

River hydrology, 7

River-run profiles, 3–6

Rockport Run. *see* Ouachita River, Lower

S

Safety and hazards, 10–12

Salado Creek
  Camp Tahkodah to US 167 Bridge, 29–30

Salem Plateau, 1, 7, 106

Saline County
  Saline River, Alum Fork, 137–138
  Saline River, North Fork, 165–166

Saline River
  Shady Lake to AR 246, 172–173

Saline River, Alum Fork
  AR 5 to Smith Ford Road, 137–138
  Smith Ford Road to Benton City Park, 138

Saline River, Middle Fork, 137–138

Saline River, North Fork, 137–138
  Steel Bridge Road to Benton, 165–166

Saline River, South Fork, 137

Searcy County
  Buffalo National River, 55–59
  Falling Water Creek, 65–66

Shepherd Mountain, 99

Shoal Creek
  Rocky Ford to Sorghum Hollow Road, 87–88

Sites of interest, Arkansas
  Buffalo National River, Baker General Store, 57
  Buffalo National River, Chimney Hole, 55
  Buffalo National River, Hemmed-in-Hollow waterfall, 53
  Caddo Gap natural springs, 147
  Clinton Whitewater real estate, 40

"Who'd a Thought It" gift shop, 72
  see also Historic sites

Sites of interest, Missouri
  Aid-Hodgson Mill, Bryant's Creek, 179
  Big Spring, Current River, 187
  Dawt Mill, White River, North Fork (MO), 200
  Merritt Rock Cave tours, Current River, 185
  Trappist Abbey, 179
  Turner's Mill, Eleven Point River, 190–191
  see also Historic sites

Smoke Rock Mountain, 143

South Fork of the Spring River. *see* Spring River, South Fork

South Fourche Lavave River
  Hollis to Deberrie, 174–175

Spirit Creek, 127

Sprada Creek
  CR 77 to Clarksville, 89–90

Spring River
  Dam 3 to Many Islands Camp, 33–35
  Many Islands Camp to Hardy, 35

Spring River, South Fork
  Cherokee Camp to Hardy, 32
  Saddle to Cherokee Camp, 31–32

Spring River, Warm Fork, 33

Springfield Plateau, 1, 7, 106

St. Francis River, 201–203
  MO 72 to SR D Bridge, 209–212
  SR E Bridge to Captain Creek, 212
  SR H Bridge to MO 72, 208–209

St. Francois Mountains, 1, 7, 201, 208

State Parks
  Bull Shoals State Park, 39–40
  Cassatot River State Park, 139
  Devil's Den State Park, 112
  Elephant Rocks State Park (MO), 208
  Millstream Gardens State Park (MO), 209–210

S *(continued)*
State Parks *(continued)*
Sam A. Baker State Park (MO),
   201–202
Withrow State Park, 132–133
Wooly Hollow State Park, 21
see also National Forests;
   Wilderness Areas
Strawberry River
Low-Water Bridge to AR 58, 37
US 167 to Low-Water Bridge, 36
Sugar Creek, 156
Knopper's Ford to Jack Creek
   Rec. Area, 176–178
Supplies. *see* Food and supplies
Swimming
Eleven Point River (MO), 189
King's River, 110
White River, North Fork (MO),
   198

T
Temperatures, Ozarks, 2
Texas County (MO)
Jack's Fork River (MO), 193–197
Topographic maps, 3
Trash and littering, 13–14
see also Etiquette, river
Turkey Creek (MO)
MO 72 to the St. Francis River,
   213–215

U
U. S. Army Corps of Engineers, 38,
   80, 181
U. S. Forest Service
Alum Creek Experimental Forest,
   137
East Fork Wilderness Area, 63
Eleven Point River (MO)
   campground, 192
landowner legal issues, 77
Marble Creek (MO)
   campground, 206–207
Ouachita River float camp, 168
South Fourche Lavave River, 175
Wild and Scenic Rivers Act, 188

U. S. Geological Survey (USGS), 3,
   7–9, 226–227

V
Van Buren County
Middle Fork of the Little Red
   River, 24–26
Vine Branch Creek, 160

W
Walker Mountain, 63
War Eagle Creek
AR 23 to Huntsville, 132
Huntsville to Rocky Ford,
   132–133
King's River and, 106
Rocky Ford to AR 45, 133
Washington County
White River, Middle Fork,
   119–121
White River, West Fork,
   134–136
Waterfalls
Baker Creek, 140
Cassatot River, 152–153
Cedar Creek, 91–92
Falling Water Creek, Falling
   Water Falls, 65
Little Missouri Falls, 158
Spring River, Devil's Shoot, 35
Spring River, High Falls, 35
Spring River, Horseshoe Falls, 33
Spring River, Saddler Falls, 33
Wayne County (MO)
Big Creek (MO), 201–203
Weather, Ozarks, 2
West Cedar Creek. *see* Cedar Creek
White Oak Mountain, 176
White River, 38–43
Buffalo City to Norfolk, 42
Buffalo National River and the,
   50
Bull Shoals to Cotter, 38–40
Calico Rock to Sylamore, 43
Cotter to Buffalo City, 40–41
Norfolk to Calico Rock, 42
White River, Middle Fork
Arnett to CR 32, 120–121

Pascal Road Bridge to Arnett, 119

White River (MO), North Fork
Hammond Camp to Patrick Bridge, 199–200
MO 14 to Hammond Camp, 198–199
Patrick Bridge to Norfork Lake, 200

White River, Upper
Crosses to Durham, 130
Durham to AR 74, 131
St. Paul to Crosses, 130

White River, West Fork
Road Side Park to West Fork, 134–135
West Fork to Fayetteville, 136

Wild and Scenic Rivers
Eleven Point River (MO), 188–193
Hailstone River, 67
Illinois Bayou, North Fork, 80
North Sylamore Creek, 27
see also Buffalo National River; Ozark National Scenic Riverways

Wilderness Areas
Caney Creek Wilderness Area, 139, 144, 149, 158, 172
Hurricane Creek Wilderness, 70
Ponca Wilderness, 129
Richland Creek Wilderness Area, 65

U. S. Forest Service, 63
see also National Forests; State Parks

Wildlife
Big Creek (AR), 17
Bryant's Creek (MO), 179
Buffalo National River, 55
Eleven Point River (MO), 189
Interior Highlands, 2
King's River, 107
Saline River, 172
Saline River, North Fork, 165

Withrow State Park, 132–133

Wooly Hollow State Park, 21, 23

World Wide Web (WWW). *see* Internet rescources

NOTES

NOTES

NOTES

Making the World
a Better Place to Paddle

The American Canoe Association
Canoeing, Kayaking and Whitewater Rafting

Membership $40 per year

Join Today!

To join the ACA call
(540) 907-4460 or visit
www.acanet.org

American Canoe Association